MORALITY & MARKETS

MORALITY & MARKETS
The Ethics of Government Regulation

Edward Soule

ROWMAN & LITTLEFIELD PUBLISHERS, INC.
Lanham • Boulder • New York • Oxford

ROWMAN & LITTLEFIELD PUBLISHERS, INC.

Published in the United States of America
by Rowman & Littlefield Publishers, Inc.
An Imprint of the Rowman & Littlefield Publishing Group
4720 Boston Way, Lanham, Maryland 20706
www.rowmanlittlefield.com

P.O. Box 317, Oxford OX2 9RU, United Kingdom

British Library Cataloguing in Publication Information Available

Library of Congress Cataloging-in-Publication Data
Soule, Edward, 1952–
    Morality and markets : the ethics of government regulation / Edward
Soule.
        p.   cm.
    Includes bibliographical references and index.
    ISBN 0-7425-1358-0 (alk. paper) — ISBN 0-7425-1359-9 (pbk. : alk.
paper)
    1. Trade regulation—Moral and ethical aspects.   2. Commercial
policy—Moral and ethical aspects.   3. Economic policy—Moral and ethical
aspects.   4. Communitarianism—Moral and ethical aspects.   5. Business
ethics.   6. Trade regulation—United States.   7. United States—Commercial
policy—Moral and ethical aspects.   8. United States—Economic policy—
Moral and ethical aspects.   9. Communitarianism—Moral and ethical
aspects—United States.   10. Business ethics—United States.   I. Title.

HD3612 .S676   2002
172'.2—dc21   2002013416

Printed in the United States of America

∞ ™ The paper used in this publication meets the minimum requirements of
American National Standard for Information Sciences—Permanence of Paper for
Printed Library Materials, ANSI/NISO Z39.48-1992.

To Jonathan and Ana

Contents

Preface

I FIRST ENCOUNTERED the subject matter of this book as a high-school student in 1967. The setting was a large discount store in suburban St. Louis where I worked part-time unloading trucks, stocking shelves, and operating a cash register. One Sunday afternoon, hours before the scheduled closing time, an announcement was made for the customers to halt their shopping and exit the premises. Moments later, St. Louis County Police Officers entered the store and escorted several of my coworkers from their stations at the cash registers to the backseats of patrol cars idling outside. Others trailed behind the store's manager as he went through the closing routines, after which he was shown to the backseat of another police cruiser. Then, as television crews and newspaper photographers crowded about, a thick chain was snaked through the handles of the front doors and secured with a cartoonishly large padlock.

After more than thirty years this little drama remains surprisingly vivid to me, perhaps because my father was the store manager. But also, later that day I participated in my first serious discussion of the topic of this book: the rightful role of government authority in the commercial lives of individual citizens. By my present standards of political philosophy it was a primitive affair—my father hyperbolically analogized the day's events to ones from a certain period in Germany's fascist past. My mother bemoaned the arbitrary enforcement of the law, the way some stores were singled out but not the more politically connected ones. To place our collective outrage in the context of the present investigation, we objected to the arbitrary discharge of state power to intervene in the innocent commercial affairs of private citizens.

In 1967, the sale of most goods on Sunday was a violation of St. Louis County's "blue" laws. I have since discovered that such laws (reputed to refer to the color of the paper the Puritans wrote theirs on) have a contentious history stretching from the colonial period to the present.[1] Years later, Missourians modified this law although Sabbatarianism lives on relative to the sale of alcoholic beverages on Sunday. But from a personal standpoint the damage was done. Now that I am a political philosopher pondering the rightful use of state authority in commercial life, this experience lingers as a reminder of the stakes involved in this subject. Although the study of commercial regulation draws upon lofty theories from any number of academic disciplines, it ultimately resolves into public policies and laws that affect ordinary people going about their daily lives. Getting it right matters.

This episode could have predisposed me to the ideals of laissez-faire capitalism, and I confess an early infatuation with it. But later experiences would intervene to complicate matters. To explain and in the interest of putting what few intellectual biases I have on the table, a very brief biographical sketch is in order.

My undergraduate studies involved the impossible combination of philosophy and accounting. Upon graduation I practiced public accounting for nine years, after which I served for another nine years as the chief financial officer of a securities firm. I read Robert Nozick's *Anarchy State and Utopia* as a senior executive, not as a philosopher, and came away with two impressions. First was the seemingly impregnable intellectual fortress Professor Nozick constructed around the minimalist state. Second was the impracticality of the libertarian project in my corner of the commercial world. I knew from experience and from studying the history of U.S. capital markets that regulatory oversight was essential. I reasoned that whether the libertarian argument was right or wrong, it could not be instantiated in the world I was familiar with. It was, I thought, dangerously utopian.

Years later, as a Ph.D. candidate in political philosophy, I studied alternative approaches to regulating commercial life. I had a similar reaction to the communitarian project, albeit for different reasons. This brief biographical note explains the motivation for this project. Unsatisfied with the extremes, I sought an alternative from the middle ground of the liberal moral tradition. However, this is a sprawling mass of vital moral insights, undifferentiated between political and commercial life. Accordingly, in what follows, I will abstract from this tradition a few moral principles crucial to commercial activity as the foundation of a systematic justification of government regulation—a Regulatory Strategy for short.

Note

1. For the account of St. Louis blue laws see Walter Ehrlich, *Zion in the Valley* (Columbia, Mo.: University of Missouri Press, 1997), 119. For a history of U.S. Sabbatarianism see Jonathan D. Sarna and David G. Dalin, *Religion and State in the Jewish Experience* (Notre Dame, Ind.: University of Notre Dame Press, 1997), 139–65.

Acknowledgments

TOWARD THE TAIL END of my business career I began dabbling in philosophy by taking graduate-level evening courses. When I suspended entirely my capitalist exploits and became a full-time graduate student, I was fortunate to be taken seriously by the faculty of the philosophy department at Washington University in St. Louis: in particular, Roger Gibson, Claude Evans, Pauline Kleingeld, Bob Barrett, Mark Rollins, and Bill Bechtel. Several of the ideas in this book originated in a doctoral dissertation directed by Larry May (chair), Marilyn Friedman, and Carl Wellman. I am indebted to each of them for their patient guidance of what must have been a most unconventional student. In particular, Larry May extended himself professionally as a mentor and coauthor and personally as a friend. It made all the difference. The present volume bears little resemblance to that dissertation and it is possible that Larry, Marilyn, and Carl would be horrified by the conclusions I now defend, but I hope not.

I teach at Georgetown University and benefit from wonderful students and the "reality checks" so important to work of this kind. I also benefit from colleagues across the range of disciplines touched on in this book. I thank Dennis Quinn, Bennett Zelner, John Mayo, and Cathy Tinsley for tolerantly guiding my excursions into their disciplines, and Tom Beachamp for straightening me out on my own. Especially, I thank my friend and colleague, George Brenkert, for unselfishly giving time and energy to my endeavors. I thank John Danley, Norman Bowie, and Patricia Werhane for reading and commenting upon this manuscript. And finally, I am indebted to my friend and intellectual foil, Craig Baker, for his unabashed willingness to provide trenchant criticism, whether solicited or not.

Portions of the discussion in chapter 5 regarding the precautionary principle were previously published in "Assessing the Precautionary Principle," *Public Affairs Quarterly* 14, no. 4 (October 2000): 309–28 and subsequently republished in the *International Journal of Biotechnology* 4, no. 1 (January 2002). (An electronic version of the *International Journal of Biotechnology* is available online at www.inderscience.com.) They appear here courtesy of the editors of those publications.

This is the place in many books where authors transmogrify into a mound of sentimental schmaltz by fawning over their undyingly supportive spouse, without whom neither their book nor any other of their adult undertakings would have been possible. Donna, in your case it's true; thanks!

Introduction

The interference of the government is, with equal frequency, improperly invoked and improperly condemned.

John Stewart Mill[1]

LEGEND HAS IT THAT *laissez-faire* entered the vernacular as the battle cry for free-market capitalism early in the nineteenth century during an interchange between a French merchant and a trade minister. The minister had solicited ideas on how to stimulate the then moribund French economy (some things never change), and one can only imagine his surprise and chagrin upon hearing the merchant's rebuke. After all, the French economy was still governed by mercantilist policies and various forms of protectionism that had been encouraged by the same business people who now wanted to be left alone.[2] True or not, this story speaks volumes about the unstable relationship between commercial life and state authority. Even in this primitive setting, limited as it was to commercial interests and an eager-to-please state, an enduring consensus was elusive. Consumer advocates, environmentalists, and other interested newcomers have done nothing to simplify the formulation of economic policy. Simply put, specifying the legitimate use of regulatory power over commercial activity is an ongoing and contentious work in progress.

It is not surprising that the relationship between government and business is contested; commerce presents a dodgy target. New goods and services appear routinely; familiar ones disappear. Virtually every business practice undergoes constant modification if it has not already been abandoned and replaced by a different mode of organization. And the pace at which commercial life changes can be breathtaking. Some of these changes are long overdue and are welcomed, but others are destabilizing and feared. Particularly unsettling is the competitive and sometimes pernicious struggle that pits individuals and groups of people against one another: producers against consumers, importers against exporters, employers and investors against workers, and so forth. Adam Smith observed that market forces tend to harmonize self-interests in socially beneficial ways. But his counterintuitive claim was tempered by his warning that sometimes the invisible hand is all thumbs. Smith recognized that market forces defuse some, and perhaps most, commercial conflicts but that government authority is needed to mediate others.

Specifying which commercial circumstances demand which regulative mechanism is the subject of ongoing debate. According to Ronald Dworkin, liberal thinkers endorse the following general proposition:

> Government should intervene in the economy to promote economic stability, to control inflation, to reduce unemployment, and to provide services that would not otherwise be provided, but they favor a pragmatic and selective intervention over a dramatic change from free enterprise to wholly collective decisions about investment, production, prices, and wages.[3]

This passage describes accurately the status of commercial regulation in the United States, where federal, state, and local authorities intervene statutorily in either specific industries (e.g., public utilities, airlines, and banks) or across industry groups (e.g., environmental protection, occupational safety, and antitrust). In the extreme, states block commercial trade entirely (e.g., narcotic drugs), but more commonly, intervention involves oversight (e.g., food safety or professional licensure), pre-approval (e.g., pharmaceuticals), or coordination (e.g., monetary policy). And in addition to direct statutory regulation, governmental authority is exercised indirectly by monitoring the judicial institutions that mediate private differences. In sum, far from the ideal of laissez-faire or free-market capitalism, commercial life in the United States occurs freely—but only within boundaries established by government authority.

This arrangement satisfies the key adjectives in Dworkin's description of the liberal attitude toward commercial regulation because it is pragmatic and selective. But these terms are too vague to either guide or criticize the moral legitimacy of state intervention. Under what specific circumstances are states justified to morally intervene in seemingly private commercial affairs? More specifically, in light of the coercive element of commercial regulation, what reasons morally justify its use? The purpose of this book is to formulate a systematic approach to answering that question. I proceed by briefly examining the objects and risks of commercial life. Based on those observations, I propose two moral principles. One, Negative Commercial Liberty, justifies intervention to reduce the risk of certain varieties of commercial harm. The other principle recognizes that some commercial practices present obstacles that prevent some people from pursuing their reasonable commercial plans. Commercial Autonomy justifies market intervention to remove or to diminish the effectiveness of these obstacles. These two principles serve as categories of morally justified reasons to regulate the practices that constitute commercial life. Their meaning is elaborated by defending them against several alternative doctrines of market intervention. And they are developed further in the context of two chapter-length case studies. The completed formulation is intended as a coherent theoretical account of morally justified commercial regulation or, for short, a Regulatory Strategy.

This is a study in political philosophy, but not to the neglect of history or the natural and social sciences—economics in particular.[4] Empirical insights matter a great deal, but not so much that they provide dispositive moral reasons to regulate. Consider this shorthand account of the way two economists justify market intervention:

> The key, it seems to me, is "Will the marketplace perform its function, and if it won't perform its function, why won't it and will regulation help do the job a little better?"[5]

The way markets function is a crucial consideration that an account of market regulation (moral or otherwise) should recognize. And were it not for the coercive element of intervention, efficiency might be unobjectionable. But when coercion is taken into account, another question needs answering: "Why should coercive state power be put to the service of making markets perform better?" Said another way, "As regulation forces some people to alter their behavior or suffer a punishment, why is market performance more important than individual liberty or some other human value?" The coercive element of regulation does not make economic efficiency a wrong or a bad reason for intervention, but it requires regulators to tell a longer story that includes the morally legitimate use of authority. The truncated version of that story is that coercive state authority is justified if it can be rationally and reasonably justified by those upon whom it is imposed.

Of course there are primitive cases in which this burden of political legitimacy seems to be satisfied on the basis of economic efficiency or in virtue of some empirical finding in medicine or some other natural science. But when these cases are particularly compelling, they are also enthymematic; some unobjectionable normative reason that justifies using coercive state authority has been assumed. In more complex and contentious cases it is often necessary to expose these normative reasons and debate them independently of the empirical facts. But, by the same token, these normative reasons do not diminish the importance of empirical findings. Normative and empirical reasons to regulate are mutually dependent at the level of concrete cases. Regulatory initiatives conceived in empirical darkness or moral vacuums are prescriptions for social disasters of one kind or another.

This investigation focuses on a single variety of economic organization, imperfectly described as free-market capitalism or free enterprise. When used here, these terms refer only to the most general recognition of private property and contractual freedom by the legal and political institutions of state and not to any particular ideology. Market intervention or commercial regulation refers to state initiatives that alter the terms and conditions of property rights or contractual liberty. And in an era that is putatively dominated by deregulation, privatization, and global acquiescence to a capitalist ideology, an investigation into the moral justification of commercial regulation may seem anachronistically quaint. The morality of state intervention seems to have been settled—regulation, bad; free markets, good—and all that remains is to dismantle the vestiges of the regulatory state. Moreover, it is arguable that multinational corporations, uninhibited by national political attachments, override the power of national regulation. But these claims are deceptively exaggerated. Although several initiatives during the last third of the twentieth century sought to rationalize and thereby thwart a certain kind of regulatory control, these efforts did not signal the death knell of market intervention. The Airline Deregulation Act (1978) set in motion an end to restricted routes and airfare controls that had shaped the industry since its infancy. But commercial aviation remains subject to rigorous regulatory oversight. The Financial Modernization Act (1999) relaxed the Depression-era barriers of the Glass-Stegal Act (1933), but no one would reasonably suggest that insurance companies or banks operate in a deregulated environment. The same could be said of telecommunications, transportation, energy, and other industries that have been "partially deregulated" or whose regulatory authority has been "reformed." But deregulation, if it is meant to imply the absence of government oversight, is not an apt description of the present state of affairs.[6] Likewise, governments have divested state-run companies (e.g., French banks) and depend increasingly on private sector providers for everything from trash collection to education. But the firms that provide these services are subject to regulatory oversight of one kind or another. It is equally naïve to exaggerate the power of multinational corporations vis-à-vis national regulators. Firms can escape some regulatory initiatives by relocating their offending operations; however, corporate production decisions involve factors other than regulatory climate, several of which limit this flexibility.[7] And finally, some international treaties (e.g., NAFTA) can conflict with and even override national or state regulatory authority. However, it is wrong to extrapolate from such instances the demise of national regulatory sovereignty. Although the nature of commercial regulation is constantly changing, both in design and intensity, at least in the United States it is alive and well.

As contentious as some debates over market intervention can be, at least two categories of "easy cases" have been settled. One is that states are justified to intervene in markets that pose serious threats to national security. No one seriously questions whether there should be a free market in weapon-grade plutonium. The other is the constraint of goods, services, or commercial practices that are demonstrably dangerous. No one challenges a local zoning restriction against the production of deadly toxins in densely populated neighborhoods. But disputes erupt on the very wide margins of commercial life, where the risks are less explicit and the consequences of intervention less predictable. What environmental controls are appropriate for cultivating genetically modified (GM) crops? Should GM ingredients be subject to mandatory labeling requirements? Should the U.S. Congress promulgate some new Bills of Rights, say, for customers of commercial airlines or for members of health maintenance organizations? Should Wall Street analysts be insulated against the organizational pressures of their colleagues in investment banking? Should public accounting firms be prohibited from providing consulting services to their audit clients? Or should the federal government take responsibility for auditing publicly registered firms? Each of these questions was stimulated by public outcries loud enough to provoke congressional hearings and, in some cases, legislative proposals.[8]

It is of great interest here that these public controversies are mirrored philosophically. The clamor in the halls of Congress, on editorial pages, in classrooms, and in boardrooms has an intellectual corollary in political philosophy. Most of these debates can be recast as being between libertarians, communitarians, welfare liberals, and others. And at the next higher level of abstraction, where these political theories gain their justificatory moorings, moral theorists are engaged in yet another dispute. Deontologists, utilitarians, and virtue theorists criticize one another's projects, although never so decidedly as to banish a contender to the depths of philosophical humiliation. Rather, such criticism inspires creative defenses or provokes impassioned counterattacks.[9] This study is not intended to engage in, much less settle, this internecine battle. I mention it as a way of defending an approach to the justification of regulation whereby none of the serious contenders in contemporary political philosophy are either ruled out or followed assiduously. Rather, I urge a morally pluralistic approach.

The failure of philosophy to coalesce around any single moral theory or political philosophy is only one reason for urging moral pluralism. Another is the complexity of commercial controversies. Consider but one significant tension in political philosophy—the tug of war between individual rights and social or community welfare. Now consider a concrete case—real-estate condemnation under powers of eminent domain. Some political philosophers criticize the practice because it violates property rights—regardless of the compensation. Others approve of it because it contributes to the welfare of the community. Both of these perspectives are valuable, but neither is ideal in terms of the range of possible eminent domain cases. On the one hand, an appeal to rights appears to be very feeble in the case of a real estate speculator standing in the way of a much-needed sanitary treatment facility where the only feasible alternative imposes a crushing burden on the community. In that case it would seem that the speculator's rights would be respected appropriately if the property were acquired for adequate consideration, even if the transfer took place under threat of condemnation. That is, it would appear that in some important sense, the speculator's property rights should yield to the community's welfare. However, this intuition changes with the facts of individual cases. Imagine a building situated in a marginal commercial area that is crucial to the viability of a small family business. And suppose further that a national retailer is willing to locate in this area provided the city acquires a large enough tract of land and razes the existing structures, including the one that houses the family business. The community that includes this area might derive significant benefits from this transaction but the lack of alternative sites will bring the family business to an end. In this case the appeal to community welfare is enfeebled and the property rights assume greater importance. Additional facts could complicate this case even further and this is but one mechanism of market intervention. A political philosophy anchored in a single moral precept (e.g., rights or welfare) is far too rigid to be applied systematically to the range of complex commercial practices.

Although moral pluralism is a necessary criterion for an adequate theory of justified government regulation, there are no satisfactory doctrines. An obvious candidate is the tradition of liberal political philosophy—a host of thinkers, bracketed in time by Locke (or Hobbes) and Rawls with Kant, Rousseau, Mill, and many others in between. However this corpus of thought is pitched (rightfully) at a level of abstraction that is suitable for the lofty goal of justifying the foundational purposes and basic institutions of nation states. Historical liberal thinkers could not have contemplated present-day commercial life and many prominent contemporary figures either confront it piecemeal or at a very general and abstract level, if at all.[10] Moreover, liberalism is overly rich in moral content and therefore hobbled by inconsistencies and contradictions. To fashion a coherent doctrine out of this intellectual sprawl requires that extraneous ideas be culled and that vital ones be specified, contextualized, and harmonized with one another. This effort is undertaken in chapter 1, beginning with a brief explanation of the purpose and limits of moral theorizing in the domain of commercial life. Next, the moral anatomy of commercial disputes is examined and, based on this description, it is then argued that moral pluralism is an unavoidable criterion of an adequate Regulatory Strategy. Moral principles are proposed (and defended) as the mechanism to satisfy this criterion, after which two such principles are formulated.

I do not dwell on the moral justification of these principles but refer instead to the justificatory heavy lifting performed by John Locke and John Stuart Mill. In an effort to construct a theoretical account of justified market intervention my challenge is threefold. First, I must overcome the objections of those thinkers that reject combining the positive and negative conceptions of human liberty in an account of government authority. Specifically, I must give an account of these principles that harmonizes their operation in a single doctrine. My second challenge is to clarify the meaning of these general principles in the special context of contemporary commercial life. And my third challenge is to explain how justice intersects these principles and

defend against not explicitly including social justice as a morally justified regulatory objective.

The remainder of the book elaborates, defends, and, where necessary, modifies these principles and the Regulatory Strategy they comprise. Chapter 2 considers the function of values as a reason to
regulate, beginning with Michael Walzer's communitarianism. For
Walzer, commercial regulation should serve the ends of distributive
justice and offset the allocative power of money and market fiat. I discourage appeals to justice in the regulation of markets but argue that
in the case of some goods—those that are vital to achieving any recognized version of a good life or avoiding a bad one—an appeal to personal autonomy will provide similar results. However, I also argue
that these results can be achieved without some of the personally disruptive consequences of communitarian regulation. Additionally in
this chapter, I address Elizabeth Anderson's project, one that can be
understood as successfully repairing some of the more worrisome
aspects of communitarianism. She formulates a highly sophisticated
account of personal autonomy, one based on the expression of rational
values, that is advanced as a reason to constrain some commercial
behavior. I raise some normative objections but also identify some
empirical impediments to instantiating Anderson's ideas in regulatory policy. The upshot of this chapter is that values are a useful heuristic device for the formulation of regulatory policy but they rise to
the level of legitimate reasons to regulate in only a very limited category of commercial practices.

Not everyone agrees that a Regulatory Strategy should be pluralistic—morally or otherwise. Several prominent projects emphasize a
single factor as the only justified reason to regulate or to forebear
intervention. Some authors of monistic projects urge a minimalist regulatory state in which the defense of individual rights is the only legitimate use of government authority (e.g., philosophical libertarians
and free-market economists). But others are less explicit about the limits of state authority (e.g., some welfare economists). What binds these
thinkers together is their refusal to recognize the legitimacy of more
than one regulatory objective whether it is individual rights, economic
efficiency, wealth maximization, or something else. I defend my pluralistic strategy against some of the better monistic arguments in
chapter 3.

In chapters 4 and 5, I provide extensive case studies. Chapter 4
investigates U.S. capital markets. The well-documented history of this
regulatory regime offers the opportunity to contrast the Regulatory

Strategy formulated here with the most likely alternative, libertarianism. This case illustrates the important roles of economics and history in regulatory decision making. And because the present-day regulatory regimes emerged out of several well-chronicled debates, it is possible to observe and evaluate the consequences of different moral postures without speculating. Chapter 5 presents a case involving an individual firm, Monsanto, and its efforts to commercialize GM crops. This technology raises different regulatory concerns than securities markets: environmental and human health being the most prominent risks. And unlike U.S. capital markets, this case is still in the formative stage. Accordingly, it provides an opportunity to clarify an ongoing controversy of international dimensions. Finally, many popular commentators and activists urge what is best understood as a communitarian approach to GM regulation. This case provides an opportunity to probe that doctrine in greater detail, but it also provides insight into some of the arguments advanced under the banner of "antiglobalism." Accordingly, those appeals will be evaluated in contrast to the moral principles of this Regulatory Strategy.

This is an exercise in practical or applied ethics whose findings matter only if they can be applied in the context of actual commercial disputes.[11] The disputes considered here are subject to resolution through a regulatory decision, the morality of which depends upon its impact upon the life prospects of those affected by it. This will be a successful endeavor if (and only if) it clarifies the moral stakes in commercial life and provides the intellectual resources from which a morally justified reason to regulate can be distinguished from an illegitimate use of state power. I approach this effort with a humility in proportion to the scope of the challenge. Of necessity I have struck a compromise between theory and practice, knowing full well the sacrifices and risks of doing so. But I bear in mind Aristotle's sage advice regarding the realistic ends of ethical investigations: "as much clearness as the subject-matter admits of, for precision is not to be sought for alike in all discussions, any more than in all the products of the crafts."[12]

I urge that readers grant me similar latitude.

Notes

1. John Gray, ed., *On Liberty and Other Essays* (1859; reprint, New York: Oxford University Press, 1991), 13.

2. Mark Blaug defines mercantilism as "the doctrine that a favourable bal-

ance of trade is desirable because it is somehow productive of national prosperity . . . protective duties on imported manufactured goods; encouragement
of exports, particularly finished goods; and an emphasis on population
growth, keeping wages low." See, Mark Blaug, *Economic Theory in Retrospect*
(Cambridge, Mass.: Cambridge University Press, 1996), 11.

3. Ronald Dworkin, *A Matter of Principle* (Cambridge, Mass.: Harvard
University Press, 1985), 187.

4. My emphasis on economic history is reflective of Annette Baier's admo-
nition that "Unless our moral reflections are historically informed, they will
be mere speculation." See "Some Thoughts on How We Moral Philosophers
Live Now," *The Monist* 67, no. 4 (October 1984): 490–97, 494.

5. Alan B. Morrison and Arthur A. Shenfield, "Government Regulation
and the Consumer," in Bernard H. Siegan, ed., *Regulation, Economics, and the
Law* (Lexington, Mass.: D.C. Heath and Company, 1979), 57.

6. The myth that regulatory reform or privatization means the end of
market intervention is exploded in Willis Emmons, *The Evolving Bargain: Strategic Implications of Deregulation and Privatization* (Cambridge, Mass.: Harvard
Business School Press, 2000). For an analysis of particular instances of regulatory reform, see Leonard Weiss and Michael Klass, eds., *Regulatory Reform:
What Actually Happened* (Boston: Little, Brown and Company, 1986).

7. For lucid and fair accounts of international trade and its effect on
national authority, see Robert and Jean Gilpin, *Global Political Economy: Understanding the International Economic Order* (Princeton, N.J.: Princeton University
Press, 2001), and Joseph Stiglitz, *Globalization and Its Discontents* (New York:
W. W. Norton, 2002).

8. The final query is not hypothetical. A Federal Bureau of Audits was
proposed in H.R. 3795 (107th Congress, 2d Session).

9. As evidence, consider how some recent scholarship in ethical theory
has become highly defensive. Tim Mulgan's contribution in *The Demands of
Consequentialism* (New York: Oxford University Press, 2001) is motivated in
large part by the savage criticism endured by consequentialist thinkers. Likewise with Rosalind Hursthouse's new work, *On Virtue Ethics* (New York:
Oxford University Press, 2000).

10. For instance, John Rawls, the towering figure in twentieth-century
political philosophy, addresses commercial life in the context of distributive
shares and concludes with these comments:

> Which of these systems [capitalism and socialism] and the many intermediate
> forms fully answers to the requirements of justice cannot, I think, be determined
> in advance . . . since it depends in large part upon the traditions, institutions, and
> social forces of each country, and its particular historical circumstances. The the-
> ory of justice does not include these matters. But what it can do is to set out in
> schematic way the outlines of a just economic system that admits of several varia-
> tions. The political judgment in any given case will then turn on which variation
> is most likely to work out best in practice.

See, *A Theory of Justice* (Cambridge, Mass.: Harvard University Press, 1971),
274. Fair enough, considering the extraordinary challenge Rawls undertook in

this book. But his findings cannot be drawn upon as a critical guide to market regulation in any straightforward way.

11. Tom Beauchamp rejects the distinction between theoretical and applied or practical ethics in "On Eliminating the Distinction between Applied Ethics and Ethical Theory," *The Monist* 67, no. 4 (October 1984): 514–31. I employ the distinction in the limited sense, distinguishing between the ultimate basis for morality and contributing to the resolution of commercial disputes. The moral principles employed here are morally justified in terms of one or more moral theories, and they are accepted uncritically. The task here is to justify their use in a critical account of commercial regulation and to weave them into a coherent strategy.

12. *Nicomachean Ethics* 1094:3, *The Basic Works of Aristotle*, Richard McKeon, ed. (New York: Random House, 1971), 936.

1

A Strategy for Justifying Market Intervention

In democracies nothing is greater or more brilliant than commerce;
it attracts the attention of the public and fills the imagination of the
multitude; all energetic passions are directed toward it.

Alexis de Tocqueville[1]

I think that there is nothing, not even crime, more opposed to
poetry, to philosophy, ay, to life itself than this incessant business.[2]

Henry David Thoreau

UNDER WHAT CIRCUMSTANCES are states justified to intervene in
putatively private commercial affairs? What distinguishes legitimate market intervention from unreasonable interference? More specifically, in light of the coercive element of commercial regulation,
what moral reasons justify its use? These questions cannot be
answered adequately in the abstract; they require detailed investigation into the goals and risks of commercial life generally as well as
those applicable to specific practices within individual markets.[3] But
theory can contribute to this investigation. This chapter sketches a theoretical account of morally justified market intervention or, for short, a
Regulatory Strategy, to guide those examinations and to answer those
questions. It begins by defining the goals of such a framework: what
it is intended to accomplish. Next, it examines the nature of commercial life and the moral dimensions of commercial controversies. This

description establishes criteria for and guides in the formulation of the theoretical account that follows.

A Job Description for a Regulatory Strategy

G. J. Warnock believed that moral theorizing was worth the effort if it contributed to the relief of what he called the "human predicament."[4] Relative to commercial life, this predicament consists first in a competitive struggle among individuals for scarce resources (e.g., material possessions, positions, status, power, and so forth). Second, as with most human competition, opportunities abound for harmful wrongdoing, injustices, and dangerous accidents. But third, because many of the rewards of commerce are indispensable, most people have little choice but to engage in and become directly vulnerable to the risks of the struggle. And everyone else is indirectly vulnerable to the extent that they live in a world where commerce flourishes. In sum, commercial life is the source of vital resources that are produced under conditions of unavoidable risk. Most generally, market intervention, say to constrain a commercial practice, is morally justified (or legitimate) if it is done for the reason of minimizing risk and if it is consistent with the productive objectives of the commercial practices it constrains.

A theoretical account of legitimate market intervention would be valuable if it clarified the morally salient factors of commercial practices, so as to systematically direct attention to those deserving of forceful change. For the sake of brevity, I refer to such a theoretical account as a Regulatory Strategy.

The Moral Terrain of Commercial Life

For conservative columnist George Will, free enterprise encourages civility and moral rectitude, a veritable "culture of commerce—contracts, lawfulness, transparency, promise keeping."[5] But according to environmental activist Jeremy Rifkin, free enterprise debases moral life, common decency, and "the very social foundations that give rise to commercial relations."[6] Obviously, both men cannot be right. But neither of these attitudes is idiosyncratic, because commercial life provides ample cause for both giddy optimism and somber regret. On the one hand, free markets respond to the unavoidable dependencies of social life or, in Charles Lindbloom's words, "People need the help of others."[7] Free markets cunningly transmit those needs, and producers "deliver the goods." Moreover, under competitive conditions, free markets encourage the moral values that Will applauds; consumers tend to reward integrity and punish deceit.

But free enterprise is neither perfect nor free in the sense that it works these wonders without exacting a price. Individuals pay a portion of the price, but market freedom also takes its toll on the social landscape. James Willard Hurst illustrates vividly the menacing factor of social drift:

> Thus fifty years of mass production and mass marketing of automobiles and trucks, heavily subsidized by public spending on hard-surfaced roads, contributed to reduce the role and financial health of the country's railroads, to promote the sprawling growth of urban areas and socially divisive separation of central city and suburbs, to multiply costs of personal injury, to imperil health through air pollution, and to increase the society's dangerous dependence on oil as a source of energy.[8]

Hurst does not relate this story to condemn the automobile industry, mass marketing, or highway subsidization. He simply identifies a phenomenon—free-market activity induces incremental and subtle social changes, the cumulative effect of which is exposure to new risks and a social world that was neither contemplated nor willed by those obliged to live in it. This unsettling realization inspires efforts to intervene and influence the outcomes of commercial activities.

So, although free-market capitalism occupies a well-deserved place in contemporary life, its place is bound to be an insecure and, at times, contentious one. The most serious contention, evident in the angriest of commercial controversies, can be understood as the collision of two varieties of morality—duties and welfare. Free enterprise, or free-market capitalism, can be understood as a form of economic organization emerging from the institutional recognition of private property and contractual freedom. As such, it is conditioned morally upon individual freedom (or liberty) as instantiated in a system of rights (primarily property and contract). Market intervention (or commercial regulation) is the use of state authority to alter those liberties and rights through statute. Some statutory intervention simply clarifies or provides formal structure to rights (e.g., the Uniform Commercial Code). These initiatives can trigger quarrels over the priority of one right holder over another, but the tension is usually limited by there being only a single moral category that affects more or less equally the interests of all commercial actors. These "rules of the game" do not produce clear winners and losers. However, regulation that constrains commercial rights on the basis of social welfare is another story. Land development ordinances, mandatory disclosure requirements, antitrust, equal employment opportunity, eminent domain, and some environmental regulations are examples in which someone's (or some group's) liberty is limited on the basis of someone else's (or some other group's) welfare. Although rights are invoked rhetorically in these disputes (e.g., a consumer's right to know food ingredients), proponents of these initiatives are typically claiming that a property right or a contractual liberty should be altered in favor of a welfare consideration. The way these disputes are settled can produce winners, runners-up, and the occasional losers. Consequently these disputes tend to be nasty, brutish, and protracted.

Moral Pluralism

The moral characteristics of commercial disputes dictate a key criterion for an adequate Regulatory Strategy. If its purpose includes clarifying the moral dimensions of a particular dispute, then the strategy must take seriously the legitimate moral intuitions of the contestants. It is dogmatic or arbitrary to disqualify (as wrong or as unimportant) either of the competing moral intuitions that dominate commercial controversies. Fortunately, there is evidence in commercial life that the clash between individual rights and community welfare is often resolved peacefully. Indeed, it is noteworthy that some commercial conventions embody both. For instance, Western patent law provides a right to enjoy the rewards of one's discoveries. However, that right is qualified in two significant ways (i.e., public disclosure and limited duration) in recognition of the public welfare aspects of innovative knowledge. Now, it might be argued that such knowledge should not be the province of any single owner, but a competing case could be made that it is wrong to force a patent holder to surrender it after the passage of time. The tension between these two moral outlooks is compromised and reconciled in contemporary patent law.

Détente between morality as rights (in defense of individual freedom) and morality as welfare (in defense of the quality of community life) has not been achieved in moral philosophy, where the hostility makes it tempting to simply pick a side and be done with it. Doing so—committing to, say, libertarianism—avoids the moral schizophrenia of trying to straddle the theoretical divide. But there is a prohibitively high price to pay, both philosophically and in terms of contributing to the clarification and resolution of contemporary controversies. Joining either of these camps is philosophically perilous because it requires that one or the other of the orthodox outlooks is theoretically right (or at least better or preferable) and the other is theoretically wrong (or inferior). And this assumes that there is some modicum of philosophical consensus regarding the "right" theoretical meaning of morality, or the right moral theory. But far from consensus, there are several candidate theories (most prominently deontological and natural rights theories, several consequentialist welfare theories, and virtue ethics), each of which enjoys formidable canonical standing.[9] And each such theory boasts prominent advocates engaged in an internecine struggle for decisive authority. Lately, as hopes for dominance fade and enthusiasm for the struggle wanes, moral pluralism is gaining increased acceptance, albeit reluctantly. Charles Larmore coined the phrase "heterogeneity of morality" to capture this compromise—that morality involves more than one irreducible element or constitutive meaning.[10]

This state of affairs explains Tom Beauchamp's belief that "[n]o theory adequate to serve as the foundation for application to concrete moral problems has ever been devised."[11] In contemporary American affairs, in which rights share their moral authority with concerns for social welfare, his observation is particularly poignant. Rights and welfare are not only prominent moral intuitions in contemporary society; they both share impeccable historical pedigrees. As evidence, consider the portion of the Preamble to the U.S. Constitution that describes the purpose of the document it introduces:

> to form a more perfect union, establish justice, insure domestic tranquility, provide for the common defense, promote the general welfare and secure the blessings of liberty to ourselves and our posterity.

Critics are fond of pointing out the fundamental conflict or internal inconsistency in this language or in the liberal moral tradition generally.[12] And they are right because promoting the "general welfare" usually requires encroaching on the rights that confer the "blessings of liberty." But as inconvenient and frustrating as this conflict may be, it is also unavoidable. Individual liberty (rights) and welfare (social in particular) are both cherished ideals. To dismiss either one in the formulation of a theory of justified market intervention risks irrele-

vance in the application stage. Contestants in rule-of-law liberal
democracies muddle through this quagmire and construct stable solutions. It is necessary for a theoretical account of this "muddling" process to accommodate the widest possible range of legitimate moral
intuitions. Moral principles are proposed as the mechanism for this
book's Regulatory Strategy.[13]

Moral Principles and Commercial Life

Moral principles comprise the layer of moral reasoning between moral
theories and moral rules. Unlike theories about the ultimate justification of morality or about what morality ultimately consists in, moral
principles are much humbler affairs. They stake claims about what
morality demands in a particular context. They are (metaphorically
speaking) between theories and rules because in one direction, principles can be justified by moral theories, but in the other direction, they
serve to generate context-specific rules. If formulated properly, moral
principles are sufficiently general to provide substantive moral
authority across the diverse range of commercial practices.

In recognition of the complexity and novelty of contemporary commercial life, the principles formulated here are proposed as revisable.
That is, their formulation is subject to ongoing modification through
application. Moreover, the principles are proposed as prima facie in
recognition that one principle can yield to the other, but the diversity
of commercial experiences makes it impractical to prescribe a rigid
application protocol (e.g., priority rules). Rather, application of these
principles must be guided by the facts and circumstances of individual cases. Sometimes this means carefully specifying the factors of a
case until such time as it is apparent what is required.[14] In other cases,
the magnitude or urgency of some factor will guide in their application. As messy as this would appear, it is not realistic to do otherwise
in an area of life that includes services as diverse as finance and entertainment, products as varied as pharmaceutical drugs and Chia-Pets,
and practices that range from shopping to employment. And as this
Regulatory Strategy is elaborated through cases it should become
apparent that this is not a crippling difficulty.

Philosophers in two domains of practical ethics have criticized the
use of moral principles in ethical decision making. In business ethics,
Buchholz and Rosenthal propose a pragmatic approach to problem
solving that, in the words of the subtitle to their 1998 book, seeks to

go "beyond principles." However, it is apparent from the text that the principles they seek to transcend are more accurately described as philosophical moral theories (e.g., Kantian ethics, utilitarianism, and so forth) or as moral rules (e.g., to always tell the truth). They reject moral theories on the same pragmatic grounds that disqualify eternally immutable accounts of anything, including accounts of moral authority. And they reject moral rules as an impossibly narrow basis upon which to erect a robust account of business ethics. However, depending on the way they are formulated, neither Buchholz and Rosenthal nor other pragmatists need to reject the systematic use of moral principles. Their criticism should instead be directed at the principles themselves and whether they conform to or violate tenets of pragmatic ethics. Alternatively, pragmatists such as Buchholz and Rosenthal could object to a rigid application of moral principles—one constrained unreasonably by priority rules or the like. But so long as the principles are designed as revisable in light of experience, and provided they do in fact identify morally salient factors that deserve consideration, pragmatists should be sanguine toward their use.

Lynn Jansen criticizes a project in the domain of medical ethics dubbed "clinical pragmatism."[15] Advocates of this approach—Joseph Fins, Franklin Miller, and Mathew Bacchetta—have responded convincingly to some of her criticism.[16] But there remains a sticking point relative to the role of moral principles in ethical problem solving. Jansen criticizes Deweyan experimentalism as all procedure and no content, and she urges a wider role for moral principles. Fins, Miller, and Bacchetta recognize the importance of moral principles but deny them a substantive role in their project. Their resistance relates to the rigid application of principles and the faulty and premature clinical judgments they supposedly encourage. But a careful reading of the initial formulation of clinical pragmatism[17] and the subsequent controversy suggests an opportunity to resolve this controversy to the satisfaction of both parties. First, Fins, Miller, and Bacchetta are wrong to resist a more substantive role for moral principles. Their objections would be understandable if the principles urged on them were overly narrow or simplistic. But otherwise, their stated worry, the cognitive influences of predetermined normative content or the idea that principles undermine the suspended belief they think is necessary for genuine critical thinking, is unreasonable. Although skepticism is vital, it need not require that the values and beliefs one brings to an investigation, moral or otherwise, be sidelined. Indeed, this may be theoretically desirable but it is a practical impossibility. Investigations will unavoidably draw upon principles and clinical pragmatists should be concerned with which ones they invoke. The careful formulation of moral principles in advance of investigations should contribute to and not diminish the results of critical thinking. And it would fend off criticism like Jansen's that clinical pragmatism lacks content.

Now, consider that Fins, Miller, and Bacchetta and Buchholz and Rosenthal are pragmatic thinkers resisting moral principles. Both sets of thinkers express an attachment to John Dewey and reject moral principles as the wrong devices for solving moral problems. This passage summarizes their views:

> Although invoking one ethical principle or rule may seem to provide structure to a case analysis, this move can actually constrict the emerging ethical discourse at the outset of a case when it most needs to be expansive. At its worst, such a mechanical approach could lead to orchestrated outcomes in which the selected ethical principle predetermines what counts as an important fact or reasonable question.[18]

Of course this is a serious risk, but it does not follow that properly formulated moral principles have this tendency. At least this would not be Dewey's assumption. Dewey would not have advised physicians to ignore principles of medical science and start from scratch by treating every patient's symptoms as novel phenomena. Surely he would allow that the germ theory of disease is a useful tool that survives from patient to patient. A psychological predisposition to frame phenomenon to the detriment of sound judgments is a reason to be careful, but it is not a good reason to suspend whatever knowledge is important in the context. It should not matter that such knowledge is formulated in theories or in principles.

It is highly unlikely that Dewey would take the position that these pragmatist thinkers ascribe to him. It is noteworthy that one of Dewey's more prominent applications of pragmatism draws upon moral principles. Education was a major focus of Dewey's prodigious intellectual life, and in a book aptly entitled *Moral Principles in Education*, he urges that "[w]hat we need in education is a genuine faith in the existence of moral principles which are capable of effective application."[19] He proceeds to carefully formulate four such principles that are justifiable in terms of the requirements of democratic citizenship. The principles are intended to promote intellectual curiosity and independent thinkers capable of applying knowledge to solve social problems. His use of moral principles seems to contradict his criticism (elsewhere) of overarching moral principles. However, Dewey is not being inconsistent if his criticism is understood as applying to rigid ethical principles intended to apply eternally to all of human experience. He does not invoke his moral principles of education and apply them to other domains of life. Accordingly, it would seem that his pragmatic commitments are consistent with his use of moral principles in the limited domain for which he applies them, if it can be shown that such principles advance the agreed-upon goals and objectives of education.

A final example should dispel the notion that moral principles are out of step with pragmatism. Perhaps Dewey's strongest moral commitment was to democracy, not as just a form of government but as a mode of inquiry. He condemned as "treason to the democratic way of life" anything that got in the way of open discourse, including "intolerance, abuse, calling of names because of differences of opinion about religion or politics or business, as well as because of differences of race, color, wealth or degree of culture."[20] Kloppenberg observes that James and Dewey could not separate their pragmatism from their democratic ideals and, specifically, "their principles of social equality and individual autonomy."[21] In sum, moral principles played a significant role in these two of the three progenitors of American pragmatism. Criticism of moral principles by self-described contemporary pragmatists is, I believe, unnecessary.

Negative Commercial Liberty

Market intervention to reduce the risks of harm is justified; unless such risks were understood and accepted by those vulnerable to them under circumstances conducive to rational deliberation and self-interested decision making. (author's definition)

The idea that it is a legitimate use of government authority to insulate citizens against the harmful behavior of others (i.e., the harm principle) is not controversial. However, the harm principle provokes significant controversy when applied to commercial practices, many of which will be addressed in subsequent chapters. But one major issue deserves consideration in the course of formulating the meaning of this principle of Negative Commercial Liberty. Some have argued that the only meaning of liberty deserving of government attention is this negative variety—the freedom to be left alone.[22] The minimalist regulatory state, limited in power to the protection against uninvited aggressors, is reflective of this attitude. Shortly I will introduce a second principle, Commercial Autonomy, which affords moral importance to positive liberty or the capacity to act purposefully in satisfaction of one's self-determined economic goals. Importantly, it is not unusual to compromise someone's negative liberty when states act on the basis of furthering someone else's positive liberty. Consequently, some explaining is in order. Specifically, it is incumbent on me to justify this enlargement of regulatory power beyond the minimalist regulatory state. The following arguments are intended to demonstrate that at least in the context of commercial life, negative liberty can share moral authority with personal autonomy.

Many libertarians justify the exclusivity of the harm principle on the basis of ideas associated with John Locke.[23] In what follows, I will appeal to Locke for a different conclusion: that defending negative liberty (or rights) does not exhaust the legitimate ends of regulatory authority. Rather, states are also justified to intervene in defense of a particular account of positive liberty or personal autonomy in commercial life. I do so by way of a brief excursion into the second of Locke's *Two Treatises of Government*[24] to isolate two arguments for property rights. One is the familiar natural law case, and the other is consequentialist. I argue that the consequentialist argument is attractive because it is easily harmonized with Locke's economic thinking. This is not a criticism of the natural rights argument and, indeed, the consequentialist one can be read as bolstering it. However, in the limited domain of commercial life, there are compelling reasons to prefer the consequentialist case. The importance of this finding is that, unlike the natural rights argument, the consequentialist one does not require a minimalist regulatory state.

I begin with the familiar story that for Locke, government should act as a fiduciary[25] for certain interests and rights that individuals enjoyed in a prepolitical state of nature (§4).[26] Two crucial such interests—that nobody has a right to harm anyone else and the fundamental human ambition for "self-preservation"—give rise to Locke's "Law of Nature": "[T]hat being all equal and independent, no one ought to harm another in his Life, Health, Liberty, or Possessions (§6). And such prepolitical Laws of Nature survive into civil society and serve to test the legitimacy of government authority. Laws that preserve "Lives, Liberties, and Estates" (§123) are in accord with the fiduciary powers granted to legislators. This is Locke's statement of negative liberty, and it clearly authorizes states to defend against unwelcome violations of persons and their property. But it is not obvious what the second interest, "self-preservation," means or implies in a commercial context. In particular, it is not clear whether state fiduciary powers extend to initiatives that advance the cause of individual self-preservation or whether they are limited to punishing those who violate individual rights.

The libertarian minimalist state assumes that punishing violators is what self-preservation means. This interpretation can be derived from Locke's natural law argument for property rights. That familiar argument will not be rehearsed here, but a second one will.

To put this second argument in context, it is important to bear in mind that private property was not at stake when Locke penned the *Two Treatises*. It is not the case that private property did not exist or that it was limited to a select class of landowners. The second half of the seventeenth century was a period of vigorous commercial and agricultural development in which property rights played an important role. Larkin notes that early in the century, "the majority of English peasants both are personally free and have a direct interest in the soil."[27] However, it was also a period of tumultuous political upheaval, owing to the struggle for power between Parliament and the Crown. A significant portion of this struggle, motivated by taxation and property rights, became a means to "sharpen ideas" about its fairness.[28] The major idea requiring sharpening was the residue of theological meaning that still attached to property—that it was God given and that the Crown had a divine right to tax it.[29] Countering this right was the doctrine of: "improvement" that McRae describes as "a dominant force in seventeenth-century culture."[30] Improvement was the intellectual consequence of the innovative agricultural practices (e.g., enclosures, crop rotation, and so forth) that Locke was personally involved in and sympathetic to.[31] Improvement had political implications, because increased productivity of human origins challenged the spiritual nature of agriculture output and the legitimacy of taxing it. Improvement was also politically attractive, because it made a causal connection between human ingenuity and material well-being and it eliminated what was left of the connection between the divine Crown and human welfare.[32] But Locke argues that productivity requires some assurance that productive efforts will be rewarded. Property rights, as a defense against arbitrary taxation, serve that function. So in the context of the improvement debate, property rights are a necessary condition for self-preservation (§48).[33] And since gov-

ernment serves as a fiduciary for each individual's interest in self-preservation, the defense of property rights follows.

I emphasize that in contrast to the natural law argument, this one is
consequentialist. That is, property rights are morally justified because
they promote the conditions for material well-being. The argument is
nominally "natural" in the sense that it derives from a psychological
predisposition to preserve one's self. But its moral standing depends
utterly on consequences measured in terms of human welfare. The
natural law argument does not. Satisfying the conditions of Locke's
Proviso justifies ownership, and what results may or may not contribute to material welfare. So although both arguments drive toward a
similar conclusion—the moral justification of private property—they
get there in different ways. And this matters because it shades the conclusions they prove. The natural rights argument enables the minimalist state, but it is not clear that it requires or permits anything beyond
the defense of title and contractual rights. But if, instead, property
rights are important not as ends in themselves but as elements of productive incentives, then the story changes somewhat. If productive
incentives are the morally important endpoint, then defense of property rights might not be sufficient to discharge government's fiduciary
duty. For example, do states overstep their legitimate fiduciary duties
when they regulate a national money supply? According to the minimalist account, they clearly do because central banks and other monetary institutions are doing much more than defending property rights.
But if self-preservation is interpreted broadly as including the necessary conditions whereby productive incentives are meaningful, then
these institutions are justified. As Huyer explains, Locke took as

the sure sign of preservation . . . a protracted bout of material progress—
i.e., prosperity. Its precondition is a diligent application of industrious
energy. In modern terms, we can say it is an ethic of production, not a
craven life ruled by "conspicuous consumption" that Locke wishes to
recommend.[34]

There is ample authority to read Locke as recommending regulatory initiatives that go beyond the minimalist state although they are
not within the Second Treatise. They can be found instead in his policy
recommendations.[35] For instance, when Locke opines on the regulation of interest rates, he is concerned first and foremost with lender
incentives and the adequacy of investment capital.[36] He objects to
lending agreements that exploit vulnerable borrowers and advocates

a legal rate of interest to protect "young men, and those in want," from being "too easily exposed to extortion and oppressions."[37] Note that Locke does not simply advocate punishment for the crimes of extortion. He goes beyond this to suggest usury caps. Likewise, when Locke writes about international trade, he advocates a variety of protectionist measures in keeping with his Mercantilist leanings. Generally speaking, Locke contemplates an activist, not a minimalist, regulatory state.[38] His concern is for the material well-being of the English people and not directly with their commercial liberties. Indeed, many of his policy prescriptions interfere with contractual liberties. The salient point of these economic writings is that they are easily derived from an understanding of self-preservation that legitimates authority to do much more than defend rights. If property rights are treated as crucial to achieving material improvements, and if government exists to further the preservation of its citizens, then market intervention is subject to a different test of legitimacy than a natural right would be. Specifically, a property right justified on the basis of productive incentives could be modified or overridden for reasons of furthering the chances for material prosperity. Importantly, a consequentialist justification of private property does not require that government authority over commercial affairs be limited to a minimalist state.

This nonminimalist interpretation is plausible for reasons other than its harmony with Locke's economic thought. It is also consistent with the historical accounts of the purpose for which Locke wrote the *Treatises*. By one interpretation, Locke sought to justify British colonial interests in North America.[39] By another, he spoke in opposition to the arbitrariness of church-inspired taxation.[40] Although arbitrary taxation can be objected to on the grounds of a natural right, seventeenth-century colonization cannot.

As mentioned earlier, many libertarian arguments for the minimalist regulatory state and laissez-faire capitalism are justified on the basis of Locke's natural rights argument for private property. My goal here is not to impugn those projects but to urge an alternative interpretation of Locke's thinking, one that provides a slightly broader range of legitimate government authority. I emphasize "slightly" because furthering the possibilities for individual self-preservation in the context of commercial life imposes a significant regulatory limitation, one that I attempt to formulate with the following moral principle.

Commercial Autonomy

Market intervention to constrain commercial practices that present formidable obstacles to pursuing one's realistic commercial opportunities is justified when those obstacles are not of one's own making. Market intervention to create the necessary institutional conditions for the pursuit of realistic commercial opportunities is justified when market participants lack the capacity to create those institutions on their own. (author's definition)

Locke's commitment to negative liberty is complicated by his economic policies, some of which could run roughshod over individual property rights and contractual liberty. The above discussion attempted to relieve this tension by elaborating the meaning of the regulatory goal of individual self-preservation and by my suggestion that this goal might necessitate efforts in the name of positive liberty or autonomy. However, significant ambiguity remains. It should be noted that Locke's failure to specify unambiguously the rightful limits to state authority, over and above the respect for property rights, is understandable Locke was urging formal recognition of property rights at a time when they were not respected as seriously as they would be in the future. His failure to specify carefully the institutional contours of a regulatory state makes sense insofar as that wasn't a lively debate. Locke and other economists of the time were struggling to discover the proper institutional arrangement to sustain prosperity. The arrangement they arrived at, Mercantilism, provided the grist for the minimalist state mill. But that would be a hundred years in the making. Therefore, I turn to the work of John Stuart Mill[41] to fill in the meaning of this principle of Commercial Autonomy.

Mill is an appropriate source insofar as he shares Locke's staunch commitment to negative liberty. However, unlike Locke, Mill is explicit that negative liberty does not exhaust the universe of justified reasons for market intervention. First, consider Mill's unambiguous statement of the harm principle:

> The sole end for which mankind are warranted . . . in interfering with the liberty of action of any of their number is self-protection. That the only purpose for which power can be rightfully exercised over any member of a civilized community, against his will, is to prevent harm to others. His own good, either physical or moral, is not a sufficient warrant. (9)

This passage seems to limit government authority to the protection of rights although, as was the case with Locke, it depends upon how "self-protection" is cashed out. I will argue that it is plausible to cash it out such that market intervention in defense of positive liberty or autonomy in commercial life is justified. And as I did with Locke, I defend this interpretation on the basis of Mill's economic writing.

Mill's commitment to positive freedom or autonomy can be constructed out of several comments in *On Liberty*: to choose one's own life plans (56) on the basis of a conscious will guided by strong feelings that have been developed through vigorous critical evaluation and self-development (67). Or, "the sovereignty of the individual over himself" (73) in all those activities necessary for human development. Obviously, the ability to do these things—to achieve an autonomous life—requires the negative liberty that Mill describes metaphorically as a sphere of human activity (the province of liberty) wherein state interference is hardly ever legitimate (e.g., the expression of ideas, the determination of preferences, tastes, life plans, associations, and so forth). But outside of this sphere of self-regarding behavior, he describes a social sphere (the realm of morality or law)[42] in which one's behavior affects the interests of others and states are justified to intervene. And for Mill, commercial life falls (largely)[43] in the social sphere. He emphasizes that "trade is a social act" and it is "undeniable" that it can be "legitimately controlled" by the state. But this "can control" translates into "morally permissible" and not morally required. Indeed, as a general rule, Mill argues for free markets on "grounds . . . different from, though equally solid with, the principle of individual liberty" (94). Unfortunately, he does not say what those "grounds" are. However, from his examples of permissible and impermissible intervention it is apparent that he contemplated self-development and personal autonomy. For instance, he treats practices like "sanitary precautions" and worker safety as obvious candidates for regulation. But he argues against regulating the terms of trade through schemes that affect prices or production guidelines. Mill is particularly critical of guild restrictions because of the way they limit individual career choices. In general, Mill believes that the autonomous decision making of individual market participants should prevail. And he believes that this is more likely to happen where trading conditions are "under the sole check of equal freedom to the buyers for supplying themselves elsewhere" (94). So although Mill considers any instance of market intervention prima facie morally justifiable, regulatory legitimacy is ultimately judged by its impact upon individual autonomy.

This sketch could be interpreted as a utilitarian appeal to human welfare or well-being and not to individual autonomy. This is a subtle distinction but one of great importance in terms of the goals of and limits to regulatory policy. The important difference is that if market freedom is important because of its welfare consequences, then markets that perform suboptimally are candidates for intervention. That, as I will explain in chapter 3, is the position of some neoclassical economists. Alternatively, if market freedom is viewed as an important aspect of leading an autonomous life, then to a certain extent market performance (aside from harmful practices) is secondary. This comes very close to Mill's view. Consider his arguments against "voluntary" slavery, in which he argues that states are justified to block the sale of one's self into slavery because such agreements naturally and necessarily undermine one's ability to lead an autonomous life (101). It is noteworthy that Mill does not appeal to welfare, even though slaves lead demonstrably wretched lives. Rather he makes autonomy an end in itself, and he justifies market intervention on that basis.

Mill's commitment to individual autonomy is also evident in his *Principles of Political Economy*[44] when he endorses a qualified version of laissez-faire regulatory policies.[45] His skepticism regarding the regulatory state and his account of the virtues of free enterprise would seem to lead inexorably to laissez-faire capitalism,[46] but they do not. Rather, he rejects the idea that unconstrained commercial activity is the same as or would produce all the happy outcomes he associates with commercial life. It is more accurate to say that his enthusiasm was for the ideal of free markets, but he was a realist. He again refers elliptically to "counter-considerations of still greater importance" [952] that justify government intervention. These counter-considerations are not described but spelled out in six categories of conditions that warrant intervention. And their wording is easily confused with market failures of welfare economics. Although there is some overlap, there are some important differences as well. To distinguish the two and to illustrate Mill's emphasis on autonomy and not welfare, I analyze one of them here.

Mill places great stock in consumer self-interest as the best general guide in the market. But he recognizes that some consumers are not the best judges of their interests. He emphasizes that this is not the case with goods intended to "supply some physical want, or gratify some taste or inclination, respecting which wants or inclinations there is no appeal from the person who feels them" [953]. But intervention is justified when there is more at stake. Specifically, he limits intervention to those goods, services, and practices that involve control over one's own life, citing the choice of education and unconscionable employment contracts as candidate examples. So, states are justified to cure any information asymmetries in education offerings. And they are justified to abrogate unconscionable employment contracts. Now, it could be argued that an appeal to welfare would arrive at the same conclusion, and in these two cases it would. But welfare is far too broad a reason to regulate for Mill's purposes. Information asymmetries are ubiquitous, and Mill is not intent for states to correct the whole lot of them. He accepts inefficiencies in the market and treats them as learning opportunities. To rid the market of every inefficiency might improve consumer welfare but, in Mill's view, it would come at too steep a price.

The above formulation of Commercial Autonomy is stated in terms of removing obstacles and creating institutional conditions.[47] Sometimes these measures are aimed at specific practices (e.g., information disclosures), and other times they mean using the law as a coordinating device (e.g., monetary systems).[48] Fully elaborating the meaning of these principles and harmonizing them in application cannot proceed in the abstract. There is undeniable conflict between principles of positive and negative liberty. But at least in the commercial sphere they are both essential. Subsequent chapters present concrete illustrations as a way of filling in the meaning of these principles and the practical resolution of the theoretical conflicts.

Commercial Life and the Political Process

The markets contemplated in this study are those within liberal democracies and the rules applicable to commercial practices considered here are assumed to have emerged through legislative bodies subject to democratic control. Two ideals of liberal democracies are assumed to regulate the formulation of commercial policies. They are treated here as background conditions and regulative of the interpretation and application of the above moral principles. One is a heavily qualified version of the principle of liberal neutrality. This is not intended as the extreme and much-maligned principle of liberal neutrality or the belief that states should not endorse any particular account of the good life; this has been seriously criticized as unnecessary and probably wrongheaded. It is thought to be unnecessary because popular sentiment seems to press states to take actions in furtherance of a good life. And it has been called wrongheaded because it is impossible to avoid acting on behalf of some notion of good lives. This criticism seems right insofar as the target is an idealized notion of neutrality. However, like all liberal and probably most any moral principle, neutrality admits to degrees of rigidity. There is a fundamental difference between life in liberal democracies and life in theocratic tyrannies. There are many factors that account for this difference, but neutrality—state respect for different versions of good lives and individual freedom to pursue them—is one major factor.

States should not necessarily be paralyzed by a commitment to be impartial with respect to interpretations of the good life. At least in the commercial sphere, it is possible to endorse a variety of market intervention without running roughshod over any particular interpretation of what makes life, commercial life in particular, worth living. The reason this is possible is that every reasonable interpretation of a good life would include some modicum of material prosperity and economic stability. Stated in the negative, universal consensus can be achieved with regard to some factors that cause lives to go badly. Lives of abject poverty and conditions of economic chaos characterize universally agreed-upon bad lives. State initiatives to relieve these conditions do not favor one version of the good life over another because there is no reasonable version of the good life that includes them. Rather, such initiatives instantiate aspects of life that complement every possible version of a good life.

Although the meanings of "material prosperity" and "economic stability" are nebulous and complex, their common-sense meanings are clear enough for citizens to grasp and for legislators to act upon. And both concepts are so widely endorsed that acting upon them is not only acceptable in a liberal democracy; voters demand that legislators pursue policies that promote prosperity and stability. This demand is a well-documented finding in economics and political science beginning with evidence that democratic elections serve to transmit and realize the preferences of median voters.[49] It includes research that documents the way that contested elections anticipate those preferences, regardless of whether they are made manifest in the political process or not.[50] And it concludes with comparative voting studies that document a similar "vote function" or response among citizens of democracies worldwide—a decided response to economic performance. Specifically, voters modestly reward incumbents for increased growth,[51] but they punish them severely for economic instability.[52] Domestically, economic stability has ranked as one of the top two or three fears of voters in public opinion polling since the inception of such polls.[53] These findings do not imply that prosperity and economic stability exhaust the universe of voter preferences. Others such as crucial post-Material values (e.g., environmental safety) are important as well. But they do suggest that state initiatives to secure wealth and economic stability will not violate a principle of neutrality.

The second ideal assumed to be regulative of policy formulation is the equality of interests among all affected parties. This does not imply a strict equality of outcomes that would taint as unjustified any instance of market intervention that advantaged a particular firm or consumer group. Virtually any instance of commercial regulation can be viewed as creating benefits and imposing burdens disproportionately. However, there may be good reasons for doing so. Equality of interests requires that anyone affected by regulatory action is entitled to participate in the rule-making process and have his or her interests considered equally with those of others similarly situated. In general, this condition can only be satisfied through a transparent process where the state's justificatory burden is on clear display.[54]

Social Justice and Commercial Life

The use of state power, whether in the regulation of markets or otherwise, cannot avoid concerns for justice. Indeed, the foregoing principle of neutrality and equality of interests are appeals to justice. But social justice or "[h]ow the good and bad things in life should be distributed among the members of a human society," is not an explicit element of this Regulatory Strategy.[55] And the obvious inequities in commercial life make this a glaring omission; especially as social justice is often invoked as the reason for some extant regulations. However, I will argue that principles of social justice are unnecessary and undesirable in this context. They are unnecessary because many of the goals of social justice in commercial life can be achieved through an appeal to Commercial Autonomy. But also, I will argue that regulating on the basis of social justice cannot be generalized across the range of commercial practices without intolerable results. Examples of Commercial Autonomy substituting for principles of social justice are presented in the next chapter. These arguments are not intended to apply outside of the realm of commercial regulation in which principles of social justice are clearly justified, so my arguments are silent relative to programs of income redistribution or other mechanisms that do not affect commercial rights or liberties.[56]

I begin with the difficulty of generalizing a principle of social justice across the range of commercial practices. Difficult commercial disputes take place at what could be called a postconstitutional level or after the basic terms of justice and the institutional arrangements have been settled. It is assumed that voluntary commercial activity enjoys prima facie moral standing by virtue of two institutional arrangements, private property and contractual liberty. Both of these institutions, qua rights and liberties, derive their moral legitimacy from what thinkers as diverse as John Rawls (a liberal egalitarian) and James Buchanan (a libertarian political economist) would describe as "basic social institutions" or "foundational rules," respectively. As Rawls says, "Justice is the first virtue of social institutions, as truth is of systems of thought."[57] Buchanan endorses a different conception of justice, but he shares Rawls' view that justice is the primary concern in formulating social institutions or what he calls "rules,"—"What justice requires depends on what particular rules individuals happen to have agreed to."[58] So, justice plays the vital role of morally justifying the institutions that define the rules of engagement for contemporary commercial life. But this application of justice is antecedent to the specific practices and disputes under investigation here.

Now, if private property and contractual freedom derive their prima facie moral standing from one or more theories of political justice, how are commercial outcomes that violate reasonable accounts of social justice (e.g., distributive inequities, unfair advantages, and so forth) to be justified or criticized? The quandary is this: Certain commercial outcomes might do violence to social justice but are nonetheless sanctioned behavior under a theory of political justice. Correcting them, that is, making them conform to a principle of social justice can be accomplished in isolation, but that principle cannot be generalized systematically such that all commercial behavior is required to conform to them. And the problem is not limited to distributional inequalities. Perhaps the more profound obstacle springs from the inherent conflict between free markets and most any account of social justice. Private property and contractual freedom set in motion the flurry of what Adam Smith called trucking, bartering, and exchanging, a great deal of which is based on individual preferences. These preferences in turn can be understood as a function of nearly any motive or attitude—from the account found in welfare economics (i.e., rationally self-interested utility maximizing) to the idiosyncratic, impulsive, irrational, eccentric, or benighted motives found in real people everywhere. What is certain is that the most important elements of social justice—fairness and equity—are occasional casualties of individual behavior based on human preferences. However, remedying this situation on anything other than a piecemeal basis requires wholesale changes in one of two things: individual attitudes (values, beliefs, and so forth) or contractual liberties.

This observation does not mean that employment discrimination or other insults to social justice should be tolerated or that correcting them is not a morally justified use of state power. However, it does imply that equality of opportunity or other principles of social justice are too blunt a reason for doing so in any systematic or general fashion. Consider this problem: In the domain of commercial life, where inequities are ubiquitous, how should those instances of unfairness that warrant market intervention be singled out? Brian Barry's commendable analysis of employment discrimination provides a clue.[59] He explains that employment discrimination in the United Kingdom is a mixed bag; it is illegal to discriminate on the basis of religion in Northern Ireland but not in Britain proper. Barry explains the difference in terms of the special function of religion in Northern Ireland, that it constitutes a "community." But I doubt whether Barry (or anyone else) would deny that religious discrimination takes place in London (e.g., toward Sikhs or Muslims) or that when it does, it, too, is an insult to social justice. So why is Barry sanguine toward this differential treatment of religion if his concern is one of equality of opportunity? Why do other egalitarian liberals in the United States worry about the job prospects of gays, lesbians, and African Americans but not those of unattractive or obese women, some of whom receive the shabbiest of treatment from prospective employers? If equality of opportunity is the goal, then it would seem that any such instances deserve equal condemnation and corrective action.

One possibility is that there is a practical limit to realizing ideals of any sort; society needs to "pick its shots," so to speak. The marketplace cannot be fortified against every bigoted or merely careless attitude that interferes with equal consideration of one's ability. Fair enough. So how should cases be distinguished and selected for regulatory relief: by the numbers of disadvantaged victims, by duration of their having been excluded, by the severity of their disenfranchisement, by their geographic location,[60] or by some other metric? A principle of equality (opportunity or otherwise) does not seem to have anything interesting to say about this. Insofar as equality is just the condition of being the same, every instance of job discrimination represents an identical event. Differences of magnitude, duration, or any other such factor should not matter if "equality" is at stake. Political equality seems to honor this logic. Violations of civil rights (say, voting) are candidates for correction; equally, all of them, and without regard to the severity or the duration because that is what it means to be politically equal. Accordingly, equality of opportunity requires that religious discrimination in Britain proper and in Northern Ireland be condemned equally because so far as such violations go, they are the same thing. And so is the treatment of the well-qualified but short, obese, tongue-tied, and bald male job applicant who competes against a slightly less qualified but tall, dark, handsome, and glib competitor.

Of course, there is something significantly different about religious discrimination in Northern Ireland versus that in London. And there is an important difference between racial discrimination in the United States and the shabby treatment of short, bald guys. But the difference cannot be explained in the language of equality alone. Rather, it requires appreciating the way Protestant business owners had systematically rejected Catholic job applicants or the way African American workers were denied access to entire categories of jobs or refused membership in labor unions prior to the passage of Title VII of the Civil Rights Act of 1964. The important difference is not only a function of the social pathology associated with these episodes, but also the nature of the harm done to individual members of these groups. Racial discrimination in the United States, by employers and by organized labor, created formidable obstacles against achieving any semblance of an autonomous commercial life for most African Americans. To be sure, their treatment was inequitable. But this factor does not begin to describe the systematic, prolonged, widespread, and therefore unavoidable nature of their treatment. The result—lives spent in low-wage jobs or chronic unemployment, an inability to exploit their abilities, and so forth—is substantively different from other instances of inequality in labor markets. Unattractive bald guys who miss out on an occasional job opportunity can work around their "bad" luck in the physical attribute lottery and lead otherwise rewarding commercial lives. The same could not be said for African Americans in the early 1960s. Focusing on obstacles to achieving commercial autonomy makes explicit the differences in these cases in a way that equality of opportunity does not.

I urge this principle of Commercial Autonomy over a principle of justice as a more realistic way to understand and correct for discriminatory attitudes. For states to remove obstacles to autonomy that are not of one's own making automatically qualifies the profound instances upon which general consensus can be achieved and disqualifies the frivolous cases. And unlike appeals to social justice, a principle of autonomy can be generalized and realized juridically throughout commercial life. Consequently, many of the same goals of social justice can be achieved without generating the distractions and nuisances that come from the unrealistic goals of achieving equality in commercial life.

I emphasize that this principle is intended as a part of a strategy for regulating commercial practices. Therefore, this discussion is not relevant to other domains where appeals to social justice may be perfectly appropriate. Efforts to redistribute income, promote educational opportunities, or other such mechanisms fall outside the boundaries of this study.

I do not suggest that this is the only Regulatory Strategy that warrants consideration or that mine is the only reasonable interpretation of these philosophical principles. There are other interpretations, alternative principles, and different methodological approaches to this topic. The remainder of this book evaluates this Regulatory Strategy in comparison to some of those other approaches.

Notes

1. Phillips Bradley, ed., *Democracy in America*, 2 vols. (1835; reprint, 1945, New York: Alfred A. Knopf), 2: 155.

2. Lewis Hyde, ed., *The Essays of Henry D. Thoreau* (New York: North Point Press, 2002), 197.

3. The inextricable relationship between circumstances and moral obligations is argued by Marcus Singer, *Generalization in Ethics* (New York: Knopf, 1961).

4. G. J. Warnock, *The Object of Morality* (London: Methuen & Co., 1971). In a similarly consequentialist vein, it is argued that promoting "some kind of cooperation or social activity between human beings" is the proper end of morality in W. K. Frankena, *Ethics* (Englewood Cliffs, N.J.: Prentice-Hall, 1970), 158.

5. George Will, "Reading China," *Washington Post*, 5 April 2001, 27A. Popular Chinese views diverge on this matter. See John J. Hanafin, "Morality and the Market in China," *Business Ethics Quarterly* 12 (January 2002): 1–18.

6. Jeremy Rifkin, *The Age of Access: The New Culture of Hypercapitalism, Where All of Life Is a Paid-For Experience* (New York: J. P. Tarcher, 2000), 11–12.

7. Charles E. Lindbloom, *Politics and Markets* (New York: Basic Books, 1977), 88.

8. James Willard Hurst, *Law and Markets in United States History* (Madison, Wis.: University of Wisconsin Press, 1982), 61.

9. See Marsha Baron, Phillip Petitt, and Michael Slote, *Three Methods of Ethics—A Debate: For and Against: Consequences, Maxims, and Virtues* (Oxford, U.K.: Blackwell Publishers, 1997).

10. See Charles Lamore, *Patterns of Moral Complexity* (Boston, Mass.: Cambridge University Press, 1987), 131–52. Virginia Held stakes a similar position in *Rights and Goods* (Chicago: University of Chicago Press, 1998). Andrew Oldenquist minimized these differences in "Rules and Consequences," *Mind* 75 (April 1966): 180. But the distinction has endured and would appear to be a reasonable and important one.

11. Tom Beauchamp, "On Eliminating the Distinction between Applied Ethics and Ethical Theory," *The Monist* 67, no. 4 (October 1984): 521.

12. Cf. John Kekes, *Against Liberalism* (Ithaca, N.Y.: 1997).

13. I discuss the role and use of principles in moral problem solving in "Managerial Moral Strategies: In Search of a Few Good Principles," *Academy of Management Review* 27, no. 1 (January 2002): 114–24. Also, see Tom Beauchamp and James Childress, *Principles of Biomedical Ethics*, 4th ed. (New York: Oxford University Press, 1994) for perhaps the most complete account of what has been described as specified principlism.

14. See Henry Richardson, "Specifying Norms as a Way to Resolve Concrete Ethical Problems," *Philosophy and Public Affairs* 19, no. 4 (Fall 1990): 279–310. Richardson criticizes other ways of resolving conflicting moral obligations in "Specifying, Balancing, and Interpreting Bioethical Principles," *Journal of Medicine and Philosophy* 25, no. 3 (June 2000): 285–307.

15. Lynn A. Jansen, "Assessing Clinical Pragmatism," *Kennedy Institute of Ethics Journal* 8, no. 1 (March 1998): 23–36. Also, Beauchamp and Childress are criticized by Carson Strong in "Specified Principlism: What Is It, and Does It Really Resolve Cases Better than Casuistry?" *Journal of Medicine and Philosophy* 25, no. 3 (June 2000): 323–41. This criticism is answered, adequately in my view, in Tom Beauchamp, "Reply to Strong on Principlism and Casuistry," *Journal of Medicine and Philosophy* 25, no. 3 (June 2000): 342–47.

16. Joseph J. Fins, Franklin G. Miller, and Mathew D. Bacchetta, "Clinical Pragmatism: Bridging Theory and Practice," *Kennedy Institute of Ethics Journal* 8, no. 1 (March 1998): 37–42.

17. Joseph Fins, Matthew Bacchetta, and Franklin Miller, "Clinical Pragmatism: A Method of Moral Problem Solving," *Kennedy Institute of Ethics Journal* 7 (June 1997): 129–45.

18. Fins, Bacchetta, and Miller, "Clinical Pragmatism: A Method," 141.

19. John Dewey, *Moral Principles in Education* (New York: Houghton Mifflin, 1909), 57.

20. John Dewey, *Creative Democracy—The Task before Us*, in John Dewey, *The Later Works, 1925–1953*, ed. Jo Ann Boydston (Carbondale, Ill.: University of Southern Illinois Press, 1981–1990), vol. 14, pp. 226–28. Cited in James T. Kloppenberg, "Pragmatism: An Old Name for Some New Ways of Thinking?" in Morris Dickstein, ed., *The Revival of Pragmatism* (Durham, N.C.: Duke University Press, 1998), 101.

21. Kloppenberg, "Pragmatism," 100.

22. Cf. Isaiah Berlin, *Two Concepts of Liberty* (Oxford, U.K.: Clarendon Press, 1958).

23. Most famous, perhaps, is Robert Nozick in *Anarchy, State, and Utopia* (New York: Basic Books, 1974). Whether that is an appropriate interpretation or not is questioned by many including Virginia Held, "John Locke on R. Nozick," *Social Research* 43 (Spring 1976): 169–95, and perhaps most damningly is Nozick's own *The Examined Life* (New York: Simon and Schuster, 1989): 286–89. But also, there is a popular appeal to Locke as well. James Gattuso, vice president of the Competitive Enterprise Institute, describing his libertarian think tank, says, "We're card-carrying, Locke-reading, Hayek-following lovers of liberty" (*CEI UpDate* 14, no. 6 [August 2001]: 2). Likewise, economic historian R. M. Hartwell makes reference to "political theories, owing much to Locke, that emphasized 'the natural right of life, liberty and property' and this provided the philosophical basis of *laissez faire*" in *The Industrial Revolution in England* (London: Historical Association, 1965), 8. This reference is repeated uncritically by Douglas North, "The Evolution of Efficient Markets," in *Capitalism in Context: Economic Development and Cultural Changes*, ed. John James and Mark Thomas (Chicago: University of Chicago Press, 1994): 257–78.

24. John Locke, *Two Treatises of Government*, ed. Peter Laslett (Cambridge, Mass.: Cambridge University Press, 1997). All parenthetical references in this section are to Book II of *The Second Treatise*.

25. Several commentators on Locke (cf. Robert A. Goldwin and Peter Laslett) have characterized the relationship between the state and the governed as a fiduciary one. However, a fiduciary relationship might imply different duties depending on the sort of fiduciary relationship intended by the grantor principal. In one case the fiduciary ought to act according to what is in the best interests of the principal (i.e., citizen). In another case the fiduciary ought to act in such a manner as the principal would have wanted, chosen, or willed. Commentators on Locke do not specify the sort of fiduciary relationship that Locke had in mind. Considering what it is that government is entrusted to care for on behalf of the governed, it is reasonable to impute the latter meaning, although for purposes of this discussion that is not vital.

26. For an expansive explication and subtle discussion of the state of nature in Locke's work, see A. John Simmons, *On the Edge of Anarchy: Locke, Consent, and the Limits of Society* (Princeton, N.J.: Princeton University Press, 1993).

27. Paschal Larkin, *Property in the Eighteenth Century: With Special Reference to England and Locke* (London: Cork University Press, 1930), 34.

28. Larkin, *Property*, 41.

29. See Laura Brace, *The Idea of Property in Seventeenth Century England, Tithes and the Individual* (Manchester, England: Manchester University Press, 1998). In particular, Brace points out that the Crown asserted its divine relationship with the Church and made a de facto claim on property as being God given. This idea served to justify state-imposed tithe-like taxes that fell heavily upon agricultural producers. Although direct ecclesiastical power

had been largely usurped by Parliament and the monarchy, its influence was still felt.

30. A. McRae, "Husbandry Manuals and the Language of Agrarian Improvement," in M. Leslie and T. Raylor, eds., *Culture and Cultivation* (Leicester and London, U.K.: Leicester University Press, 1992), 48.

31. Neal Wood, *John Locke and Agrarian Capitalism* (Berkeley: University of California Press, 1984), 13, goes so far as to describe Locke as a "theorist of early agrarian capitalism."

32. Locke emphasizes that "'tis *Labour* indeed that *puts the difference of value* on every thing"(§40). Though this may seem exaggerated, Locke explains that *everything*, from apples—God given but worthless until picked—to uncultivated fields, requires human effort to be of practical value.

33. The complexity of these claims and conflicting outlooks are discussed at length in Jerome Huyler, *Locke in America: The Moral Philosophy of the Founding Era* (Lawrence: University of Kansas Press, 1995). Huyer recognizes the pragmatic aspects of Locke's economic thinking as concerned with "the maximization of trade and wealth." But he also believes that these "prudential" considerations are "wholly consistent with the juridical conceptions adumbrated in his natural law and political writings" (169). Huyer reconciles these two seemingly disparate positions by way of a more expansive reading of Locke's natural law account of private property that leans heavily on Locke's theological commitments.

34. Huyer, *Locke in America*, 110, 111.

35. Karen Iverson Vaughn provides insightful commentary in *John Locke, Economist and Social Scientist* (Chicago: Chicago University Press, 1980).

36. Cf. Patrick Hyde Kelly, ed., *Locke on Money*. (Oxford, U.K.: Clarendon Press, 1996).

37. See Larkin, *Property*, 68.

38. See Karen Iversen Vaughn, *John Locke, Economist and Social Scientist* (Chicago: University of Chicago Press, 1980) and the collection of essays, *Locke on Money*, ed. Patrick Hyde Kelly (Oxford, U.K.: Clarendon Press, 1991).

39. Barbara Arneil, *John Locke and America, The Defence of English Colonialism* (Oxford, U.K.: Clarendon Press, 1996).

40. Laura Brace, *The Idea of Property in Seventeenth Century England, Tithes and the Individual* (Manchester, England: Manchester University Press, 1998).

41. Throughout this section, all parenthetical references are to J. S. Mill, *On Liberty* (Indianapolis, Ind.: Hackett Publishing, 1978) and all bracketed references are to his *Principles of Political Economy* (New York: August M. Kelley Publishers, 1969).

42. Cf. Section V of *On Liberty*.

43. I say "largely" because there can be no doubt that commerce involves personal tastes and preferences or that it factors into one's life plan. But commercial behavior itself is at minimum a binary affair, and therefore government has a legitimate interest in how it occurs.

44. Book V, *Of the Influence of Government,* and Chapter XI, *Of the Grounds and Limits of the Laissez-Faire or Non-Interference Principle.* There are two rea-

sons that support reading this text in conjunction with *On Liberty*. For one, they are generally consistent on commercial issues, although the *Principles* will push the issue much further than Mill does in *On Liberty*. But moreover, in Mill's *Autobiography* he confirms his strong attachment to *On Liberty*, which was published in 1859. Therefore, this text would overlap with the *Principles*, which was first published in 1848 but as a standard economics text went through seven reprintings, the last of which was in 1871.

45. In one place he says, "[L]*aissez-faire*, in short, should be the general practice: every departure from it, unless required by some great good, is a certain evil" [950]. In another he says,

> [A]s a general rule, the business of life is better performed when those who have an immediate interest in it are left to take their own course, uncontrolled either by the mandate of the law or by the meddling of any public functionary. The persons . . . who do the work, are likely to be better judges than the government, of the means of attaining the particular end at which they aim. . . . [T]he individual agents have so much stronger and more direct an interest in the result, that the means are far more likely to be improved and perfected if left to their uncontrolled choice. [953]

46. Mill *feared* the influence of commercial regulation on government generally. He worried that it would swell in size and stifle opportunities for personal development. For Mill, a spirit of freedom and distrust of tyranny were crucial factors in proper cultivation. He believed that such attitudes were likely to emerge from unconstrained human interaction, and the marketplace is as appropriate a venue as any. Alternatively, he feared that too much commercial regulation would not inculcate a spirit of freedom but "an unmeasured appetite for place and power; diverting the intelligence and activity of the country from its principal business to a wretched competition for the selfish prizes and the petty vanities of office" [950].

47. This formulation is more or less consistent with David Miller's responsibility view of freedom, "according to which an obstacle to someone's action counts as a constraint on their freedom if and only if another agent (or set of agents) is responsible for the existence of that obstacle" (*Principles of Social Justice*, Cambridge, Mass.: Harvard University Press, 1999, 14).

48. Brian Barry criticizes what he refers to as "Millian liberals" or those that interpret Mill as claiming "that it is the job of the state to promote autonomy." He grants that Mill recognized a connection between liberal institutions and the development of autonomous personalities. But he rejects the idea that Mill thought that states should engage in the "compulsory inculcation of autonomy" (*Culture and Equality*, Cambridge, Mass.: Harvard University Press, 2001), 120. The principle of autonomy formulated here does not contemplate compulsory autonomy or the inculcation of autonomous life, only the removal of obstacles.

49. See S. A. Baba, "Democracies and Inefficiency," *Economics and Politics*, 9 (July 1997): 99–114; D. Wittman, "Why Democracies Produce Efficient Results," *Journal of Political Economy* 97 (1989): 1395–1424; and D. Wittman,

The Myth of Democratic Failure: Why Political Institutions Are Efficient (Chicago: University of Chicago Press, 1995).

50. See J. A. Stimson, R. S. Erikson, and M. B. MacKuen, "Dynamic Representation," *American Political Science Review* 89 (1995): 543–65; and R. D. Arnold, *The Logic of Congressional Action* (New Haven, Conn.: Yale University Press, 1990).

51. See G. B. Powell Jr. and G. D. Whitten, "A Cross-National Analysis of Economic Voting: Taking Account of the Political Context," *American Journal of Political Science,* 37 (1993): 391–414.

52. D. P. Quinn and J. T. Woolley, "Democracy and National Economic Performance: The Preference for Stability," *American Journal of Political Science* 45 (2001): 634–57.

53. Quinn and Woolley, "Democracy and Performance."

54. For a detailed justification of this principle see my "David Hume and Economic Policy" in *Hume Studies* 26, no. 1 (April 2000): 143–58.

55. David Miller, *Principles of Social Justice* (Cambridge, Mass.: Harvard University Press, 2001), 1.

56. For instance, there is an undeniable imperative for equality of opportunity in what Jennifer Hochschild defines as the "socializing domain" (e.g., education). See *What's Fair? American Beliefs about Distributive Justice* (Cambridge, Mass.: Harvard University Press, 1981) and *Facing up to the American Dream* (Princeton, N.J.: Princeton University Press, 1995).

57. John Rawls, *A Theory of Justice* (Cambridge, Mass.: Harvard University Press, 1971), 3.

58. James Buchanan, *The Reason of Rules* (Cambridge, Mass.: Cambridge University Press, 1985), 98.

59. Brian Barry, *Culture and Equality: An Egalitarian Criticism of Multiculturalism* (Cambridge, Mass.: Harvard University Press, 2001), 54.

60. Many urban planners would prefer this one. In *Places Matter* (Lawrence, Kans.: University of Kansas Press, 2001), Peter Dreier, John Mollenkopf, and Todd Swanstrom make a compelling argument that a range of inequalities including income, education, and crime victimization are best understood in terms of geographic isolation. Importantly, their analysis controls for race and other such factors that are the basis of equal employment opportunity legislation.

2

Competing Reasons to Regulate: Values

The Communitarian Challenge

COMMUNITARIANS CRITICIZE what they see as an overemphasis (philosophically and otherwise) on individuals, including their rights and liberties to the exclusion of concerns for the communities in which individuals thrive. According to some advocates of the doctrine, communities are prior to, more fundamental than, and constitutive of individual selves and therefore are deserving of moral and political standing.[1] Generally speaking, communitarian literature is both critical and prescriptive. The critical variety identifies liberal weaknesses (inconsistency, ambiguity, contradictions, or some other such malady) and is largely theoretical and abstract in nature.[2] Liberals have responded to this literature by pointing out where communitarians either misunderstand or misinterpret liberalism in general and specific liberal thinkers in particular.[3] The prescriptive variety goes further and advocates specific government initiatives that would realize communitarian ideals.[4]

The focus here is on this second variety because it is difficult to impute substantive projects from abstract criticism of liberal thought. But also, the prescriptive variety of communitarianism provides philosophical underpinnings for a strain of popular thinking about commercial life. For instance, although they do not identify themselves as such, advocates of so-called smart growth development are best defended philosophically along communitarian lines. Likewise, those opposed to national retailers in defense of local merchants or the character of a small town voice a communitarian sentiment. And arguments against large-scale agricultural organizations and their threat to the viability of family farms and farm communities are often communitarian. Each of these instances, and many others, press the case that property or other commercial rights should not trump concerns for communities and the sort of people that are produced by them. Liberalism does not ignore commonwealth values or put individual freedom ahead of it in each and every case. However, it is fair to say that in the context of commercial life, community concerns only enter the picture when commercial practices affect it in pernicious ways (e.g., toxic discharges). Otherwise, there is a bias toward contractual freedom, and an assumption that communities will either benefit from economic activity or otherwise adjust to an altered landscape.

It might be appropriate to ignore communitarianism in light of the theoretical scholarly criticism it has endured. However, doing so fails to address its popular appeal: Why ought not members of Small Town, U.S.A., draw upon government authority to protect their way of life and the values they hold dear from the changes that a new Wal-Mart store will bring about? The Regulatory Strategy formulated here tends to ignore this refrain as a legitimate reason to regulate, so it behooves me to consider such appeals and argue against incorporating a communitarian principle as a morally justified reason to regulate.

Michael Walzer's Communitarian Project

I selected Walzer from the universe of communitarian thinkers because he is concerned with market regulation *and* distributive justice. This Regulatory Strategy is not a theory of distributive justice and claims that justice is not an appropriate moral principle by which to regulate commercial behavior. However, Walzer raises unavoidable concerns about the operation of markets, and it is incumbent upon me to see whether his claims are sound. I have also chosen to focus on Walzer because he is specific. Criticism of market activities must ultimately contend with particular goods and specific services, and Walzer addresses a host of them. Therefore, he provides a clear vision of commercial affairs guided by communitarian principles.[5] And Walzer is not a "straw communitarian" by any stretch of the imagination. His work is thorough, and his specific policy recommendations are argued clearly.

Although Walzer does not explicitly describe or label his work as communitarian, I treat it as such because his policy recommendations will often place social valuations ahead of individual rights. This is partly due to his understanding of freedom in a negative sense as the absence of domination or tyranny. To avoid tyranny, he calls for the distribution of goods based on their social meaning within a particular community. For Walzer, social meanings are shared understandings and commitments that can be gleaned from extant institutions and practices of a given community. He believes that to understand the social meaning of a good is also to understand its "distributive logic" or the appropriate way for it to be produced and distributed. Sometimes a good's distributive logic will conflict with distributional patterns based on individual rights, and in some such cases Walzer argues that rights ought to yield to social meanings.

In its most general formulation, Walzer's project aims to prohibit economic power from dominating the lives of others. To realize this end it will be necessary for states to ensure that goods do not distort, disrupt, or otherwise encroach upon socially determined patterns of distribution. That is, the community's values or shared understandings should determine how a good should be produced, to whom it should be distributed, and in what amounts. For Walzer, money is the primary culprit or subversive good because of its propensity to disrupt socially determined patterns of distribution. A word about Walzer's methodology may illuminate these abstract principles. First, he conceptualizes various "spheres" of life—work, leisure, the marketplace, office, communal provision, and so forth. He rejects the idea that there is any inherent quality of a given good that determines its rightful placement within any given sphere. Rather, he believes, placement should be based on the social meaning that a community attaches to a good. And Walzer recognizes that social meanings can change over time such that goods might shift from one sphere to another. Second, he claims that goods should circulate within a given sphere according to one of three different modes or "logics": free exchange, need, or desert. And this implies that goods should not be permitted to migrate into other spheres where they could corrupt the social meaning of the goods circulating in those spheres. For instance, the office of bishop in the Catholic Church should not be sold to the highest bidder because simony, which embodies free exchange, violates the distributive logic of desert, which is applicable to ecclesiastical affairs. Likewise, one's piety and knowledge of ecclesiastical law should have no bearing on one's access to commodities in the sphere of the marketplace. Walzer believes that if spheres of life are carefully differentiated and goods are segregated according to their rightful spheres then it will be difficult for people to dominate one another. Financial resources might be held unequally, but they would also be rendered useless with respect to goods outside the sphere of the marketplace. This idea is formulated into the rule that

> [n]o social good[6] x should be distributed to men and women who possess some other good y merely because they possess y and without regard for the meaning of x. (*SOJ*, 20)

It may appear that free markets would epitomize Walzer's rule insofar as most every free exchange expresses an individual understanding of the meaning of the good received and of that exchanged. But Walzer notes that although the individual agent expresses a personal interpretation of the meaning of a good in a market exchange, he or she does not necessarily express the social meaning of the good; "[f]ree exchange leaves distributions entirely in the hands of individuals, and social meanings are not subject, or are not always subject, to the interpretative decisions of men and women" (*SOJ*, 22). In particular, Walzer believes that money has a unique ability to contaminate the social meaning of some goods when they are "bought and sold." He goes so far as to say that "Money . . . is in practice a dominant good, and it is monopolized by people who possess a special talent for bargaining and trading—the green thumb of bourgeois society" (*SOJ*, 22). This idea is perhaps best illustrated when money has free rein in the political sphere. Vote buying contaminates the meaning of political goods (e.g., elected offices) and could undermine or debase the meaning of democracy. Money not only imports a foreign meaning to the shared understanding of democratic institutions; it also allows those with substantial resources to dominate others (*SOJ*, 22).

The key nonliberal aspect of Walzer's account is the nature of the reasons he gives for subordinating individual liberty—shared or community values. And it may seem from this that Walzer is therefore unconcerned for the welfare or liberty of individuals. However, that is too strong a reading, because at its base Walzer's project is designed to shelter the individual from tyrannical practices. His worry that property rights can sometimes undermine shared commitments is not simply a move to put the community ahead of the individual to the point that an individual would be worse off (although some might be). Rather, he believes that when people are allowed to use one good to monopolize, horde, or to gain exclusive access to other goods, then there is a significant risk that individual citizens could be tyrannized in the process. Walzer does not limit the role of a tyrant to political rulers but believes that in an advanced capitalist society it is possible for individual citizens to become tyrants through economic power. He emphasizes community as the starting point, with the ultimate goal being the insulation of individuals from tyrannical practices—be they of state or private origin.[7]

Defending against Communitarianism: The Electoral Marketplace

At this juncture, I pause to consider Walzer's use of the spheres in which he conceptualizes social experience. His example of vote selling is a poignant one that suggests a serious role for the way a community values various goods. His claim amounts to this: free-market ideology, in which one is free to buy and sell with abandon, implies an intolerable political system. Therefore, it is incumbent upon liberals to either construct a liberal reason against vote selling or admit that liberalism fails to adequately contend with some goods because it lacks the key intellectual resource, the way communities value goods. In the following I will provide that reason and shortly explain why it is preferable to an appeal to community valuations.

To better understand Walzer's position, it is helpful to unpack exactly why he worries about the practice of vote selling. Walzer's concern stems from his belief in or his commitment to a particular feature of democratic governance: majority rule. He believes that this is a shared understanding of American culture and worries that vote selling is antithetical to such a belief. And he worries that by undermining majority rule, vote selling opens the door for domination or, as he puts it, a tyrannical regime. So, Walzer's worry about vote selling makes two basic assumptions. One is that majority rule is a defense against tyranny. The other is that vote selling would destroy this feature of democracy. Some (e.g., J.-J. Rousseau) might argue with Walzer's analysis by claiming that majority rule does not protect against tyranny. Others might claim that the practice of vote selling does not jeopardize majority rule.[8] In order to respond to Walzer on his own terms I will not challenge either of these assumptions. Rather, I will assume that he is right and present a response cast in terms of this Regulatory Strategy.

The starting point is Mill's idea that states can legitimately intervene in a commercial transaction that causes a serious loss to an individual's liberty or autonomy. Vote selling might be conceived in these terms by recalling the reasons why Mill thought that one should not be allowed to sell oneself into slavery, that doing so defeats the chances for living an autonomous life. Now, selling one's vote is not nearly as straightforward an autonomy-defeating practice as selling one's self into slavery is. Unlike slavery, it is possible to sell one's vote without any diminution in one's liberty or autonomy—life might very well be unchanged (or even improved upon) for any given vote seller in an isolated election. The sale of a few votes here and there might not affect the outcome of an election. But this is not the scenario that motivates Walzer's worry. Rather, it is the wholesale destruction of the institution of democracy by undermining majority rule. And if Walzer is even close to being right—that a loss of majority rule could produce tyrannical political conditions—then this Regulatory Strategy would be equally anxious to block such a practice. However, the concern would not be based on the way in which the community values political goods but on the connection between majority rule and Negative Commercial Liberty and Autonomy.[9]

This Regulatory Strategy can respond to Walzer's concerns about vote selling by direct reference to individual liberty and autonomy. Walzer's worry about a free market in political goods is misplaced because according to this construction, such a market is not free so much as it is unconstrained. And this Regulatory Strategy is not blindly committed to unconstrained markets. It may be argued that I have simply changed the rules in midstream, and in a sense I have. Where communitarianism takes aim at radically unconstrained markets I am substituting and defending the idea of markets that are not candidates for intervention on the basis of the principles of Negative Commercial Liberty or Commercial Autonomy; I call them Ideally Free Markets. My move would be unfair if I were intent on impugning communitarianism, however, that is not my goal. Rather, I am only trying to determine whether this Regulatory Strategy can withstand communitarian criticism.

In this chapter I will also be interested in determining whether this Regulatory Strategy has anything to recommend it over the communitarian approach to market regulation. As the policy recommendations in the foregoing example were identical, it is not apparent that there is any such advantage or disadvantage. However, there is one aspect of this example that might favor the approach of this Regulatory Strategy over communitarianism. This Regulatory Strategy applied a fairly abstract, albeit empirical, test to the commercialization of voting practices—the reasonably expected consequences for individual liberty and autonomy. In contrast, communitarianism applied a standard that was embedded in the community and evident in extant institutions. The concern that the communitarian method raises in this case is this: What would the answer be if American attitudes drifted away from these values? Would communitarianism have any basis for objecting to the practice of vote selling? That is, if the American community became enamored with, say, Platonic guardianships or rule by a wealthy aristocracy, it is not clear that Walzer would have a communitarian objection to vote selling. At least it would not seem to be a quarrel based on communitarian ideals. In such cases, majority rule would no longer be valued and vote selling might be the best expression of the way the community valued political power. I do not mean to suggest this possibility as a wholesale condemnation of communitarianism, because Walzer might have respectable responses to the picture I am painting. However, I would suggest that there is at least a methodological advantage to the liberal response, insofar as it makes a direct appeal to the more objective standards of liberty and autonomy. And if Walzer's worry is with tyranny, then it would seem that direct appeals to liberty and autonomy would be more effective defenses against oppression than would appeals to potentially unstable community values. My point is that this Regulatory Strategy may offer a more resilient defense against tyranny because it does not try to contend with or placate community values.[10]

I now turn to another example that will illustrate other points of departure between the two approaches and further aspects of communitarianism that are critical of this Regulatory Strategy.

Defending against Communitarianism: Legal Aid

I provide the following lengthy quote relative to the provision of legal aid because it further reveals Walzer's use of values and justice in the regulation of commerce.

> If accused men and women are to receive their rightful share of justice, they must first have a rightful share of legal aid. Hence the institution of the public defender and the assigned counsel: just as the hungry must be fed, so the accused must be defended; and they must be defended in proportion to their needs. But . . . [t]he rich and the poor are treated differently in American courts, though it is the public commitment of the courts to treat them the same. The argument for a more generous

provision follows from that commitment. If justice is to be provided at all, it must be provided equally for all accused citizens without regard to their wealth. . . . I don't mean to underestimate the practical difficulties here; but this, again, is the inner logic of provision . . . Legal aid raises no theoretical problems because the institutional structures for providing it already exist, and what is at stake is only the readiness of the community to live up to the logic of its own institutions. (*SOJ*, 85)

For Walzer, extant institutions of public legal defense (aid) provide evidence of and satisfy the logic of the shared understanding that the indicted ought to be defended, regardless of their ability to pay for it. That is, the sphere of life that includes criminal justice demands that legal defense be meted out according to need and not desert or market exchange. And Walzer bemoans the inequalities in the U.S. criminal justice system—that those with substantial personal resources can procure a higher-quality defense. The culprit in this scenario is money and the way it violates the logic of need. Money, Walzer believes, should be restricted to the sphere of the marketplace (where commodities circulate) and not be allowed to trespass into other spheres. Although Walzer is not explicit as to what should be done, the only possibility that comports with his project is this: States must ensure that legal defense services are provided on an equal basis to every defendant. In a nutshell, this is what it means to segregate activities and goods into their socially determined spheres.

The antiliberal feature of this methodology is the lack of recognition of the liberty to contract for legal services. Of course, liberals would agree with communitarians that defendants deserve to be defended regardless of their ability to pay. But this does not require that legal defense services be treated outside of market practices. Rather, it requires that the market for legal services function in an Ideally Free fashion. A primary consideration in criticizing the market for legal services is whether it functions in such a way that threatens the liberty or autonomy of individual citizens. Such a threat could come about if poorly trained or incompetent practitioners were permitted to sell their services to unsuspecting consumers. So the licensing and policing activities of state boards and bar associations comports with the principles of this Regulatory Srategy. Moreover, one's inability to pay for legal services poses a grave threat to one's liberty by increasing dramatically the odds of being incarcerated wrongfully. Consequently, the market for criminal defense services is not one that should be allowed to operate without intervention.

The question is, beyond licensure and oversight, what sort of intervention is appropriate to the risk borne by the indigent defendant? To satisfy this Regulatory Strategy, it must be selective and limited to alleviating the violation of the principles of Negative Commercial Liberty and Commercial Autonomy. And in doing so, it must not run roughshod over the rights and liberties of others. The solution involves state provision of funds or services to those in need (probably more so than at present) but would not involve anything else. In particular, it does not prevent those with substantial personal resources from using them to mount a defense. How does this seemingly callous disregard for justice fare against Walzer's solution? Recall that the logic of need implies that *all* defendants be treated the *same* in terms of providing them with legal defense services. I have argued against such egalitarian appeals, here, in a domain that seems to demand one. Indeed, the wealthy stand a better chance of avoiding incarceration (O. J. Simpson jumps to mind). But recall, the overarching objective of Walzer's project is to eliminate opportunities for domination, and inequality of criminal defense services does not contribute to that end. That is, although Simpson's extraordinary defense could be seen as "buying" his way to freedom, his doing so was not at the expense of someone else's liberty. There is no straightforward way for Walzer to get from the claim that need ought to control the distribution of legal services to his call for the egalitarian treatment of the accused.

This point deserves some elaboration. Walzer recognizes that any strict egalitarian distribution of goods is utopian but believes that justice can be realized when no one possesses the means of domination. Equality is not a good in its own right but only insofar as it prevents the opportunities for domination.

> [N]o more bowing and scraping, fawning and toadying; no more fearful trembling; no more high-and-mightiness; no more masters, no more slaves. It [equality] is not a hope for the elimination of differences; we don't all have to be the same or have the same amounts of the same things. Men and women are one another's equals (for all important moral and political purposes) when no one possesses or controls the means of domination. (*SOJ*, xiii)

This means that O. J. Simpson's use of his wealth to provide for his defense should not insult Walzer's notion of equality. As Simpson did not use his personal funds to leverage himself into some advantage that subjugated or dominated others, it is unclear why it would offend Walzer's notion of justice.[11] Disparate treatment of similarly situated defendants might offend one's sense of fairness, but communitarians are highly critical of justice as fairness, at least the variety proposed by Rawls.

However, there are other reasons why community valuations might be a flawed way to regulate markets. First, as others have pointed out, a shared belief is an empirical matter and subject to possibly contentious interpretations.[12] State-provided legal aid would appear to be a fairly uncontroversial shared understanding, yet it is not beyond the realm of honest disagreement as to what is implied or entailed by it. The exact nature of that shared belief—its specific content and limits—is not obvious from the (some might say) fairly shabby institutions of public defense in some jurisdictions. Walzer claims that we have a commitment to legal aid and that what remains is for us to live up to it. But that assumes that we agree on what it is that we are supposed to live up to. Whatever that shared belief might be, it is not clear that it involves a commitment to providing all defendants with the *same* level of legal defense. It might, but even then it is not clear that the shared belief or value is one that prohibits individuals from using their resources to enhance their chances for success in a criminal trial. A shared belief is at best a starting point and an ambiguous one at that.

Second, if a shared value of a defined community could be specified and shown to be universally shared, it is likely that it would conflict with some other equally well-defined and shared value. If so, then there is little reason to hope that such values could serve to mediate contentious commercial disputes. In the case of criminal defense services, Walzer's methodology leads to the conclusion that wealthy and indigent defendants deserve equivalent criminal defense services, implying that wealthy defendants should not be allowed to purchase additional services. While the provision of criminal defense services to those lacking in resources can be located in a shared belief, the denial of the wealthy defendant's contractual freedom cannot. Indeed, another widely shared community value is that individuals should be free to expend their resources as they see fit, provided that doing so does not harm others. Among the visceral reactions to the O. J. Simpson trial, Simpson's right to use his personal resources to engage counsel was not among them. Walzer's remedy solves one problem (aligning the values within the sphere of justice) while creating another of the same variety (imposing an inappropriate value within the sphere of the marketplace). This relatively straightforward case suggests that shared beliefs may be tangled up with others that present intractable conflicts. And this is not an isolated case. Virtually every policy prescription Walzer and several other communitarians advance conveniently ignores their impact upon the way people value their market freedom.

This criticism of communitarianism leaves open the question of whether a Regulatory Strategy based on principles of freedom and autonomy would fare any better in resolving this issue. Walzer's call for the regulation of criminal defense services to achieve an egalitarian result is laudable but not justified, even within the confines of communitarian thinking. On the other hand, this Regulatory Strategy ignores egalitarianism and is concerned only with the liberty and autonomy of criminal defendants. As callous as this sounds, it might be more desirable in terms of the criminal defendants whose interests are at stake in this example. The ambiguities involved in interpreting the shared understandings with regard to legal aid do not necessarily argue for the outcome that Walzer thinks they do. In all probability there are only two unimpeachable community values relative to the indigent defendant: that some defense is required and that the resources to provide O. J.-type defenses for every accused defendant impose an unrealistic financial burden on states. Every other value would seem to be subject to dispute. This Regulatory Strategy avoids these ambiguities by ignoring community valuations and focusing instead on the criminal defendant, his or her liberty and personal autonomy. I do not mean to imply that it is precisely clear what is involved in respecting the defendant's liberty and autonomy, but divining the community's attitudes is not necessary. Determining what counts as respecting the defendant's liberty and autonomy lends itself to an objective determination based on the skill and experience of legal counsel. Moreover, this determination permits the state to selectively intervene in the market for criminal defense services without impinging on the liberty of wealthy defendants and lawyers alike.

Nonetheless, there *is* something unfair about the O. J. Simpson scenario, and this Regulatory Strategy seems to just avoid the issue. And that is a fair criticism. A noncommunitarian view of justice, one rooted in fairness, argues for treating similar cases similarly. However, intervention to achieve such fairness creates injustices of its own, perhaps worse ones. This Regulatory Strategy advocates that the state should provide vigorous defenses that are deemed to be adequate on the basis of experts in criminal justice. But wherever that level would be set, there will always be some additional service that the legal profession will make available to those with the resources to buy it. The question is whether such purchases ought to be blocked. Doing so would achieve an egalitarian outcome but at the price of subjecting those willing and able to pay for it to the risk of wrongful incarceration. The suggestion here is that states ought to concede an element of unfairness in deference to permitting individuals to mount the most vigorous defense possible. The inegalitarian outcome seems to be justified by the absence of any viable alternatives.

Defending against Communitarianism: Medical Care

I now consider Walzer's communitarian treatment of the healthcare market, in which he affords his reader a more detailed understanding of his communitarian ideals. I will respond critically to his conclusions but also present an argument that justifies government provision of some goods based on a commitment to Ideally Free Markets.

Based on his identification of a shared understanding, Walzer defines the distributive logic of healthcare goods (or services) "proportionate to illness and not to wealth" (*SOJ*, 86). So, as was the case with legal aid, the distributive logic of health care is need and not desert or free exchange. The basis for this logic is our shared belief that "longevity is a socially recognized need; and increasingly every effort is made to see that it is widely and equally distributed, that every citizen has an equal chance at a long and healthy life: hence doctors and hospitals in every district, regular check-ups, health education for the young, compulsory vaccination, and so on" (*SOJ*, 87). Walzer believes that this commitment follows from another shared belief that is a feature of American culture, that disease is tantamount to plague and if it "can be dealt with, it must be dealt with" (*SOJ*, 88). The *must* in the preceding sentence is a moral one based on a want "so widely and deeply felt that it can plausibly be said that it is the want not of this or that person alone but of the community generally—a human want." According to Walzer, this want implies that healthcare should not circulate in the market but, rather, states should deliver care directly. He fears that so long as a system of free enterprise exists, medical care will be distributed based on one's ability to pay as opposed to one's need (*SOJ*, 89). Otherwise, chances of realizing the social meaning of healthcare cannot be realized.[13]

The fact that wealth influences the distribution and quality of health care in the United States flies in the face of the distributive logic that

Walzer believes is imbedded in medical care. He believes that physicians are the culprits in this matter.

> [A]ny fully developed system of medical provision will require the constraint of the guild of physicians. Indeed, this is more generally true: the provision of security and welfare requires the constraint of those men and women who had previously controlled the goods in question and sold them on the market . . . For what we do when we declare this or that good to be a needed good is to block or constrain its free exchange . . . Needed goods cannot be left to the whim or distributed in the interest of some powerful group of owners or practitioners. (*SOJ*, 89)

So, consistent with other national needs such as defense, "ownership is abolished" and physicians should be "conscripted" into public service in order to deliver medical care in accordance with the needs of people and not the personal ambitions of physicians. Walzer sees no need to "respect the doctor's market freedom. Needed goods are not commodities" although he thinks there might be a case for allowing them to be traded above a "level fixed by democratic decision making" (*SOJ*, 90).

I will not engage in a detailed criticism of Walzer's case for nationalizing the American health care industry. For one thing, his analysis is dated, and although the problems he cites remain troubling, recent developments might influence his conclusion were he writing today. My concern is more with the nature of the reasons that he believes justify the intervention he advocates. Again, the problem of conflicting and ambiguous values infects this case in the same way as that of legal aid. The failed Clinton healthcare initiative and the ongoing debate thereafter brought to the surface a number of incompatible attitudes. But also, nationalization would seem to conflict with at least three other shared beliefs. First, the Clinton healthcare reform also revealed a generally held belief or fear of the federal and state governments taking over the healthcare industry. Whether the fear was justified or not is not as important as is its existence. Walzer ignores it. Second, as in the case of legal aid, there would seem to be a shared understanding that individuals should be able to use their funds to acquire extraordinary or superior medical care. Walzer mentions this as a possibility but as values go, it is secondary at best. And third, there would seem to be a widely held belief that medical practitioners ought to be able to sell their services. The notion of state conscription conflicts with a shared belief about ownership of one's labor and the freedom to deploy it with some modicum of market freedom. Walzer makes an analogy with national defense and other services whose provision should be based on need. Whether his analogy goes through is not of concern. But it is relevant that a call to nationalize the services of medical practitioners runs counter to a deep-seated sentiment that respects market freedom.

In short, Walzer is right to recognize that the market for healthcare ought in to be responsive to human health needs. However, his policy prescriptions ignore or severely diminish the regulatory importance of every other competing value. Setting aside the illiberal nature of his recommendations, this is an arbitrary move on strictly communitarian grounds. The shared understandings of the American community he deals with offer too many ambiguous and conflicting sentiments to steer abruptly in any single direction—compromise is essential. However, Walzer is right to criticize a market that distributes a crucially important good like healthcare such that some people get as much of it as they need or want while others may not receive any at all or receive care of an inferior quality. Such a market fails to satisfy the moral principles of this Regulatory Strategy and is therefore a candidate for intervention. The question is whether these principles can respond to the defects of the market for medical care any better than communitarianism does. In particular, I am challenged to determine whether this Regulatory Strategy can satisfy what is a clear violation of distributive justice without doing violence to the liberty and autonomy of producer and consumer alike.

To respond to the distributional defects of the market in medical care requires expanding or following to their logical conclusion the moral principles that inform Ideally Free Markets. In the case of legal aid I argued that the state ought to fund the costs of legal defense for indigent defendants but otherwise leave the legal services market unmolested. I might have elaborated that case and traced my argument to Locke's claim that the state serves as a fiduciary to protect individuals from the harms of others. In the case of indigent defendants, the risk protected against is that of the criminal justice system. Medical care parallels the legal aid case, but it is also substantively different. It is similar in the sense that one's failure to receive adequate medical care can sometimes be harmful and imperil one's autonomy. However, it is harmful in a different way than the failure to receive legal representation. The harm associated with the lack of legal representation seems consistent with Locke's call for the state to protect citizens against the harms of aggressive others—in this case the prosecution. However, medical care is different because there is not necessarily an identifiable aggressor. There is no responsible agent to be constrained, no foreign aggressor, no violent or coercive intruder to be turned away or punished. Consequently, the provision of medical care does not seem to follow in any straightforward way from a principle of negative liberty or the right to be left alone.

The importance of medical care is best thought of in terms of one's ability to lead an autonomous life. The victim of a life-threatening disease or injury is clearly in danger of losing that capacity. Most recognize that states ought to intervene in the medical care market to provide life-saving emergency care—hence state "antidumping" laws applicable to hospitals. And at the other end of the spectrum, no one seriously argues that the state ought to fund the cost of Botox treatments. The controversy is focused on the wide swath of services between the two extremes and whether the market distribution of those services jeopardizes the capacity to function autonomously.

The moral dimension of medical services depends upon how they are characterized. Norman Daniels describes the central function of healthcare as its ability to "keep us functioning as close to normal as possible."[14] For Daniels, such "normal functioning" is crucial not just because it affects "our opportunities to gain access to education, jobs, or offices . . . but also our opportunities to carry out the kind of goals or tasks in life that all reasonable people may want to pursue, including engaging in meaningful social interaction with friends, family and colleagues; carrying out the tasks of daily living; and engaging in avocations . . ."[15] Daniels makes this claim in his argument for universal access to a "basic tier of services." I am not so much interested in his argument for universal access as much as I am in the apt connection he draws between healthcare and the possibility of leading an autonomous life in contemporary American society. This Regulatory Strategy describes an Ideally Free Market as one that does not interfere with one's Commercial Autonomy. However, putting this in the negative does not impugn the healthcare market—the market does nothing to imperil one's autonomy and is not deserving of intervention. Rather, the lack of financial resources puts someone's autonomy at risk. Rectifying this failure is not a matter of intervening in the market, because it is not the causal agent in diminishing personal autonomy. That does not mean that action is not required. However, it does mean that such action should not be directed at the healthcare providers.

Eliminating the healthcare market as the culprit leaves but one alternative: state provision of financial resources or services to those denied access to the market. The basis for provision is the nature of the good itself, what could be called "essential" goods (or services). This concept is an extension of, or a more specific instance of, the notion of the state's interest in the autonomy of individual citizens. However, it makes this principle specific to the provision of some goods not delivered to some citizens by way of the market. It is justified on the basis of a prior commitment to personal autonomy. Call a good or service essential if it meets the following criteria. First, it is something without which it is highly unlikely that any recognized version of a good commercial life can be achieved. Said another way, lacking access to essential goods and services virtually guarantees that one will live a bad commercial life. And second, it is something for which there is no substitute or alternative good (or service). At perhaps the most primitive level, food is clearly an essential good because unless one's nutritional needs are satisfied it is impossible to achieve any version of a good life, commercial or otherwise.

I recognize that the concept of a "good life" is a contentious idea whose meaning has been debated ad infinitum. However, the goal here is not to try to determine its meaning or to deny the multitude of meanings in a pluralistic society. For my purposes, it is only necessary that there is such a thing as recognized good lives. Defining essential goods in this way does not endorse one of these interpretations over the other or suggest that there is an ideal one. So long as there are such things, then the concept of an essential good has a referent. It might better be said that so long as there are notions of "bad lives," something upon which agreement can be reached more easily, the concept of essential goods has substance. It is also important to note that an essential good is relative to the society in which it is being evaluated. So a good that is essential to contemporary life in America would not necessarily be essential in a seventeenth-century colonial setting. (And this stands to reason, as goods come and go, the meaning of a good or a bad life is subject to change.) In this way the principles of this Regulatory Strategy do not preclude efforts to achieve distributive justice or the welfare aspirations of liberalism writ large.[16] But they preclude direct market intervention as a means of achieving them. This Regulatory Strategy is concerned to regulate the operation of markets such that they do not impinge upon individual liberty or autonomy. When markets in essential goods fail to distribute their goods to those in need of them then state provision of funds to the needy, not market intervention, is called for.

Repairing Communitarianism:
Elizabeth Anderson

The flaws in Walzer's communitarianism undermine it as a justificatory theory of market intervention. But in *Value in Ethics and Economics*[17] (subsequently referred to as *Value*), Elizabeth Anderson advances
a novel and thoughtful approach that retains a regulatory role for values while sidestepping the normative defects of communitarianism.
Her thinking is subtle and hard to classify, but it is perhaps the best
hope for rescuing communitarianism. She de-emphasizes the way a
community values things and seeks instead to discern and confer regulatory authority to rationally determined values. And unlike Walzer,
she does not countenance market intervention as a means of achieving
social justice first and individual liberty second. Rather, her objective
is the more straightforward liberal[18] commitment to individual freedom and autonomy. However, it should be noted that Anderson's
understanding of these terms is somewhat idiosyncratic: freedom is
"access to a wide range of significant options through which [one] can
express [one's] diverse valuations" (*Value*, 141); autonomy is "govern
[ing] [oneself] by principles and valuations [one] reflectively
endorses" (*Value*, 142). Anderson's concern for commercial life is that
market norms can insinuate themselves into areas of life in which they
do not belong and thereby interfere with the way noncommercial
goods and practices should be valued. Her greatest worry is that these
rogue norms would undermine the possibility for expressing fully
one's values or governing one's self according to one's reflectively
endorsed valuations. In either event, given her account of autonomy,
Anderson fears that inappropriate norms imperil personal freedom.
Although she claims the mantle of liberalism, Anderson's emphasis
on values warrants consideration in the context of communitarianism.
It should be emphasized that I am only concerned with a narrow slice
of her wide-ranging project. In particular, I focus on Anderson's theoretical and practical account of markets but ignore a large portion of
her account of practical reasoning.[19] Hers is a formidable effort that
has deservedly received considerable attention.[20] However, the present
discussion is limited to her proposal to treat rational values as reasons
to intervene in commercial markets. First I will uncritically sketch her
ideas, and in the next section I will evaluate her conclusions.

The key to Anderson's approach to market regulation can be
located in her "rational attitude theory of value" and her "expressive

theory of rational action" (*Value*, 17), and in her belief that attitudes about goods can be subjected to rational criticism. She is not interested in the spontaneous experience of positive attitudes, tastes, or preferences. Rather, she is concerned with thoughtful judgments that something is valuable. Consequently, for Anderson, attitudes are not simply a "given" in the sense that economists treat preferences. For her, a proper valuation is one in which the object of valuation conforms to the reflectively endorsed standards applicable to the good. The idea that the way we value things can be rationally determined or criticized provides the framework for Anderson's approach to regulating commercial life. Unlike Walzer, Anderson endorses the liberal commitment to pluralism and its call for a system of rights ensuring a private sphere of life. But for her, pluralism can be understood as applying to goods that differ from one another in virtue of the way they should be rationally or properly valued. This means that in addition to Mill's private/public demarcation, Anderson argues for further differentiation within the social sphere based on categories of goods and the norms that guide their proper valuation. For instance, buying and selling things like votes or children perverts the ways in which democracy and human beings respectively should be valued. Cordoning off these goods into protective spheres—free of commercial influence—makes their proper valuation possible. If Walzer's project is intended to achieve justice through a multiplicity of protective spheres, Anderson's aim is freedom and autonomy through protective spheres that allow goods to be properly valued.[21]

Anderson is interested to discover those goods and services that should circulate according to market norms and those that should not. She wants to align the norms that control the production and circulation of a good with the norms that guide its proper valuation. For example, she describes the norms that govern the production and circulation of goods in markets and finds them to be consistent with the way we properly value commodities or "use" goods. These goods are properly valued as instrumental or as a means to achieve some other end. Accordingly, they are subordinated to one's private (or exclusive) use. But other goods are properly valued in terms of norms that are wholly different than those that guide (and should guide) markets. These goods might have intrinsic (as opposed to use) value (e.g., a family heirloom) or may be nonexclusive or shared things (e.g., a historic site). Also, Anderson cites "goods embodied in the person," such as a woman's reproductive labor or personal relationships that are properly valued by norms that are inconsistent with those that guide market activities. Accordingly, these goods should not circulate in markets but in "gift exchanges"[22] or according to some other methodology. For instance, the norms that guide gift exchanges are consistent with the way shared goods are properly valued. And Anderson recognizes that some goods are valued according to several different modes of valuation. Legal services are properly valued for their intrinsic *and* their instrumental worth. Mixed goods require creative solutions. She suggests creative thinking about quasi-market institutions (e.g., private nonprofit organizations) for their production and distribution.

The regulatory importance of this analysis is the link Anderson makes between valuations and individual autonomy. She believes that autonomy is at stake when the norms that govern the production or distribution of something conflict with the way the good should be properly valued. This follows from her understanding of personal autonomy as the expression of reflectively endorsed valuations, because the hegemony of market norms could deprive one of his or her ability to express such a value. Consequently, Anderson advocates market intervention for one of two reasons. For one, "[c]onstraints [of the market] may be needed to secure the robust sphere differentiation required to create a significant range of options through which people can express a wide range of valuations" (*Value*, 143). For instance, if friendship were bought and sold, the opportunity to express the proper value toward friendship would be destroyed; indeed, the good would be debased and unavailable for proper valuation. Secondly, Anderson urges market intervention "to protect individuals or collective autonomy" (*Value*, 143). This reason sounds different from the first, but given Anderson's account of freedom and autonomy as linked to the expression of rational values, it appears to be essentially the same.

Anderson provides three stages of analysis for deploying this abstract framework to concrete cases. First, if the proper valuation of a good is the starting point for understanding its rightful mode of production and distribution, then such valuation must be determined. Second, the norms that govern market behavior and those that are operative in nonmarket institutions must be specified. Finally, a comparison must be made between the two and examined for agreement or conflict. If the norms governing the way a good is properly valued agree with those guiding its production and distribution, then market intervention is not justified. Alternatively, if there is a conflict, then corrective action may be required. This might mean removing the good from market circulation and producing and distributing it in some more appropriate fashion. She encapsulates this analysis as follows:

> First, do market norms do a better job of embodying the ways we properly value a particular good than norms of other spheres? If not, then we shouldn't treat them as commodities but rather locate them in nonmarket spheres. Second, do market norms, when they govern the circulation of a particular good, undermine important ideals such as freedom, autonomy, and equality, or important interests legitimately protected by the state? If so, the state may act to remove the good from control by market norms. (*Value*, 144)

Anderson does not provide a detailed empirical study beyond this sketch.[23] But her approach can be illustrated with her example of professionals who sell their services. She worries that selling such services compromises the norms that should control the way legal and medical services are delivered. That is, when professional services are provided for profit, market norms might crowd out or contaminate the norms that determine excellence in professional services. Her worry is that the way, say, legal services should be valued—according to norms internal to the law—can be perverted by external ones such as profitability. Rather than aspire to the high ideals of the profession, lawyers in profit-making firms might become "hired guns" for malicious clients who want to use the law to bully or harass others. Likewise, if artists were employed in profit-making firms, they might pander to popular tastes and ignore the norms that define artistic merit; doctors might perform unnecessary procedures; and so forth. But Anderson does not condemn the commercialization of professional services, because she also recognizes that the alternatives to market freedom (e.g., artistic and medical patrons or state provision) are sometimes antithetical to the autonomy of artists or physicians. Consequently, she promotes hybrid or not-for-profit institutions that would uphold the proper valuation of professional or artistic services but also respect the market freedom of producers.

This overly brief account of Anderson's project is intended to describe her methodology and illuminate the way she justifies market intervention. The following criticism is offered gingerly, insofar as she admits that applications of her theory are tentative and ultimately dependent upon rigorous empirical analysis. In that spirit I will first express an objection of an empirical nature: the veracity of her descriptive account of market norms. This matters because conflicting norms are the basis upon which Anderson would block the commercialization of a good. But this is not intended as a debate about the precise nature of market norms.[24] Nor do I debate whether commercial life is normatively distinct in comparison with other nonmarket realms.[25] Rather, I recognize that market behavior exhibits elements of the norms Anderson cites. And I grant that a substantive differentiation can be made between commercial and noncommercial life. However, I will argue that the normative overlap between these two worlds is too profound to arrive at any meaningful generalization about the normative logic of either. If my account is even partially accurate, then there is faint hope of granting values any normative importance that rises to the level of regulatory justification. Alternatively, if I am wrong and commercial norms are distinct and different from those in other walks of life, then another problem arises. Anderson bases her case to regulate on the basis of conflicts in values on the damage that inappropriate norms do to noncommercial goods (e.g., market norms as applied to friendship). But this claim is also subject to empirical analysis, and I will argue that it is but a prima facie reason to regulate. Whether such fears truly warrant coercive intervention depends upon whether there is actually some change to the character of the good itself. The upshot of this criticism is that, in most cases, norms and values do not provide justified reasons to regulate. They signal the need for investigation but, except in those rare instances bereft of contention (e.g., neighborhood aesthetics), they should not be treated as conclusive.

Proper Values and Market Intervention

Anderson characterizes commercial life as guided by this cluster of norms: impersonal and egoistic,[26] want-regarding,[27] exclusivity or rivals in consumption,[28] and exit and not voice.[29] Although she suggests these norms as a tentative sketch, it is improbable that this or any other such idealization can be plausibly formulated. Simply put, commerce is far too complex to generalize a single description across the range of goods and services. At best, this analysis would need to be carried out on a case-by-case, market-by-market basis. But it is unrealistic that the norms that guide the behavior of a currency trader or a hedge fund operator in New York City are the same ones that motivate a veterinarian in Omaha. Consider the first one, that the behavior of commercial actors is governed by egoistic norms. In many instances, treating customers, suppliers, employees, and so forth according to a norm of impersonal egoism—as a mere means—is not rewarded but punished by the market.[30] The extent of actual egoistic behavior observed in any given market is mediated by countervailing forces. Perhaps commercial actors shun egoism out of prudential concerns, although their motivation is difficult to determine.[31] More important, their reasons for moderating their egoistic behavior are irrelevant to the question at hand: the descriptive veracity of a norm of egoism. At a minimum, the ubiquitous exceptions to this ascription prohibit generalizing it across the range of commercial behavior. Consider this utter rejection of egoism as expressed by Benjamin F. Edwards, Chief Executive Officer of A. G. Edwards, Inc.:

> Our philosophy is that the only legitimate purpose of any corporation or institution is to benefit its customers. If we had financial goals, too often the client would be "used" to achieve them. Our clients should be served and not used. It is our challenge to deliver value for what we charge and to do it so efficiently and cost effectively that we can have "profit" left over which we can use to reward our employees and our shareholders and to reinvest in our business.[32]

I do not belabor this point in an effort to denigrate Anderson's descriptive account of market norms. Nor do I suggest that the norms evidenced by Mr. Edwards can be generalized throughout the securities industry—they cannot be. The point is that *any* descriptive account of market norms, or even the norms within an isolated market, will be grossly imperfect. And it is not feasible to accommodate this factor into regulatory schemes that apply without exception to classes of products or participants within a market.

A similar inability to generalize hobbles the norm of exclusivity. However in this case the distinction is not one of corporate behavior but the very nature of goods themselves. Anderson draws upon the idea of rival goods to contrast it with shared goods, whose value is increased the more the goods are shared. The value of friendship is realized in the course of sharing it, but the same cannot be said of groceries. This surely applies to most commercial goods, but it is problematic with regard to commercial goods that are not "rivals in consumption." The availability and value of broadcast media and computer software is not affected negatively by consumption. Watching (consuming) a television show or downloading software does not diminish the availability of the commodity. Rather, as described by economists as network effects, increased "consumption" (i.e., adoption or use) of some goods increases their value.[33]

The notion that markets afford exit but not voice is also flawed when applied across the range of commercial markets. Anderson draws on a distinction made famous by Albert Hirschman[34] to explain certain commercial and political phenomena. But it is a distinction that has been seriously challenged, most notably by Arthur Okin's[35] claim that exit is an accurate description of auction-type markets but less so in the case of customer markets. His distinction is based on the idea that the impersonality of auction markets is not desired by most merchants. Rather, they try to develop enduring relationships with consumers that will encourage repeat business. And they create such relations by dropping the "take it or leave it" of exit and replacing it with receptivity to consumer demands. In short, some consumer markets grant consumers a voice that modifies or limits the impersonality of auction markets.

Graham Dawson[36] challenged Anderson along similar lines to these, provoking a response that emphasis on consumer voice is overblown, that "[t]he moral benefits of participation in consumer markets accrue mostly to well-to-do customers, less to sellers and poor customers, and least of all to workers."[37] If I understand her point, Anderson interprets the lack of reciprocity as evidence that commercial relationships are not genuinely interpersonal. But her quarrel with Dawson is telling—she identifies examples bereft of reciprocity to counter his evidence that voice is prevalent in some markets. Might they both be right, that some markets afford voice but that others do not?

In sum, generalizing about the values of "the market" is problematic. It is so problematic that comparisons between market and non-market values will be fraught with systematic inaccuracies. Granted, egoism is at work in markets, but it is naïve to suggest that it is absent from personal relationships. And egoism is at work in government and nonprofit organizations as well. If there is overlap and consistency—perhaps distinguished only by a matter of degree—between the norms that are operative in various spheres of life, then norms will not provide a useful tool for parsing activities between different spheres. Anderson seems to recognize this problem when she admits that a particular good might be properly valued according to norms from various spheres or modes of valuation. But I am suggesting that each of those spheres or modes of valuation is also comprised of norms that are typically or ideally associated with other spheres. The nomadic nature of some norms may interfere with making use of them as standards for regulatory action because they cannot perform the work Anderson hopes they can.

It would appear that Anderson has employed an ideal type characterization similar to those stylized by Max Weber. If so, then her characterization of market norms is a necessary simplifying assumption to operationalize her theory. But simplifying in this manner brings risks of sacrificing empirical accuracy. It is noteworthy that many late-twentieth-century sociologists eschew grand narrative descriptions like those Weber elaborated and instead investigate individual organizations as a way of understanding society. Their methodology has become more bottom-up than top-down, and although their scope has of necessity narrowed from that of Weber, it is arguably more illuminating in the areas chosen for study.[38] And this is a positive trend insofar as there is a fine line between sweeping generalizations of dubious accuracy and false caricatures. When the above quote from Benjamin Edwards is read in the context of Anderson's description of market values, the man appears to be delusional or intentionally misleading. But if A. G. Edwards were not automatically presumed to be characterized by those values but understood instead along the lines of one contemporary organizational theorist as "systems of interdependent activities . . . dependent on continuing exchanges and constituted by" the "environment in which it operates," the quote is perfectly reasonable.[39]

But what if a more substantive investigation were undertaken and it turned out that Anderson's normative description was accurate? In that case, would the threat that these norms would contaminate one's proper valuation of noncommodity goods justify regulatory intervention? Without a very large condition or qualification, it is hard to see where it would, and even then it is not clear that values are what is at stake. Casual observation reveals that many goods that are properly valued by nonmarket norms are traded in markets without any discernable harm or degradation of the way these goods should be valued. Most pets are acquired in markets—through a transaction in which the pet is treated as a commodity. We buy dogs and cats, but we also afford them the "consideration" that Anderson rightfully believes they are due.[40] The fact that pets are the subject of market exchanges but loved nonetheless implies that something else is needed to justify intervention. Perhaps market exchanges should be forbidden when commercial values *actually* (or are highly likely to) damage the way a good should be properly valued. So, if buying a pet destroyed its value as a lovable companion, then the practice would be suspect. However this appears to be a roundabout way to identify and selectively correct for the abuses in the market of domesticated animals. The ways in which animals can be denied due consideration—inhumane living conditions, puppy mills, animal fighting, and so forth—can be (and are) criticized and regulated without regard to rational attitudes of valuation. That is, these practices inflict suffering on sentient creatures; therefore, squabbles over the proper way to value domesticated animals and whether they should circulate in markets seem beside the point.

Popular Value Appeals

I have argued that values, whether shared by communities or rationally derived, are insufficient reasons to regulate commercial behavior. But this discussion has focused on the philosophical literature and ignores a popular sentiment—call it a "value appeal"—that some things (e.g., education) should be insulated against the corrupting influences of rampant commercialization. This less sophisticated version of Elizabeth Anderson's project is vulnerable to similar objections: that it is based upon sweeping generalizations that cannot withstand empirical scrutiny and therefore breaks down in the face of complex concrete cases. In particular, many value appeals ignore the way commercial relationships can adapt to and thereby embody the values of the good or service being traded. The relationships between a patient and a doctor and that between two anonymous stock traders are both commercial relationships. But, apropos the differences between healthcare and securities, there are salient differences between these two relationships. The value appeal ignores these differences because it lumps them together as members of the class of rationally self-interested profit-maximizing commercial relationships.

To be compelling, value appeals need to go beyond these sweeping generalizations and, for instance, recognize the complexity of these terms. Arguments against for-profit firms engaged in primary, secondary, or even higher education focus on the possibility that profit motives will override concerns for educational excellence. But the profit motive cannot be safely treated as an indicator of the importance that any particular organization will attach to educational excellence, any more than it can predict the importance that any given pharmaceutical firm will attach to scientific scholarship. Simply put, some firms (e.g., Merck) encourage and reward publishing in scholarly journals regardless of their impact on profitability; some do not. Superficially, the "defining aim" of an organization would seem to determine whether it is an appropriate venue for producing various goods and services. As commercial firms must include profitability as one of their objectives, they would seem to be disqualified from some activities whose quality cannot be compromised, say, primary education. Alternatively, since not-for-profit organizations or government agencies are immune to the potentially corrupting influences of profitability, they would seem to be the ideal organizational types for delivering these crucial goods and services.

However, it is wrong to draw any definitive conclusions from an organization's defining aims or its organizational type. For one, it is not the case that not-for-profit firms are immune to the sorts of pressures that bear upon their commercial cousins. Assuming otherwise glosses over the very real need that not-for-profit organizations have for covering their costs and reinvesting in their activities—it is simply called something different (e.g., the excess of revenues over expenditures, or an operating surplus). Some not-for-profit organizations are subject to budgetary pressures comparable to the profit expectations heaped upon some publicly traded corporations. Both categories of firms are locked in competitive struggles—one for sales, the other for contributions or grants. This is not to suggest that there are no differences between them, because there is a large one—ownership. But it is not clear that this difference translates into a substantive difference that is predictive of how individual groups of managers within different institutions will behave with regard to the intrinsic value of any particular good or service. Some goods and services are likely to suffer for the sake of stockholders and their unrealistically high quarterly earnings expectations. But others are vulnerable to the irrational demands of major donors, foundations, and so forth. And we should not ignore the third possibility: elected officials have been known to bully government agencies with similarly undesirable consequences. So long as "outsiders" can inflict unreasonable demands on management, there is no prima facie reason to favor any particular organizational type over the others. And there are reasons to be concerned about the risks, regardless of the institutional type.[41]

This is a counterintuitive and contentious position that deserves a bit more defense. Surely, it might be argued, the distinctions between these organizations are real and should not be blurred. A case gleaned from personal experience in the animal welfare "industry" may illustrate better why these differences are often exaggerated. Consider the typical humane society consisting of an animal shelter and adoption center, a veterinary clinic, and perhaps more exotic functions like public education, animal rescue, or abuse investigations. Based on their defining aims and the lack of a profit motive, one would expect veterinary clinics operated by not-for-profit animal welfare organizations or government agencies to differ substantively from for-profit ones. In particular, one would expect that the not-for-profit clinics would pay less attention to the pet owner's ability to pay for services or, for that matter, whether the pet had an owner or not. But this is not the case. Indeed, it is not even possible to generalize about not-for-profit veterinary clinics. Some live up to the highest ideals of animal welfare and provide care based strictly on the animal's condition. Others routinely euthanize injured but treatable strays or pets with indigent owners. And the same applies to private veterinary clinics: some care for injured animals regardless of whether the care will be paid for, but some do not. Incentives play a vital role in determining whether services will be rendered or not. It is not unusual for veterinarians to be compensated based on their production of fees. Obviously this discourages the provision of free care, but many not-for-profit clinics employ these same incentive systems. In the final analysis, the deciding factor as to whether an animal in need of treatment receives it or not is unrelated to the institutional arrangement of the clinic. And it would be wrong to assume that a profit motive—or the putative lack of one—indelibly imprints itself on organizations and determines whether precious goods or services will be respected or demeaned. The reality is not nearly that simple.

If the profit motive is not the great evil that value appeals assume it to be, then it is tempting to dismiss value appeals of any sort as wrongheaded. But values clearly count for something. I rehearsed the above example to emphasize that the values held dear by individual managers and veterinarians determined more the conditions under which treatment was rendered to injured or sick animals. However, I also emphasized an idiosyncratic factor in the market for charitable veterinary service. So while there is something crucial about values, their behavior is unpredictable and therefore of dubious standing as a justification of market intervention. Cass Sunstein struggles similarly: he recognizes that "the reference to diverse kinds of valuation gets us nowhere" and yet he says, "we cannot get an adequate grasp on the problem [of commercialized adoption services] without seeing this concern [valuation]."[42] To add to the ambiguity, he says, "a judgment about the appropriate kind of valuation, even if it can be reached and persuasively defended, need not entail a particular conclusion for law . . . any general claim about the right kind of valuation needs a great deal of supplementation to result in concrete recommendations for law and policy."[43]

Sunstein's comments are indicative of the ambiguous role of valuations in the context of regulating commercial behavior. His comments are also somewhat cryptic. Two interpretations are possible. One is to place them in the context of his work on the expressive function of the law.[44] However, Sunstein does not make that connection, and his work on the expressive function emphasizes the way norms expressed in laws influence social norms; not necessarily the other way around. Another more plausible interpretation is that a value can serve as a heuristic device by identifying potentially troubling practices that warrant investigation. This would appear to be a more plausible interpretation of Sunstein's thinking, including his reluctance to treat valuations as sufficient justifications for law.

Valuations are reasonable heuristic devices for investigating commercial wrongs. But they would seem to have another important role in crafting regulatory policy. As previously discussed, moral principles, including those of this Regulatory Strategy, are intentionally general and therefore unavoidably ambiguous. They assume maximum possible specificity when applied to concrete cases. However, that process draws upon values in terms of determining the fine-grained meaning of harm and of autonomy in the pursuit of commercial objectives. In particular, the determination of which harms and which obstacles to autonomy are worthy of government intervention require consideration of values. In sum, values do not provide sufficient reasons to regulate although they are important and perhaps essential heuristic and interpretive devices in the formulation of regulatory policy.

Values versus Principles

One final way to vindicate value appeals is found in Michael Walzer's more recent work. Importantly, he now defends the moral standing of a community's values by contrasting them with moral principles and criticizing the latter for their artificial abstraction that is supposedly unconnected with actual people and their places in the world.[45] One way to defend against this criticism is to deny the charge and claim that the two principles of this Regulatory Strategy—Negative Commercial Liberty and Commercial Autonomy—are not foreign abstractions to Westerners and perhaps most others. Western thinkers may have undertaken their formulation or their moral justification, but that does not make these policies contrivances of men such as Kant or Mill. According to this defense, Walzer's criticism is overly general; he might have a point with regard to some moral principles but not the ones upon which this Regulatory Strategy is based.

Another rejoinder to Walzer's criticism of moral principles is to challenge the plausibility of constructing a theoretical account of government regulation without reference to moral principles. Even if one concedes the moral standing of community values, they cannot provide the necessary moral content for a cogent theoretical account of morally justified market intervention. A good illustration of this difficulty is Donaldson and Dunfee's effort to construct a theory of business ethics on the basis of communitarian ideals (dubbed Integrative Social Contracts Theory or ISCT).[46] ISCT treats local agreements as prima facie morally justified business behavior. But the authors of ISCT recognize that some of these agreements are bogus: Hester Prynne, the protagonist in Hawthorne's *The Scarlet Letter*, might have questioned the moral justification of some of the micro-social contracts or local values endorsed by the good burghers of seventeenth-century Salem. These authors also appreciate that some local agreements conflict with one another. To contend with these and other challenges, Donaldson and Dunfee employ numerous devices that culminate in their formulation of "hypernorms" that ride herd over the morality of all "lower-level" norms, including those evidenced by the values of a given community. However, I have argued elsewhere that when hypernorms are invoked to override lower-level norms or to arbitrate between discordant ones, a moral principle has usually been invoked.[47] According to this defense, Walzer's criticism ignores the unavoidability of moral principles in the formulation of a Regulatory Strategy.

Is Nothing Sacred?

Notwithstanding the profound difficulties of deriving commercial restrictions out of valuations, there does appear to be a category of regulation that is both justifiable and not connected in any meaningful way with either the harm principle or personal autonomy. What I have in mind are aesthetic values that are widely, if not universally, shared within a community. For instance, some zoning ordinances, signage or architectural guidelines, as well as restrictions against residential solicitation, appear to be justifiable on the basis of values and not the moral principles of this Regulatory Strategy. That is, although these rules are coercive, they are not justifiable on the basis of relieving serious harms or of removing meaningful obstacles to anyone's autonomy. Yet there must be a place in a theory of commercial regulation to account for what appear to be nonoffensive uses of coercive state power. If a neighborhood chooses to restrict door-to-door sales between certain hours of the day (or entirely), they would not seem to be using local law enforcement power to wrongfully enforce their will on others. I would concede that little in the way of opposition can be mounted against these cases. But also, such cases are not likely to raise serious controversy. Market forces have a tendency to punish commercial actors that would defy such widely held community standards. So, while these cases represent a category of market intervention that falls outside of this Regulatory Strategy, they are not of the controversial variety this project is intended to resolve.

Communitarianism and popular value appeals will be revisited in chapter 5 when I investigate a concrete case. The arguments in this theoretical portion of the investigation have advanced two general themes. One is that apart from the exception noted above, values are not morally justified reasons to intervene in markets. The other is specific to Walzer's communitarian approach to government regulation. Note that his project is long on moral justification or the reasons why values should serve as the basis for regulatory rules that command obedience. And note as well that his project provides a methodology for locating morally justified reasons to regulate, including an elaborate taxonomy of social life carved up into spheres. But, as a theory of morally justified government regulation, it fails to specify moral content in either a systematic or a comprehensive fashion. That is, Walzer describes what counts as moral content and he explains how to go about looking for it, but except for some isolated examples, he does not say what it is. It is not overly challenging to isolate a few commercial practices, criticize them because they violate some moral factor, and then use that moral factor as a reason to regulate the practice. The more arduous challenge is to formulate substantive moral content by defending reasons to regulate against competing reasons to forestall intervention and to generalize those reasons across the range of commercial practices. Such an exercise is part and parcel of a moral theory of commercial life that specifies permissible commercial behavior and justified government regulation. Walzer and, by my estimation, no other communitarian thinker has formulated such a theory. To avoid lapsing into a similar pattern this Regulatory Strategy will be subjected to the criticism of theories where moral content is on clear display, beginning in the next chapter.

Notes

1. Generalizing about communitarians is admittedly perilous. Allen Buchanan finds "almost as many communitarian positions as there are communitarian writers." See "Assessing the Communitarian Critique of Liberalism," *Ethics* 99, no. 4 (1989): 852. The following discussion focuses on specific communitarian thinkers and avoids references to the doctrine generally.

2. Examples are Michael Sandel's *Liberalism and the Limits of Justice* (Cambridge, U.K.: Cambridge University Press, 1982) and Charles Taylor's *Sources of the Self* (Cambridge, U.K.: Cambridge University Press, 1990).

3. Able responses include those of Will Kymlicka, *Liberalism, Community and Culture* (New York: Oxford University Press, 1989); David Johnston, *The Idea of Liberal Theory* (Princeton, N.J.: Princeton University Press, 1994); and Derek Phillips, *Looking Backward: A Critical Appraisal of Communitarian Thought* (Princeton, N.J.: Princeton University Press, 1993).

4. Michael Walzer's *Spheres of Justice* (New York: Basic Books, 1983) epitomizes this style of communitarian literature. I will subsequently refer to this work as *SOJ*.

5. John Danley's survey of the communitarian literature criticizes its lack of clarity and practical guidance. See "Community and the Corporation in Contemporary Communitarianism," in *Proceedings of the Ninth Annual Meeting of the International Association for Business and Society*, ed. Jerry Carlton and Kathleen Rehbein (1998): 371–76.

6. Walzer's reference to "social" goods is meant to mark off the province of distributive justice. That is, distributive justice is concerned with social goods. However, he also claims that virtually everything derives its meaning from its social context and admits that he is "not sure that there are any other kinds of goods [than social ones]" (*SOJ*, 7).

7. For a more elaborate explanation of Walzer's project, see the introduction to *Pluralism, Justice, and Equality*, ed. David Miller and Michael Walzer (New York: Oxford University Press, 1995).

8. In *The Limits of Liberty* (Chicago: University of Chicago Press, 1975), J. M. Buchanan imagines that selling votes is an efficient expression of preferences, just like voting for real but with the extra gain from the purchase price. However, he also recognizes that political power could be shifted in favor of those with the money to buy votes (178). And it should be noted that although Buchanan mused over the possibilities for a market in votes, neither Buchanan nor Tullock pursued the matter in subsequent publications.

9. A complementary way of thinking about this problem is along the lines suggested by Robert Dahl in *Democracy and Its Critics* (New Haven, Conn.: Yale University Press, 1989). Dahl believes that a key virtue of democratic

regimes (as opposed to alternative forms of political governance) is their responsiveness to the concerns of citizens—primarily individual freedom and, to the extent possible, relief from harm. But the concern that elected officials have for citizens of a democratic republic is not automatic or just an outpouring of their virtuous leadership qualities. Rather, it is a unique feature of democratic systems in which the politicians' interest in gaining and retaining elective office makes them responsive to the electorate's interests (economic prosperity being key among such interests). Consequently, democratic regimes tend to pander to citizens in a way that other regimes do not. However, if politicians were no longer inclined to pander to citizens but could instead purchase their votes, there is reason to believe that individual liberty might not be of such a great concern to those in power. By Dahl's account, majority rule is a freedom-making practice, and anything that would diminish it would jeopardize the liberty of the electorate.

10. The normative implications of this difference are thoroughly explored by Marilyn Friedman in "Feminism and Modern Friendship: Dislocating the Community," *Ethics* 99 (1989): 275–90. Friedman raises the additional criticism of communitarianism that shared values might not be the sorts of things worthy of preservation or support—much less guides in regulating a market. Rather, they may be oppressive and harmful to some groups. I will address this issue later in this chapter in the context of Elizabeth Anderson's work.

11. I can only imagine one scenario in which money could invade the market for legal services and result in the domination or subjugation of people. This would be the far-fetched situation of someone having monopolized the market for criminal defense services. If one law firm were to employ every criminal defense attorney in a market, it would be possible for that firm to use its monopoly power to dominate criminal defendants. However, this is not the problem that Walzer has in mind and is not a problem engendered by the O. J. Simpson case.

12. Walzer's idea of shared beliefs and what he does with them has come under some pretty serious criticism. Perhaps the most scathing is the chapter entitled "What Justice Isn't" in Ronald Dworkin's *A Matter of Principle* (Cambridge, Mass.: Harvard University Press, 1985). But also see Norman Daniels, "Review of Walzer's *Spheres of Justice,*" in *Philosophical Review* 94 (1985): 142–48, and Joshua Cohen "Review of Walzer's *Spheres of Justice,*" in *Journal of Philosophy* 83 (1986): 457–68.

13. There are some obvious tensions or conflicts in Walzer's account that are difficult to reconcile. As discussed with regard to legal aid, it is not clear that there is a shared belief in the egalitarian distribution of medical care, although there might be. And it is unclear that communal distribution of a good follows from the fact that it represents a human want. However, to pursue these problems at this juncture would take me far afield from my main objective. For the time being, I will assume that there is, as Walzer puts it, a "human want" associated with medical care that any theory of markets should either provide for or explain away.

14. Norman Daniels, Donald W. Light, and Ronald L. Caplan, *Benchmarks*

of Fairness for Health Care Reform (New York: Oxford University Press, 1996), 21.

15. Daniels, et al., *Benchmarks*, 22.

16. For example, Rawls (*A Theory* 62, 92) sets forth the state's welfare obligation in terms of "primary goods." These are things that all rational people are presumed to want and include "rights and liberties, opportunities and powers, income and wealth." I do not mean to take issue with this formulation, or Rawls' account suggesting that people are owed the resources to be "reasonable and rational." He is surely right. These ideas are ignored here because they are too general to guide in the formulation of regulatory policy.

17. Elizabeth Anderson, *Value in Ethics and Economics* (Cambridge, Mass.: Harvard University Press, 1993).

18. In response to Dawson (discussed below), she says "[b]ut I am a liberal, not a utopian socialist." Elizabeth Anderson, "Comment on Dawson's 'Exit, Voice and Values in Economic Institutions,'" *Economics and Philosophy* 13 (1997): 101–5.

19. Anderson approves of this division of her work by advising, "Those who are primarily interested in markets and politics should read chapter 1, and then chapters 7, 8, and 9" (*Value*, xiii).

20. See Nicholas Sturgeon, "Anderson on Reason and Value," *Ethics* 106, no. 3 (1996): 509–24; and Adrian Piper, "Sense of Value," *Ethics* 106, no 3 (1996): 525–37.

21. This tangential link between Anderson's thinking and communitarianism is overshadowed by its differences, both in her fundamental commitments and in the subtlety of her applications to commercial disputes. First, she does not grant normative standing to community valuations unless they can withstand rational scrutiny. Then, while Walzer's spheres are hard and fast segregations, Anderson's delicately "differentiate" on the basis of multiple valuations. Sphere segregation suggests policies that tend to block market exchanges entirely, whereas differentiation suggests a place for quasi-governmental or nonprofit organizations. Another major difference is Anderson's respect for individual market freedoms. Where Walzer was dismissive of a physician's market rights, Anderson cares about an artist's market freedom.

22. Cf. Richard Titmus, *The Gift Relationship* (New York: Pantheon, 1971).

23. Adrian Walsh criticizes Anderson for her neglect of empirical analysis and for thereby skirting the difficult work in regulatory analysis. This seems unfair insofar as she is sketching a framework for conceptualizing market intervention, readily admits its tentative status, and emphasizes the need for empirical investigation. See "Teaching, Preaching, and Queaching about Commodities," *The Southern Journal of Philosophy* 36, no. 3 (1998): 433–52.

24. For those interested in the debate over the nature of market norms, Ian Maitland provides reasons to be hopeful in "Virtuous Markets: The Market as School of Virtues," *Business Ethics Quarterly* 7, no. 1 (1997): 17–31. Alternatively, for reasons to despair, see Richard Sennett, *The Corrosion of Character: The Personal Consequences of Work in the New Capitalism* (New York: W. W. Norton and Company, 1998).

25. Sociologists are fond of carving up the social world into what Niklas Luhmann describes as discrete self-referential "systems" in *Social Systems* (Stanford, Calif.: Stanford University Press, 1995). The way any given system functions—its logic—serves as a basis to (alternatively) explain, rationalize, or sometimes criticize the operative norms that supposedly operate in any given system. While this work can be illuminating, it is not clear that it can bear the normative weight that some, including Anderson, want to saddle it with. Cf. William Ossipow, "Niklas Luhmann's Sociology and the Economic System: Some Moral Implications," in *Ethics in Economic Affairs*, ed. Allan Lewis and Karl-Erik Warneryd (London: Routledge, 1994), 302.

26. In Kantian terms, impersonality means treating "the other as merely a means to the satisfaction of ends defined independent of the relationship and of the other party's ends" (*Value*, 145). And "[t]he market leaves its participants free to pursue their individual interests without considering others' interests. Each party to a market transaction is expected to take care of herself . . . each party defines and satisfies her interests independent of the other" (*Value*, 145).

27. By which she means that the market responds to "desires backed by the ability to pay for things" (*Value*, 146).

28. Anderson's idea that goods are exclusive has two meanings. One is the obvious point that property owners enjoy the good to the exclusion of others. But she makes the further claim that being an exclusive good makes it a "rival in consumption"(*Value*, 145). By this Anderson means that when one person consumes an exclusive good, the total amount that is available is reduced. So, "[t]he use-value of commodities is rival, since it is tied to the distinct ends of the person who appropriates and uses it. One cannot give the value of a rival good to another without losing it oneself."

29. Meaning that the consumer "votes with her feet" or the merchant says "take it or leave it"(*Value*, 146). She believes that "[t]he customer has no voice, no right to directly participate in the design of the product or to determine how it is marketed" (*Value*, 146).

30. James C. Collins and Jerry I. Porras provide an excellent empirical case for this point in the chapter entitled "More than Profits" in *Built to Last* (New York: Harper Business, 1997).

31. Why does a restaurateur wash his or her hands before returning to the kitchen? Because of genuine concerns over health risks? Because he or she is worried about the damage to the firm's reputation if customers contract food poisoning? Or because the law requires doing so? Or might it be a combination of these factors?

32. From his cover letter dated 9 June 1998 to shareholders of A. G. Edwards, Inc. This quote may strike some as pabulum for public consumption. However, based on the personal experience of having competed against Mr. Edwards' firm for ten years, I would argue that it is not.

33. This phenomenon is documented by W. Brian Arthur in "Competing Technologies, Increasing Returns, and Lock-In by Historical Events," *The Economic Journal* 99 (1989): 116–31.

34. Albert O. Hirschman, *Exit, Voice and Loyalty* (Cambridge, Mass.: Harvard University Press, 1970).

35. Arthur Okin, *Prices and Quantities: A Macroeconomic Analysis* (Washington, D.C.: Brookings Institution, 1981).

36. Graham Dawson, "Exit, Voice, and Values in Economic Institutions," *Economics and Philosophy* 13 (1997): 87–100.

37. Elizabeth Anderson, "Comment on Dawson," 101–5. Anderson contradicts portions of this statement further on, when she cites the example of the airline industry, one of the few cases in which the least desirable customers (i.e., infrequent fliers) pay considerably less than the most desirable ones (i.e., frequent business travelers).

38. Princeton sociologist Paul DiMagio details this trend and provides an overview of the various methodologies in "The Relevance of Organization Theory to the Study of Religion," in *Sacred Companies*, ed. N. J. Demerath, Peter Dobkin, Terry Schmitt, and Rhys Williams (New York: Oxford University Press, 1998), 7–23.

39. W. Richard Scott, *Organizations: Rational, Natural and Open Systems*, 3rd ed. (Englewood Cliffs, N.J.: Prentice-Hall, 1991), 25.

40. Of course, one can imagine circumstances that would deny pets the consideration they are due. Day trading one's pets would probably qualify. However, I have in mind here extant markets where a pet is purchased as a lifetime companion from a reputable breeder.

41. Richard S. Ruch defends the quality of a college education provided by stockholder-owned institutions in *Higher Ed, Inc.* (Balitmore, Md.: Johns Hopkins University Press, 2001). In the course of this illuminating study, he makes reference to a study by David Blumenthal and Joel S. Weissman of Harvard Medical School (published in *Health Affairs*, April–March 2000) that examines the practices of teaching hospitals sold to for-profit corporations. He says, "[N]o negative impacts were found on teaching, medical education, research, or indigent care" (Rush, *Higher Ed*, 8).

42. Cass Sunstein, *Free Markets and Social Justice* (New York: Oxford University Press, 1997): 85, 90, 97.

43. Sunstein, *Free Markets*, 97.

44. See Cass Sunstein, *On the Expressive Function of Law*, 144 U. Pa. L. Rev. 2021 (1996). For Anderson's own views on the subject, see Elizabeth S. Anderson and Richard H. Pildes, *Expressive Theories of Law: A General Restatement*, 148 U. Pa. L. Rev. 1503, 1564–65 (2000). For a critical overview of the doctrine, see Matthew Adler, *Expressive Theories of Law: A Skeptical Overview*, 148 U. Pa. L. Rev. 1363 (2000).

45. Michael Walzer, *Thick and Thin: Moral Argument at Home and Abroad* (Notre Dame, Ind.: University of Notre Dame Press, 1994).

46. See Thomas Donaldson and Thomas Dunfee, *Ties That Bind: A Social Contracts Approach to Business Ethics* (Boston, Mass.: Harvard Business School Press, 1999). The genesis for the ideas in this book are Thomas Donaldson and Thomas Dunfee, "Toward a Unified Conception of Business Ethics: Integrative Social Contracts Theory," *Academy of Management Review* 19, no. 2

(1994): 252–84 and Thomas Donaldson and Thomas Dunfee, "Integrative Social Contracts Theory: A Communitarian Conception of Economic Ethics," *Economics and Philosophy* 11, no. 1 (1995): 85–112.

47. This is a truncated version of an argument I advance in "Managerial Moral Strategies: In Search of a Few Good Principles," *Academy of Management Review* 27, no. 1 (January 2002): 114–24.

3

Monistic Theories of Commercial Regulation

Introduction

THE PREVIOUS CHAPTER considered two projects designed to increase the legitimate reasons to regulate beyond Negative Commercial Liberty and Commercial Autonomy. But others urge limitations on the range of legitimate regulatory goals to a single factor. Accordingly, these projects will be referred to as monistic Regulatory Strategies. The policy prescriptions of monistic strategies tend to endorse minimalist or "night watchman" regulatory states whose powers are limited to the defense of individual rights. The classic cases are philosophical libertarians[1] but some economists arrive at the same conclusion, albeit for the consequentialist reason that self-interested economic agents will organize themselves to society's maximum possible advantage if government interference is minimized.[2] Another body of economic literature comes to the same conclusion but does so by way of a contractarian argument.[3] But the minimalist regulatory state is not an inevitable outcome of monistic Regulatory Strategies. For instance, some normative economic theories, including some in the law and economics tradition, justify market intervention on the basis of an economic outcome: efficiency, wealth maximization, and so forth. Some of these accounts could endorse isolated regulatory actions that would favor, say, economic efficiency at the expense of individual rights.[4]

The common denominator among these monistic projects is their emphasis on a single reason to regulate in contrast to the pluralism I endorse. Although I have argued the inadequacy of monistic theories, these competing projects provide a rich source of practical criticism that deserves consideration. However, it is vital that this criticism (and my response to it) be specific to the context of commercial regulation. For instance, it might be the case that libertarianism suffers some serious or even fatal flaws as an overarching doctrine of political philosophy.[5] However, that defect does not disqualify every libertarian idea nor, depending on the nature of the flaw, undermine the authority of libertarian thinking within the limited domain of commercial life. Important arguments have been fashioned within each of these monistic doctrines and although they may fail to inoculate the whole project from serious criticism they may succeed in undermining mine. So rather than engage in a debate over the general merits of any particular monistic project, I focus on isolated ideas that are antagonistic to my Regulatory Strategy.

First, I consider four arguments within various monistic regulatory projects, each of which endorses a minimalist regulatory state: (1) free markets produce the best of all possible commercial worlds, (2) individual property rights and contractual liberties morally trump nearly every other possible reason to regulate, (3) statutory regulation that does more than protect individual rights is morally impermissible because it is anticipatory of harms and punishes commercial actors in advance of any misdeed, and (4) tort law is morally preferable to statutory regulation because it can remedy pernicious commercial behavior and therefore negate the need for anticipatory regulatory regimes. Next, I defend a stance that is usually associated with libertarianism but is much at home with this Regulatory Strategy—that states ought not to produce or provide goods and services that can be produced privately. I conclude by considering two monistic projects that do not necessarily underwrite the minimalist regulatory state—welfare economics and Richard Posner's law and economics approach to market intervention.

The Best of All Possible Economic Worlds

The idea that free markets achieve the best of all possible economic outcomes owing to a system of prices that stealthily guides production has achieved significant purchase, especially considering the dearth of lively alternatives. This mechanism achieves normative status insofar as tampering with market freedoms by limiting individual property and contractual rights retards the system and impairs economic productivity.[6] Alan Gibbard argues that libertarians have exaggerated the connection between a pricing system and the primacy of individual rights.[7] He recognizes that a system of prices "can harmonize the conflicting demands people make on limited resources, while leaving each person a wide latitude of choice."[8] So Gibbard grants the moral worth of pricing systems but not to the same extent that libertarians do. He is not committed to a system of unfettered free exchange because he makes a distinction between a system of prices and laissez-faire capitalism. Gibbard notes that pricing systems emerge from institutional settings that would not be described as unconstrained. He points to government-regulated capitalist systems with redistributive taxation and state-controlled economies. This implies that libertarians are wrong to bind the two together such that a pricing system serves to justify the minimalist regulatory state.

But while a libertarian might agree with Gibbard's observation, it would be a highly qualified agreement. In effect, Gibbard is claiming that a distinction can be made between the ideas of free exchange and a system of prices—they are different things. The libertarian might agree that they are different things but add or insist that they are not completely independent of one another—that the pricing systems that emerge from different modes of exchange are qualitatively different from one another and that some are better than others. Some, those of state-controlled economies, are pricing systems in name only but fail to perform like capitalist ones. This is largely an empirical matter and one upon which the libertarian can easily claim empirical high ground. And given the moral saliency of pricing systems, by Gibbard's or by libertarian lights, quality matters. For a nation to *have* a pricing system is not of much consolation if it is the sort that produces the wrong goods or otherwise serves to diminish welfare.

However, a dispute over the relative quality of pricing systems misses the point that Gibbard indirectly argues—that adequate pricing systems emerge from institutional conditions that can hardly be characterized as laissez-faire capitalistic. The U.S. economy is not one of free or unconstrained markets and neither is that of Britain, Holland, Australia, and so forth. Yet to a significant extent, pricing systems in most Western nations perform admirably. Of course, market distortions occur. But if the normative basis for a system of prices is its contribution to human welfare, the prosperity in these nations seems to undermine a rigid connection between unfettered trade and an adequate system of prices. So Gibbard's distinction is right although it, too, is overdone. At some point a system of prices is defeated by market intervention. In extant economies the connection is much more complicated than the libertarian "all" or Gibbard's "none." A plausible compromise position must recognize that there is some point at which the constraints upon trade will harm and even nullify the effective workings of a system of prices. Rent controls can and do stifle real-estate development, reduce the availability of housing, and, ultimately, increase prices. Other instances of market intervention seem to have little or no effect on the efficacy of a pricing system. Modest ad valoram taxes (e.g., sales or value added) applied equally across a territory do not seem to distort production. And intervention that reduces information asymmetries can improve the pricing system (e.g., mandatory certification of odometer readings).

This complexity and the lack of a rigid connection among market intervention, pricing systems, and human welfare mean that pricing systems are not moral trumps. But by the same token, a system of prices is too important to be ignored. Therefore, the facts and circumstance of each case have to be examined to determine the effect of market intervention on the relevant system of prices. However, this is hardly earth shattering. It is, in effect, a fancy way of saying that regulators must consider the impact of their decisions on the quality, availability, and price of the goods and services they regulate. But whether the impact is justified or not cannot be decided in a general way. Sometimes the market distortion will be an acceptable trade-off and other times it will be intolerable. But the minimalist regulatory state cannot be erected on the foundation of a pricing system.

Property Rights Über Alles: A Moral Argument

This section is not interested in the libertarian claim that individual rights trump other moral claims so much as it is in the practical implications of instantiating that claim in regulatory policy. I examine Tibor Machan's arguments for a minimalist regulatory state because he is bold enough to consider in detail the way such a state would be structured.[9] His overarching claim is as follows:

> [G]overnment regulation is wrong in principle because any bona fide instance of it—as distinct from instances that really amount to judicial processes or managerial functions of government—infringes upon human liberty, something to which everyone has a natural right.[10]

This generalization gains subtlety from the way Machan defines and characterizes the operative terms. "Government regulation" is the "forcible institution of legal guidelines for production, trade, and consumption" outside of those necessary to fulfill the state's managerial responsibility.[11] And "managerial responsibilities" are those that satisfy two criteria: the system subject to the rule is owned by the state ("or the public it officially represents owns"), and the state has been appointed to manage it.[12] Setting and enforcing speed limits for commercial vehicles is not commercial regulation (and therefore is not illegitimate), because states have the responsibility of managing public roadways.

So far, so straightforward. Machan condemns market intervention as morally unjustified because it infringes upon the liberty of private contractors. But he allows for rules whose purpose is to discharge specified managerial responsibilities to which government has been appointed. This second point is crucial because without it the libertarian project is a prescription for anarchy. And notwithstanding the attraction some political philosophers have for individualist or anarcho-capitalism, a sizeable portion of the general public is likely to resist the wholesale transfer of police, fire departments, and other public agencies to private industry.[13]

But this taxonomy of justified and unjustified government duties exposes a serious weakness. To illustrate, consider what is perhaps the most ubiquitous instance of market intervention in modern economies—central bank regulation of national money. According to these criteria, central bank activity is an example of unjustified regulation because it affects the value of privately held funds. And a theory that disqualifies the legitimacy of one of the primary institutions of economic organization has some explaining to do. Specifically, it must explain why nominal property rights are more important than the stabilizing effects of central banks and their ability to ameliorate the risk of a monetary crisis inflicting damage on the real economy.[14] And this explanation must include an adequate account of a realistically possible substitute mechanism that satisfies these managerial criteria. This is a tall order, one that monetary theorist and libertarian advocate Milton Friedman is not anxious to undertake.[15]

This is not a criticism of the rigors of libertarian thinking but a practical impediment to its application. It may not be realistic to emphasize property rights to the point that doing so precludes government from providing essential coordinating mechanisms. At least there are no good extant or historical examples of this model. The next chapter explores this difficulty further in the context of U.S. capital markets. But this is a serious enough problem to entertain a possible remedy here. Although Machan treats property and appointment as jointly necessary and sufficient justificatory conditions for intervention, the practical problems urge him to shift the moral weight to appointment or, in effect, consent. Sensible as this might be, it raises other problems. What does it mean or what is required to say that the government has been appointed to perform some function or, conversely, that the governed consent to its authority in this area? Unanimity is not realistic, and authorization by a democratic regime makes possible the panoply of regulatory initiatives that Machan criticizes. So a repair of this sort is possible, but to the detriment of the factors that make libertarianism distinct.

Paradoxically, if manifested in regulatory policy, Machan's project would subject individual bearers of rights to intolerable and to some extent avoidable commercial risks, for the reason of protecting their rights. To the extent that is even possible, it bears mentioning how this comes to be. The basis for Machan's project is a perfectly reasonable principle that I defended earlier: private property is a *necessary* factor in individual self-development.[16] However, by making a fetish of rights, by limiting government authority to their defense, individual rights are expected to serve as a *sufficient* condition for self-development as well. And, at least in the commercial sphere there is no good evidence that they have ever succeeded in doing so.[17] Contemporary commercial life is a thoroughly social endeavor requiring coordination, some of which is coercive. If that coordination destroyed individual property rights and imperiled self-development then there would be a case for rejecting it. Such is the case for rigidly controlled and centrally planned economies.

The Anticipatory Dimension of
Statutory Regulalation

Another way to arrive at the minimalist state is to challenge the moral standing of statutory regulation directly or to demonstrate its inferiority to other legal remedies. I will examine two sources of these arguments: one is based on the anticipatory feature of statutory regulation and the other hails from the law and economics tradition. I begin with an argument made by Machan, which is based on his distinction between a convention that prescribes behavior and punishes for the failure to conform (i.e., statutory regulation) and one that exacts damages for harms committed (i.e., the law of torts). He argues that statutory regulation is unjustified because it punishes people by imposing costs of compliance even though they may not have harmed anyone.

This anticipatory feature of statutory regulation is a factor that critics of the minimalist state must overcome. Libertarians argue that parallel logic cannot be applied to other domains of life, say, for violent criminal behavior. That is, the criminal law is only operative with regard to actual crimes. It would be an unjust violation of civil rights to imprison someone because of the *possibility* that he or she might commit a crime (leaving aside the separate crimes of conspiracy and attempt). If someone fits the personality type or background characteristics of a rapist, it would be morally wrong to invoke the criminal law against him. Rather, the individual must actually do something in order for the rape laws to be operative. Statutory regulation seems to jump the gun in terms of meting out punishment. Many statutory regulations are cumbersome, intrusive, and expensive to comply with. The question is whether, in advance of any harm to any individual, there is any basis in morality for forcing compliance. Reducing evil, even violent crime, does not warrant preemptive punishment.

This is a serious consideration that should discourage some instances of commercial regulation. However, it should not forestall all of them because it is an imperfect analogy. Criminal law and statutory regulation are similar insofar as they impinge on rights by restricting the range of options available. That is, they forbid some choices under threat of punishment. But the fact that they do so in advance of an actual harm is not necessarily morally right or wrong; it depends upon the option that is being foreclosed. More specifically, in the case of commercial regulation, it depends upon whether the option was one that individuals or firms were morally obliged to avoid in the first place. For instance, airline safety regulations reinforce the moral responsibility that a carrier already has, qua commercial carrier, to respect the lives and safety of passengers. FAA safety rules eliminate the option of operating in a reckless manner but, given the purpose of commercial aviation, doing so could not be among the options necessary to achieve any meaningful conception of commercial freedom. The commercial carrier that must comply with safety rules has not lost anything in terms of its legitimate aspirations to be free. Safety regulations do not force an airline to go beyond what is morally expected of them as an institution upon whom public safety depends. This is different than incarceration on the basis of suspicious behavior, because acting in a nonsuspicious manner (whatever that is) is not morally required. However, there are correlates in the criminal law. Driving under the influence of alcohol is punishable whether an accident occurs or not. Leaving a small child unattended or in the presence of loaded firearms is treated as reckless endangerment that is punishable without demonstrating any untoward consequences. In these and other cases, rules anticipate reasonably the probability of harm and punish in advance of them. The behavior they seek to inculcate (i.e., driving in a sober state or attending to a child's safety) is morally required to begin with. Coercively limiting one's freedom with respect to morally impermissible options does not do violence to one's freedom as properly understood.

Statutory Regulation versus Tort Law

Another objection to statutory regulation hails from scholarship in the law and economics tradition. One strand of this literature argues that statutory regulation actually inhibits the natural evolution of civil law and its effectiveness in mediating commercial conflicts. For instance, Richard Posner has argued that courts fashion property and contractual rights in a manner that reduces commercial risks.[18] Moreover, it is argued that they do so without the deadweight loss to society of a regulatory agency. This is the tip of a vast and complicated literature that cannot be addressed adequately here. Nor need it be. The findings in this scholarship deserve regulatory attention because they are often right: nonstatutory civil law remedies (i.e., contract, property, and torts) are often preferable—morally and otherwise—to statutory regulation. Some statutory regulation is little more than an expensive nuisance designed to curtail some commercial abuse that would have been remedied through the disciplinary force of tort law. And unlike tort law, regulation and its administrative enforcers linger on after the risk has been averted. So there is no debate here as to the value of nonstatutory remedies. But there is a concern over whether these findings are robust enough to be generalized to the point that they impugn every instance of statutory regulation. The following discussion identifies two classes of cases with characteristics that diminish the effectiveness of court-made law. Contrary to law and economics thinking, these appear to be reasonable candidates for statutory regulation.

The first group of candidates is those commercial practices that pose risks that cannot be remedied with money damages—life, health, environmental, and so forth. Although wrongful death settlements can replace one's earning capacity, they cannot bring someone back to life. And although the fear of such suits disciplines some commercial actors as effectively as statutory regulation, this is not universally the case. Consider commercial aviation and, in particular, the safety risks of shoddy maintenance. Neither tort law nor mandatory maintenance requirements can eliminate this risk. But as mechanisms for risk reduction, court-made law pales in comparison to the rigors of statutory regulation. According to the law and economics literature, it should not. Rather, the threat of litigation should produce the same maintenance outcomes as mandatory maintenance. As profit maximizing agents, the costs of defending against and paying wrongful death suits will discipline firms in the commercial airline industry to either provide the level of maintenance the public demands or go out of business from the cost of wrongful death suits or the dearth of paying customers. But this happy equilibrium assumes far too much. For one, firms do not make resource allocation decisions; managers do. For this argument to go through, it must be assumed that fully rational people with long-range horizons manage commercial airlines. It also must assume that these people are provided with the proper incentives to align perfectly their personal interests with those of the firm. Unless these and similar assumptions are obtained, short-term opportunism is a real possibility that impairs the discipline that tort law should exact. These assumptions are always dubious but in the case of commercial aviation they are profoundly unrealistic. On the basis of personal experience among the ranks of senior management of an ailing international carrier, none of these assumptions can be taken for granted. Rather, consistent due diligence is more likely to result from statutorily imposed maintenance requirements, independent oversight, and criminal liability applicable to individual decision makers.

An example of the second category of risks, in which money can compensate for the harms but in which defendants lack the capacity to compensate, is the securities industry. Although money can compensate for one's losses in the stock market, the magnitude of those losses can easily overwhelm the financial resources of any given market participant. This is not to suggest that underwriters, independent accountants, and corporate executives are not influenced by the threat of litigation, because they clearly are. And, again, the present regulatory framework does not screen out all violations. However, the record of monetary recovery from securities losses—usually around ten percent of the actual damages—is evidence that tort law does not compensate for losses. And simple arithmetic reveals that it cannot possibly compensate. The amount of market loss from a single instance of faulty accounting can reach into the tens of billions of dollars. Simply put, no accounting firm can sustain such losses. And since the discipline that tort law exacts is limited to the credibility of the defendant's risk, these cases present the possibility that litigation simply becomes a cost of doing business. Again, I draw here upon personal experience in both the accounting and the securities industry. Appreciating that the plural of *anecdote* is not *data*, it is my view that although tort law curbs some commercial abuses, it leaves some behavior untouched. Criminal sanctions under a statutory regime are more effective in reaching this other behavior because many (although not all) commercial actors will not subject the prospect of incarceration to a cost-benefit analysis.

Some law and economics advocates would dispute my treatment of these cases. Some argue that over time, court-made law would provide the same results as statutory regulation; only careful and conscientious accounting firms or commercial carriers would exist because the others would be forced out of business. However, that claim commits the fallacy of comparing an ideal theory to the sloppy reality of commercial markets. Agreed, in a commercial world where the full costs of wrongdoing are actually borne by the parties at fault and where the barriers to new firm entry are impermeable, market forces and court-made laws will reduce risk as effectively as would statutory regulation. And indeed, this happens. But it does not happen uniformly in a world where plaintiff's counsel can count sufficiently to recognize that one-third of a settlement for ten percent of actual damages is larger than anything that can be recovered from a bankrupt defendant, where new opportunistic entrants can replace fallen ones, and where replacing every economically irrational managerial incentive is just as likely as changing human nature. In that world it is unrealistic to forestall statutory intervention in hopes of achieving a state of economic harmony that has never emerged anywhere.

So, where tort law is a second-best response to risks that cannot be remedied with money damages, or in cases in which the prospect for recovering monetary losses is far-fetched, statutory regulation is a reasonable alternative. I rehearsed these cases to challenge as overly general the repudiation of statutory regulation by some law and economics enthusiasts. But likewise, these cases should not be generalized because there are cases of different industries with similar risks in which the discipline of tort law cannot be improved upon through statute. The complexity of markets and industries demands a case-by-case analysis and a healthy skepticism toward any sweeping endorsement or repudiation of any mechanism of market intervention in the abstract.

The Pragmatics of Libertarianism

A theme runs though my criticism of Machan and (indirectly) other advocates of the minimalist regulatory state. I have offered examples to illustrate why the doctrine is too blunt—that an overemphasis on individual rights and an exaggerated condemnation of statutory regulation ignores subtleties of actual markets and the people who comprise or are affected by them. This implies that libertarianism has nothing interesting to say about market regulation, beyond a cautionary note regarding pricing systems. But this would miss a vital element of libertarianism that, although rooted in individual rights, is more pragmatic than deontic. Libertarians could grant Gibbard (or any other critic) his theoretical claims but remain steadfast on the basis that theoretical criticism ignores the way government regulation actually functions. This rejoinder holds that no matter how well-intentioned and morally sound the case for market intervention might be, intervention has unintended consequences and, as Mill described it, creates bumbling bureaucracies fraught with all the risks of political intrigue.

Alan Gibbard defends against these worries:

> If there is anything to be said for untempered free exchange, it is its salience as a solution to a political bargaining problem. The "old-time religion" of laissez-faire is just that; its only rational support comes from an extreme skepticism about the ability of any political process to mitigate the inequities of laissez-faire. Its chief recommendation, in other words, is as an arbitrary fetish; that to settle matters by taboo may beat settling them by struggle.[19]

Gibbard's claim is that there is no prima facie reason to favor free market solutions to those that emerge through the political process. Libertarians would counter that the political process is not sufficiently removed from partisan concerns to create actual policies that are true to the philosophical theory. With this eventuality in mind, libertarians could claim that it is better to just let the market function regulation-free because the invisible hand is more likely to produce better results.

This is the public-choice doctrine associated with the writing of James Buchanan and Gordon Tullock. Gibbard counters that there are reasons to believe, based on social choice literature, that the political process is not defective in the way that libertarians claim. But in any event, he believes that the free market should not serve as a substitute for political struggle as a means of settling differences.

Since both of these outlooks are overly general, it is arbitrary to seize on either one as superior to the other. However, there is another element of the libertarian worry that deserves consideration. In chapter 1, I touched on Mill's fear of government becoming an active participant in commercial affairs by directly producing goods and services. His worry was that government is organized in a way that is appropriate for governing but not producing. Consequently, Mill set out a very narrow range of activities that would be appropriate for government to engage in, including large-scale public works that could not or would not be undertaken by the private sector. But he emphasized that such endeavors were advisable when (and only when) private sector providers were unwilling or unable to participate.

In the context of this investigation there is another reason to emphasize this point. If the critics of libertarianism are right—that it is morally permissible and sometimes even desirable for government to regulate some commercial affairs—then, to the extent possible, government ought to avoid direct participation in the production of goods and services. This would follow from the idea that when the state actively produces goods and services, then it is no longer available as an impartial regulator. Once government replaces the private sector and directly provides goods and services, then who stands to discipline the activities of the state? There are answers to this question, but they are inadequate. The question is not whether "the people" or a self-regulatory state could provide regulatory oversight but whether such a solution is preferable to a more or less neutral administrative body regulating an "outside" private concern. That is, everything else being equal, if coercive intervention is morally justified and desirable, then ideally it would come from outside of the market itself.[20]

The significance of this limited principle is that it indirectly endorses many, but by no means all or even most, libertarian projects. To illustrate, consider the libertarian case for funding primary and secondary education.[21] Some libertarians argue for a system whereby state governments would distribute vouchers that students could redeem for educational services at the school of their choice—public or private. The widespread distribution of vouchers is at least two things. First, it is a form of income redistribution. Second, a voucher system may involve a critical appraisal of direct government provision of education. Many advocates of voucher systems begin with a criticism of the public school system as it is and argue that the voucher system will improve the quality of education by introducing competition and accountability. Libertarians (or nonlibertarians for that matter) could also argue that the condition of some public schools is partially attributable to the lack of regulatory oversight of educational services. That is, in some jurisdictions, government has a near monopoly on the education market but is unable to discipline itself the way other regulated monopolies are disciplined. By directly providing education, government compromises its ability to discipline itself the way it disciplines the activities of a private commercial market. Monopolistic electric utility companies "deliver the goods" under the hand of government regulation. Such entities are disciplined by state boards that (ideally) are not connected politically or in any other way to the regulated entity. But public schools are both organs of the state and regulated by it. There is a concern that such an arrangement is less than ideal because there is no independent force acting upon the organization. Both the school and its supervisory board are subject to the same political controls of the state and therefore accountable to the same authorities. One of the motivating features of the voucher system is that it breaks this connection and imposes independent oversight (i.e., parents).

Now granted, this is a roundabout way to argue for government regulation of a market. It is, in fact, the opposite of what Mill had in mind. Writing before the advent of public education, Mill saw the need for government to establish a limited number of schools in order to ensure the quality of the education provided by proprietary schools. The point is that he viewed government as the essential regulator or insurer of quality. But for that to be possible, for government to act as a fair and impartial regulator of productive activities, a position of oversight removed from the provision of the service is probably a more desirable vantage point than that of a producer. Regulatory capture is still a very real possibility but there is a healthy tension when oversight of an activity is structurally separated from the activity itself. Ideally, the oversight function should be insulated from private and political influence through models like those of the Federal Reserve or the National Transportation Safety Boards.

As in the case of pricing mechanisms, I do not believe that too much can be made of this finding. If properly understood, it would serve only as a guide or a cautionary note and not a hard and fast rule. In some cases there is simply no choice but for government to directly take on activities to provide certain goods and services. And in other cases, government will be the provider of choice on other grounds. However, if regulation of a commercial activity is desirable and morally warranted then this prima facie principle—that government should steer and not handle the oars—should be on the list of relevant regulatory considerations.

Economic Outcomes and Regulatory Legitimacy

Economics is not a monolithic discipline, and the range of economic justifications for market intervention is vast. Several important ones will be covered here, but first, a distinction is in order between positive and normative economics. Milton Friedman described the positive variety as "the body of tentatively accepted generalizations about economic phenomena that can be used to predict the consequences of changes in circumstances."[22] In this context, positive economic findings alert regulators to risks and identify opportunities to create benefits in commercial life. The hoary debate about whether "value-free" economics is realistic need not detain us, for reasons that will be evident shortly. Similarly, the less-than-stellar predictive reputation of economics is not of concern. Economic insights that did no more than describe and explain the mechanisms of commercial life warrant regulatory consideration similar to findings in the natural sciences. They should be considered seriously although they are (usually) necessary but never sufficient reasons to intervene in markets.

However, "consider" is not the same as "determine." Economic risks and opportunities, similar to those in natural science, should influence policy makers without being dispositive of regulatory action. As a nonmarket solution, commercial regulation involves the discharge of coercive state power and, consequently, a decision to use it is a political one. Deciding whether or not an economic risk is worth taking should not be done on the basis of economic evidence alone when such decisions affect involuntarily the interests of democratic citizens. Likewise, whether realizing an economic opportunity justifies the use of coercive force should not be decided on the basis of economic "facts of the matter." Regulatory decisions would go badly if made without the benefit of economics, but they could go morally wrong if such evidence were the only reason for regulating commercial affairs. Such is the case with natural science in which, for instance, field biologists should not have the only or the final say in determining grizzly bear habitats, nor should biochemists decide among themselves the acceptable levels of arsenic in drinking water. These decisions affect the rights and interests of citizens, and the best available science is but one important factor. In sum, findings in positive economics are crucial, but they are inherently incomplete.

What about normative economic reasons to regulate? I will review several normative themes in economic thought, not with the intention of exhausting the universe of such thinking but with these limited goals: (1) to explain the monistic theme that runs through all normative economic theories, and (2) to argue the inadequacy of basing a Regulatory Strategy on a single factor, regardless of what it is. I begin with the ruling orthodoxy, neoclassical or welfare economics, and the basic assumption upon which the dictum is based: "Voluntary exchange between a willing buyer and a willing seller usually cannot make either party worse off and typically makes both parties better off."[23] This is intuitively right, insofar as people are not likely to voluntarily do things that make them worse off. If benefits received in trade improve one's position, and if society is ultimately comprised of buyers and sellers, it stands to reason that voluntary trade has a salutary social dimension. Economic efficiency or social welfare measures this dimension by isolating a market arrangement and testing how effectively it "delivers the goods" in comparison to alternative arrangements. But consider this shorthand account of economic efficiency in the language of neoclassical economics: the excess of benefits over costs where benefits are understood as the consumer's willingness to pay (and the price received by a producer) and costs are understood as the price paid by the consumer (and the cost to produce for the producer).[24] If one is interested to "benefit individual consumers and maximize efficient utilization of the earth's scarce resources"[25] then economic efficiency is a sound measurement. And regulation would only be justified in cases in which markets have failed, meaning those circumstances in which the free market does not optimize the allocation of resources (e.g., monopoly power, the provision of "public" goods, externalities, or information asymmetries). Otherwise, markets should be left alone.[26]

There can be no denying that this economic model picks out a legitimate factor deserving of regulatory attention. Human welfare cannot be reduced to consumer surplus, and the economic measurement of social welfare should not be conflated with more robust accounts of what makes a life worth living. But those worries do not undermine the importance of economic efficiency. Economic social welfare or market efficiency is a sound regulatory objective because it is an indicator of public access to and the affordability of goods and services. Ceteris paribus, a world of efficient markets is morally preferable to one that is hobbled by chronic market failures. The question is not whether economic efficiency should be afforded any importance in a moral account of regulatory authority but, rather, how much importance it deserves. Efficiency enjoys an imperious role in economics because, as Robert Gilpin says, "The basic task of economists is to instruct society on how markets function in the production of wealth and how these markets can be made more efficient."[27] But two considerations should condition society's response to these instructions. One is practical—economic analysis cannot always clarify the nature and extent of market failures nor the relative desirability of nonmarket remedies. A classic example is the seventy-five-year debate over the Radio Act of 1927 and the creation of the Federal Radio Commission (after 1934, the Federal Communications Commission). Herbert Hoover analogized the haphazard way that broadcasters chose frequencies to an unregulated highway. He feared that left to its own devices, the broadcasting industry would alienate listeners who were growing increasingly frustrated by signal interference. The decision to license and regulate broadcasters was an effort to correct a failure of the free market in the broadcast spectrum and thereby achieve a more efficient allocation of resources for broadcasters and listeners alike.

This seemingly straightforward appeal to economic efficiency is but a fraction of an ongoing dispute—among economists—regarding the regulation of U.S. airwaves. Ronald Coase argued that courts could devise a system of property rights for broadcast spectra and avoid the cumbersome and expensive interference of licensing regulation.[28] But other highly credentialed economists took issue with Coase.[29] And although both sides to this controversy cite theoretical evidence and similar market analogies, their hypotheses cannot be tested empirically. Although internal disagreement characterizes any scientific discipline, economics is particularly constrained by the nature of its subject matter—individuals, many of whom are known to defy the simplifying assumptions of self-interested utility maximization. Meanwhile, regulators may not have the luxury of awaiting the conclusion of these debates or the evolution of a suitable property rights regime.

This case also illustrates the second reason why efficiency should not take center stage in setting regulatory policy. Signal interference is but one of many concerns regarding the commercial use of radio spectra. Coase argued that property rights could solve that problem without incurring the deadweight loss of a regulatory agency. And he was probably right. But the efficiency of property rights versus regulatory licensure begs the question of whether public airwaves should be owned privately. That determination cannot be made on the numbers without ignoring the public interest in the broadcast media industry. This is not to judge one way or the other on the merits of government licensing of broadcast companies.[30] But it is to say that judgments about spectrum ownership should not be settled by debating the relative efficiency of a free versus a nonmarket solution to signal interference. Efficiency matters, particularly if licensing would have impaired the nascent broadcast industry; but it is incomplete. It is arguable that broadcasters could be obliged to satisfy a public interest requirement under a property rights regime for broadcast spectra. However, that requires speculating as to the terms of the property rights that would ultimately emerge from court-made law. For property rights to do the work that Coase expected of them, they have to be powerful. And whether that power would inhibit legislators from imposing public interest obligations cannot be determined ex ante.

In short, economic efficiency does not exhaust the universe of legitimate factors for market intervention. It may be inefficient to resist the sale of radio and television spectra to private firms, but citizens may have legitimate noneconomic reasons for not doing so. That is, it is wrong to assume that efficient markets are always more desirable than failed ones. Abstracting the FCC case illustrates this. Coase (and most other economists) claim that the legal recognition and enforcement of negotiable title to private property is conducive to market efficiency. Generally speaking, they are right, but they would also agree (I think) that sometimes market efficiency should yield to some other right, even if doing so diminishes market efficiency. For instance, protective rights against unreasonable searches and seizures are economically inefficient. So are the ones against self-incrimination that swindlers, thieves, and other violators of property rights enjoy. But being an economic nuisance is not a sufficient reason to curtail these rights. The point is that commercial life cannot avoid confrontation with legitimate moral concerns that are different from and sometimes more compelling than the benefits described in market-efficient terms—some deadweight losses might be desirable.

That economic efficiency or welfare does not exhaust the universe of possible moral concerns in life is not lost on neoclassical theorists. Two prominent responses, both associated with the Chicago School, deserve mention. The first involves placing an economic value (a utility function or, in market exchange terms, a willingness to pay) on what have traditionally been noneconomic factors (including moral and quasi-moral ones like environmental values). Once assigned a value, these factors can be made a part of a more encompassing cost-benefit analysis.[31] These efforts enlarge the normative scope of neoclassical economics, but the utilitarian roots of the project remain firmly planted. Consequently, these efforts inherit and magnify the measurement problems that hobble any utilitarian calculation. For instance, the foregoing illustrations would require placing a value on the public's interest in retaining power over broadcast spectra and on to the civil right against self-incrimination. Denominating these and similar factors in economic terms extends the normative scope of the neoclassical model, but it does so at a price. It has been argued, largely on methodological grounds, that it is not well advised to provision public goods on the basis of simulated competitive markets.[32] It is not clear that demand for things like a clean environment or safe neighborhoods, much less civil rights, can be quantified in the same way that consumer goods can be. The reason protective rights are valuable and the conditions under which market efficiency ought to yield to them could be obscured in the calculus of a cost-benefit analysis. That these simulated models provide valuable explanatory accounts largely overlooked by noneconomic disciplines is undeniable. But contrary to President Reagan's Executive Order 12291 (1981), their place in the formulation of regulatory policy should not be a commanding or a dispositive one.

The other Chicago School project that reinforces and expands the normative basis of neoclassical economics is the law and economics literature.[33] As Chicago School theorist Gary Becker[34] directed neoclassical economic analysis to putatively nonmarket domains of life—from romantic relationships to law enforcement—Richard Posner and others focused these techniques on law and justice. And they did so with an unabashed normative objective. As Kim Lane Scheppele describes it, "Ethics, in the world of law and economics, just is [limited to] simply the comparison of the overall consequences of one rule against another."[35] In particular, Judge Posner believes that rules are morally (or otherwise) good and desirable if they bring about results that are better than a steady state or the results of other rules. He construes "better" as wealth maximizing, measured on the basis of society writ large:

> [T]he wealth of society is the aggregate satisfaction of those [individual] preferences (the only ones that have ethical weight in a system of wealth maximization) that are backed up by money, that is, that are registered in a market [or that can be approximated].[36]

Law and economics advocates trumpet the precision that wealth maximization calculations afford to ethical judgments. And they reject as "vague and ill-formed"[37] other methods such as those derived from social contracts, duties, Aristotelian virtues, or any others. When this moral core is placed at the center of the neoclassical economic model, the purpose of law is strictly limited to the protection of market exchanges (qua instances of preference satisfaction) and the reduction of transaction costs that hinder market exchanges.

The law and economics literature has attracted a great deal of criticism, focused in part on whether wealth maximization is a coherent and morally justified regulatory objective.[38] Other critics take exception to collapsing law and justice into the relative desirability of various economic outcomes or in their measurement. Posner has answered this criticism with varying degrees of satisfaction. It is pointless to delve deeply into this dispute, as it will not be settled here. In the context of this study, there are reasons that recommend the law and economics project, but there are more compelling reasons to preclude its use in any general way. As was the case with the neoclassical notion of market efficiency, everything else being equal, it is hard to argue that maximizing wealth is not, in most instances, a desirable objective. And contrary to much of the criticism that Posner and other law and economics advocates have endured, the doctrine need not be staunchly ideological or lead inexorably to a minimalist regulatory state. At least in Judge Posner's formulation of the doctrine, property rights are "contingent on transaction costs and subservient or instrumental to the goal of wealth maximization."[39] Since laissez-faire capitalism is tantamount to the free exercise of property rights and contractual liberty, Posner's project is not an unqualified endorsement.

But there is an unsettling aspect of the law and economics project that is revealed in language such as this: "The economist is interested in how the machinery of justice, constituting a system of governmental coercion, is used and how it could be used more effectively to prevent wasteful private activities, such as theft and murder."[40] For economists to analyze crime and criminal justice in economic terms, a pursuit going back at least as far as Jeremy Bentham's analysis of poor laws and prison design, is a worthwhile endeavor. Crime diminishes society's limited resources, and economists, with their understanding of the mechanisms of creating and destroying those resources, provide valuable insights. But there are other connotations of crime that do not lend themselves to the language of transaction costs, efficiency, or wealth maximization. Even when Posner and Becker enlarge those terms, it is not clear that their economic analysis attains the normative standing they seem to grant it. Democratic societies pursue legal remedies in accordance with a variety of legitimate moral values, some of which yield laws and legal judgments that violate the calculus of wealth maximization. But it is not clear why these remedies should be subordinate to wealth maximization. Consider these scenarios that Posner uses to differentiate wealth maximization from utilitarianism:

> Suppose a polluting factory lowers residential property values in an area by $2 million, but that it would cost the factory $3 million to relocate (the only way to eliminate the pollution), and on this basis the factory prevails in the property owners' nuisance action. . . . Now reverse the numbers and assume that the property owners are wealthy people and that if the factory has to close down, its workers will suffer heavy relocation costs and many small local merchants will be pushed into bankruptcy. A judgment that forces the factory to close will be efficient.[41]

This example lays bare the limitations of law and economics to commercial regulation in a democratic regime. At least according to Judge Posner's rendition of the dictum, courts that hear such cases should make "a reasonably accurate guess as to the allocation of resources that would maximize wealth."[42] In these cases, he implies that justice demands continuing the state of affairs because it would be inefficient to do otherwise. The only legitimate considerations are the diminution in residential values, the costs to relocate an industrial business, and the wealth-maximizing consequences they imply with regard to alternative decisions. But this seems to be an arbitrary limitation, whether in the context of a tort action or in the crafting of statutory regulations. The reasons law and economics enthusiasts give for ruling out other considerations that might not register in local real estate values are not compelling. Of course these other considerations are vague and ill-formed, but it is wrong to assume that markets for real estate reflect everything of importance. Assuming that these examples take place in a democratic community, there are (at least) two viable and morally justifiable possibilities. First, with regard to the first scenario, pollution statutes might be drafted such that they err on the side of public health, forcing the factory owners to bear the cost of moving. And in the second scenario, policy makers might consider the economic vitality of their community of greater importance than the marginal health risks of the pollution. According to the theory of law and economics, both of these policies commit sins against wealth maximization. But, as I will argue shortly, they are both legitimate uses of state authority nonetheless. The point is not that wealth maximization is wrong or that in many cases it is not a compelling reason to regulate or to forestall regulation. I urge the more humble conclusion that wealth maximization is not the only legitimate human aspiration deserving of legal attention.[43]

Sifting the Pieces

Several features of these monistic approaches to market intervention survive critical analysis. The first is that pricing systems are vital economic mechanisms and therefore deserve regulatory consideration. The second is that direct government provision of goods and services is, prima facie, a less desirable alternative than private production with government oversight. Likewise, the goals of economic Regulatory Strategies (e.g., efficiency or wealth maximization) are important factors that neither regulators nor judges can ignore. But neither should they be enslaved to any one of them. Finally, I have tried in this chapter to put to rest the notion that property rights should trump all other moral concerns in commercial regulation. Machan serves as a good target in this effort because he illustrates clearly the logical conclusion of overemploying negative liberty. Many libertarians, such as Milton Friedman, recognize the need for some regulatory agencies whose purpose cannot be justified in terms of the defense of individual rights. The challenge for libertarians (I believe) is to articulate a Regulatory Strategy that does not preclude the possibility for the fundamental coordinating devices of a modern capitalist economy. Central banks cannot be afforded regulatory legitimacy on the ad hoc basis that they perform admirably or that they have become indispensable. If the defense of negative liberty is the only legitimate use of government authority, then these institutions should be removed from the libertarian model. However, the history of modern commercial life reveals that experimentation has been essential to human understanding of large-scale economies. Models of justified state authority based on the negative dimension of freedom alone will preclude entire categories of creative adaptations to economic risk, coordinating mechanisms in particular. The rigidity of these models puts them at risk of fossilizing into intellectual dead ends.

The previous chapter concluded with the criticism that communitarian regulatory projects failed to specify their moral content in any thoroughgoing fashion. The monistic projects considered in this chapter provide specific moral content that I have described as vitally important and deserving of a place in regulatory decision making. So none of these strategies advance bad or wrong reasons to regulate. I have criticized them as incomplete and unsatisfying because it is not the case that there is one, and only one, morally justified regulatory objective. By the same token, it is important that the reasons advanced by each of these projects be recognized in an adequate Regulatory Strategy. In the next chapter I consider capital market regulation and will emphasize the rightful influence these reasons deserve.

Notes

1. The classic formulation is Robert Nozick, *Anarchy, State, and Utopia* (New York: Basic Books, 1974). The criticism is a literature unto itself, but a good example is Jonathan Wolff, *Robert Nozick* (Stanford, Calif.: Stanford University Press, 1991).

2. Cf. Milton Friedman, *Capitalism and Freedom* (Chicago: University of Chicago Press, 1962) and, with Rose Friedman, *Free to Choose* (New York: Harcourt Brace Jovanovich, 1980). Likewise, in *Morality within the Limits of Reason* (Chicago: University of Chicago Press, 1988), 14–15, Russell Hardin describes Hayek as a utilitarian in virtue of his emphasis on outcomes. Although Hayek disagreed, there is clearly a sense in which rights have an instrumental value in some libertarian economic literature.

3. Cf. James M. Buchanan and Gordon Tullock, *The Calculus of Consent* (Ann Arbor, Mich.: University of Michigan Press, 1962).

4. For instance, Judge Richard Posner treats "wealth maximization" as the rightful goal of the law, something that could easily intrude upon individual rights. See William Landes and Richard Posner, *The Economics of Justice* (Cambridge, Mass.: Harvard University Press, 1981), 61.

5. At least one prominent (although disillusioned as of late) libertarian scholar has arrived at this conclusion. John Gray writes,

> libertarian and egalitarian doctrines are fatally flawed and are therefore incapable of serving as fundamental political moralities. The utopian models suggested by these doctrines—*laissez-faire* capitalism and egalitarian socialism—are not only impractical but also, and more importantly, philosophically indefensible.

See John Gray, *Beyond the New Right* (New York: Routledge, 1993), 66. Also, twenty-five years after the publication of *Anarchy*, Robert Nozick wrote, "The libertarian position I once propounded now seems to me seriously inadequate, in part because it did not fully knit the humane considerations and joint cooperative activities it left room for more closely into its fabric." See *The Examined Life* (New York: Simon & Schuster, 1989), 286–87.

6. Milton Friedman states,

> [t]he price system is the mechanism that performs this task [cooperative production] without requiring people to speak to one another or to like one another. When you buy your pencil or your daily bread you don't know whether the pencil was made by a white man or a black man . . . As a result, the price system enables people to cooperate peacefully in one phase of their life while each one goes about his own business in respect of everything else . . . Prices perform three functions in organizing economic activity: first, they transmit information, second, they provide an incentive to adopt those methods of production that are least costly and thereby use available resources for the most highly valued purposes, third, they determine who gets how much of the product—the distribution of income. (Friedman and Friedman, *Free to Choose* [New York: Harcourt Brace Jovanovich, 1980, 13])

The Friedmans go on to suggest that any effort to tamper with pricing systems damages the productive capacity of an economy.

7. Alan Gibbard, "What's Morally Special about Free Exchange," in *Ethics & Economics*, ed. Ellen Frankel Paul, Fred D Miller Jr., and Jeffrey Paul (Oxford, U.K.: Basil Blackwell, 1985), 20–28.

8. Gibbard, "What's Morally Special,"20.

9. Tibor Machan, "The Petty Tyranny of Government Regulation," in *Rights and Regulation*, ed. Tibor Machan and M. Bruce Johnson (Cambridge, Mass.: Ballinger Publishing Company, 1983), 259–88. Although somewhat dated, he reiterated these views in a subsequent essay, "Government Regulation of Business," in *Commerce and Morality*, edited by Tibor Machan (New York: Rowman & Littlefield, 1988) and, most recently, in his introduction to *The Commons: Its Tragedies and Other Follies*, Tibor Machan, ed. (Stanford, Calif.: Hoover Institutions Press, 2001).

10. Machan, "The Petty Tyranny," 260.

11. Machan, "The Petty Tyranny," 270. Also, regulation includes only statutory rules and regulations. Judicial decisions that are enforced by the state do not count as regulation for Machan. In the next section, I will address Machan's contentions that judicial decisions are appropriate measures to constrain commercial activity but that statutory regulation is not.

12. Machan, "The Petty Tyranny," 267.

13. David Osterfeld reviews the substitute mechanisms of anarcho-capital-ism in *Freedom, Society, and the State* (Lanham, Md.: University Press of America, 1983).

14. The ability of central banks to play this role is discussed by Lawrence Summers in "Macroeconomic Consequences of Financial Crises," in *The Risk of Economic Crisis*, ed. Martin Feldstein (Chicago: University of Chicago Press, 1991).

15. Milton Friedman, in *Bright Promise Dismal Performance* (New York: Har-court Brace Jovanovich, 1983) is among the most ardent fans of libertarianism and an eminent scholar on U.S. monetary policy and the history of the Federal Reserve. He has also been a trenchant critic of the institution as evidenced by his statements throughout Milton Friedman and Paul A. Samuelson, *The Economic Responsibility of Government* (College Station, Tex.: The Center for Education and Research in Free Enterprise at Texas A&M University, 1977). But asked whether the institution should be abolished, Friedman answers, "No." See *Milton Friedman and Paul A. Samuelson Discuss the Economic Respon-sibility of Government* (College Station, Tex.: Center for Education and Research in Free Enterprise at Texas A&M University, 1980). Rather, he sug-gests ways it could better contend with inflation. Hayek argues for a shadow private currency to discipline the policies of central banks, but he makes no suggestions about abolishing them altogether.

16. Machan writes,

> [i]f the task of every person is self-development, the right to private property is a moral prerequisite for the realization of that task within a social context. In such a context . . . the right to private property is justifiable on grounds that (a) a sphere of jurisdiction, consisting of such items, is indispensable for the moral life of human beings and (b) one (not others) ought to be the authority over items or processes one has recognized and made valuable or received from someone, or from a series of persons who have done the same. To the extent that the right to private property . . . is eroded, the prospect for a moral life will also erode. (*Indi-viduals and Their Rights*, 141–42)

17. There is an impression that twentieth-century American regulation, New Deal legislation in particular, marks a break from the laissez-faire capi-talism that preceded it. However, this is an oversimplification and, on some accounts, simply wrong. Commercial regulation was endemic in the postco-lonial period (i.e., 1776–1847), and it accelerated during the second half of the nineteenth century. As legal historian Lawrence Friedman observes, "The statute books swelled like balloons despite ideological sound and fury about individualism, social Darwinism, free enterprise, Horatio Alger, and the like, from pulpit, press and bench." See *History of American Law* (New York: Simon & Schuster, 1973), 157. The twentieth century is noteworthy for the growth of *federal* regulatory power. But this development should not obscure the regulatory zeal that preceded it.

18. See Richard Posner, *Economic Analysis of Law*, 5th edition (New York: Aspen Publishers, 1998).

19. Gibbard, "What's Morally Special," 28.

20. I ignore the issue of self-regulation in the commercial sphere, where strong incentives make it possible for a collection of firms to discipline one another. Those same incentives are not at work in the case of government.

21. I am not bringing this case up in order to thoroughly explore it or to suggest that this principle justifies the libertarian account. The issue of primary and secondary education involves concerns that go beyond a general principle that (ceteris paribus) government ought to regulate instead of provide. I only use this case as an illustration of how this principle can be arrived at without the libertarian apparatus that necessitates the minimalist regulatory state.

22. Milton Friedman, "The Methodology of Positive Economics," in *Essays in Positive Economics* (Chicago: University of Chicago Press, 1953), 39.

23. Roger Blair and David Kaserman, "The Economics and Ethics of Alternative Cadaveric Organ Procurement Policies," *Yale Journal of Regulation* 8, no. 2 (Summer 1991): 444.

24. For a more extensive formulation, see D. Kaserman and J. Mayo, *Government and Business: The Economics of Antitrust and Regulation* (New York: Dryden Press–Harcourt Brace College Publishers, 1995).

25. Robert Gilpin, *Global Political Economy* (Princeton, N.J.: Princeton University Press: 2001), 23.

26. As Kaserman and Mayo contend, "In a free enterprise economy, government intervention in market processes is generally justified by some sort of market failure. That is, unless a market exhibits some type of dysfunction, it should remain free of direct government control" (*Government and Business*, 5). And depending on the costs and efficacy of intervention, most economists would prefer for the failure to continue rather than risk the regulatory remedy.

27. Gilpin, *Global Political Economy*, 24. Gilpin continues, "How societies then choose to distribute that wealth among alternative ends is a moral and political matter lying outside the realm of economic science."

28. Ronald H. Coase, "The Federal Communications Commission," *Journal of Law & Economics* 2 (October 1959): 1–40.

29. For a recap of the debate some fifty years after the creation of the FCC, see Ronald H. Coase and Nicholas Johnson, "Should the Federal Communications Commission Be Abolished?" in *Regulation, Economics and the Law*, ed. Bernard H. Siegan (Lexington, Mass.: D.C. Heath & Co., 1979), 41–56.

30. For anecdotal evidence of the perils of government licensure of broadcasters, see Katharine Graham's account of harassment at the hands of the Nixon administration, *Personal History* (New York: Random House, 1998), 479–82.

31. I attribute this approach to the Chicago School because it can be traced to many of Gary Becker's pioneering essays compiled in *The Economic Approach to Human Behavior* (Chicago: University of Chicago Press, 1976).

32. Of special note is Amartya Sen, *Choice, Welfare, and Measurement* (Cambridge, Mass.: MIT Press, 1982) and "The Moral Standing of the Market" in *Ethics and Economics,* ed. Ellen Frankel Paul, Fred D. Miller Jr., and Jeffrey Paul (Oxford, U.K.: Basil Blackwell, 1985), 1–19; Cass Sunstein, "Disrupting Voluntary Transactions," in *Nomos XXXI,* ed. John Chapman and J. Roland Pennock (New York: New York University Press, 1989), 279–302; and *Free Markets and Social Justice* (New York: Oxford University Press, 1997). In response to some of this criticism, multicriteria decision-making models and other techniques have emerged. For a critical analysis of these efforts, see the second chapter of Stuart Hall, *Democratic Values and Technological Choices* (Stanford, Calif.: Stanford University Press, 1992), 29–54. Also, Irene van Staveren identifies other methodological flaws in the neoclassical paradigm in *The Values of Economics: An Aristotelian Perspective* (New York: Routledge, 2001).

33. See for instance Frank Easterbrook and Daniel Fischel's *The Economic Structure of Corporate Law* (Cambridge, Mass.: Harvard University Press, 1991); William Landes and Richard Posner, *The Economic Structure of Tort Law* (Cambridge, Mass.: Harvard University Press, 1987); and *The Economics of Justice* (Cambridge, Mass.: Harvard University Press, 1981).

34. Cf. Becker, *The Economic Approach to Human Behavior* (Chicago: University of Chicago Press, 1976) and *A Treatise on the Family* (Cambridge, Mass.: Harvard University Press, 1991).

35. Kim Lane Scheppele, "It's Just Not Right: The Ethics of Insider Trading," *Law & Contemporary Problems* 56, no. 3 (Summer 1993): 123–73, 150.

36. Landes and Posner, *The Economics of Justice,* 61.

37. Jonathan R. Macey, *From Fairness to Contract: The New Direction of Rules against Insider Trading,* 13 Hofstra Law Review 9, 10 (1984) at 15. Cited in Scheppele, "It's Just Not Right," 151. Also, Richard Posner, "The Problematics of Moral and Legal Theory: The 1997 Oliver Wendell Holmes Lectures," *Harvard Law Review,* vol. 3, no. 7 (May 1998), 1638–1717, goes so far as to dismiss the role of philosophical moral theory in adjudicating the law. In this same volume, Ronald Dworkin and Martha Nussbaum respond to him by, among other things, identifying how his own legal reasoning assumes a theoretical account of morality.

38. See, e.g., Ronald M. Dworkin, "Is Wealth a Value?" 9 *Journal of Legal Studies* 191 (1980), and Anthony T. Kronman, "Wealth Maximization as a Normative Principle," 9 *Journal of Legal Studies* 227 (1980).

39. Landes and Posner, *The Economics of Justice,* 70.

40. Landes and Posner, *The Economics of Justice,* 70.

41. Landes and Posner, *The Economics of Justice,* 70.

42. Landes and Posner, *The Economics of Justice,* 70.

43. For the unconvinced, for those still satisfied that normative economics provides the only legitimate reasons to intervene in commercial markets, see Don Herzog, "Public Choice and Constitutional Law: Externalities and Other Parasites," *University of Chicago Law Review* 67 (Summer 2000), 895. And for a thorough discussion of the flip side of this debate—the role of moral theory

in economics—see Daniel Hausman and Michael McPherson, "Taking Ethics Seriously: Economics and Contemporary Moral Philosophy," *Journal of Economic Literature* 31 (June 1993), 671–731.

4

U.S. Capital Markets

A continuing market presupposes that most participants find an acceptable measure of net satisfaction in their transactions.

James Willard Hurst[1]

Regulation of U.S. Capital Markets

To develop further this Regulatory Strategy requires the rigors of concrete cases—the more complex and contentious, the better. Capital markets, especially the constellation of activities pertaining to underwriting and trading of securities, are well suited to this purpose. Stocks and bonds are not essential goods (as that term was previously defined) because they are not a necessary condition for living any possible conception of a good life. Yet they contribute meaningfully to the quality of the lives of their owners, helping them achieve dignified retirements in particular. And unlike some commercial products, securities pose no danger to personal safety or the environment, issues that will be explored in the next chapter. Also, capital markets are of national importance because they channel scarce investment capital to commercial endeavors. The way such capital is allocated bears directly on the productive capacity of firms and those dependent upon them for goods, services, and jobs. Consequently, participants in capital markets deserve special regulatory consideration. As Martin Feldstein observes,

[T]he reason for social concern [over the stability and vitality of the financial services industry] is not that some individuals are financially hurt or even bankrupted by their bad investments. Individuals who take risks in the hopes of big returns must face the risk of commensurate losses. But a collapse of the financial institutions can hurt innocent depositors and, through the subsequent effect of collapse on business activity, can lead to unemployment and the loss of otherwise healthy businesses.[2]

Jonathan Glover emphasizes the social consequences that can radiate from serious capital market failures. He goes so far as to note that "the depression of 1929–31 may have contributed more to Nazism than the motives and beliefs of particular Nazis."[3] In short, the social importance of capital market efficiency cannot be overemphasized. While economic historians will debate the causal connections between capital market failure and economic depressions, the link between capital market stability and economic prosperity is undeniable. Simply put, there is no example of a national economy that has sustained a reasonable level of economic performance in the face of chronic capital market failure.

My goal here is to explore the regulatory framework of U.S. capital markets as an example of the Regulatory Strategy formulated here. This is not to say that every instance of capital market intervention can be justified according to these principles. However, the general framework, that is, the enabling legislation and the principles that guide the relevant regulatory agencies, conforms nicely. And it is an extremely controversial framework that has spawned spirited debate— libertarian, communitarian, and economic—from its inception to the present. Accordingly, it provides a rich source of resistance against which to probe the principles of this Regulatory Strategy. And focusing on extant regulation of a long-established industry provides a laboratory-like setting. Securities regulation has effected changes in the U.S. securities industry that has been scrupulously chronicled.[4] So unlike debates over some government initiatives, the regulation of the securities industry permits empirical observations of its impacts that make speculation unnecessary. Most importantly, prior to the legislation enacted in the early and mid-1930s, U.S. capital markets approximated the laissez-faire ideal. Securities firms were obliged only to maintain the standards of the clublike exchanges to which they belonged—assuming they belonged to an exchange. Those operating outside the exchanges (over-the-counter markets) experienced few, if any, controls in terms of their sales practices or the way they managed their internal financial affairs. And issuers were only obliged to divulge the meager information that the market was able to coax out of them.

The regulation that ensued transformed the structure of the securities industry as well as many of its practices. Paradoxically, U.S. capital markets—equity trading in particular—seem to epitomize freewheeling capitalism when they are actually among the most highly regulated. Consider this: upon entering a Sears store, one is confronted with the firm's motto, "Satisfaction Guaranteed or Your Money Back." But neither Merrill Lynch, nor Morgan Stanley, nor any other U.S. brokerage firm will adopt a similar slogan. Perhaps it would be suicidally foolish to do so, but even a moderate version, say, a promotion that guarantees favorable results from a single order, is forbidden by law. A regulatory framework so onerous that it limits a firm's contractual freedom so extensively warrants examination.

Finally, securities regulation is a valuable case study because it has not endured the abysmal administration of some regulatory initiatives. Evaluating regulation is often difficult because the merits, moral or otherwise, are confused by the failures of administering the law. Examples abound—public housing and employment training perhaps among the most egregious. But the congressional intention instantiated in securities legislation has been more or less effectively realized in the market. Throughout its existence, the Securities and Exchange Commission (SEC) has generally been feared but respected, both within the securities industry and by the general public. The agency has avoided scandal and by any measure is extraordinarily efficient.[5] And relative to some other New Deal administrative bodies (e.g., the Civil Aeronautics Board), the SEC has not been captured by the industry it was designed to regulate.[6] As least it has not experienced the degree of regulatory capture that has enfeebled other agencies. Therefore, the moral dimensions of this initiative can be explored without the distraction of inept implementation or administration. This is not to suggest that the SEC is the paradigm of management excellence or that it has not flirted with every manner of administrative failure, including excessive intrusiveness and timidity. Capital markets involve inordinately complex practices subject to rapid change, and anecdotal failures abound. However, the failures are not so ubiquitous that they obscure the overall success of the agency, measured by the worldwide standing of U.S. capital markets.

The Securities Industry and Its Regulatory History

Before highlighting the history of capital market regulation, a few words are in order about the industry and the terminology to be used in this chapter. The portion of the securities industry of interest here encompasses two discrete activities—retail brokerage and investment banking. Retail brokerage involves mostly secondary market (post-issuance) trading by and between individual investors with securities firms acting as their agents or trading between an individual and a securities firm where the firm acts as a principal for its own account. Investment banking involves the process whereby securities firms raise capital for commercial firms when these firms issue their securities to the public (hence the ascription "issuer") after registering them with the SEC (hence the term "registrant"). The two activities give rise to the regulatory reference to securities firms as "broker-dealers." An ancillary, but from a regulatory standpoint crucially important, service provided by broker-dealers is the lending of money on securities owned by their customers. Referred to as a "margin loan," this activity allows investors to acquire securities without paying the entire purchase price in cash. Margin loans provide owners of fully paid securities a source of liquidity to purchase other securities or to make nonfinancial purchases. The importance of this business cannot be overstated insofar as it accounts for a sizeable portion of industry profits. For some individual firms, particularly the new breed of online brokers, net interest income is the primary source of profitability. It is also a source of significant risk to individual investors, to firms making the loans, and to capital market stability. When customers are afforded liberal margin requirements (i.e., very small down payments—only ten percent was required prior to 1934), relatively small declines in the price of a security can cause brokerage firms to liquidate individual stock holdings to repay outstanding loans. When this occurs simultaneously to a great number of investors, the results can destabilize the market temporarily. Accordingly, the amount of money that customers are allowed to borrow against their securities is regulated by way of statutorily imposed margin requirements.

Prior to the advent of twentieth-century regulation, the activities described above were neither rigorously policed nor segregated in any meaningful way. Most importantly, demand deposits in commercial banks were used to fund the operations of broker-dealers, including their highly leveraged margin loans. The financial crisis of 1929 revealed the structural risks inherent in such an arrangement. In effect, customer deposits in commercial banks financed speculative purchases of volatile securities. Since neither the banks nor the securities firms were sufficiently capitalized to bear the risk of precipitous declines in stock prices, the ultimate risk was passed along to the unsuspecting bank depositor. In October of 1929, this scenario became painfully obvious. But it was doubly devastating insofar as the sharp drop in the price of many securities was not a temporary setback due to panic selling. Rather, many of the issuers were not and had never been viable businesses. Moreover, the individuals whose margin loans were being "called" (i.e., a demand for repayment) could not satisfy the loans from their personal resources. So the high degree of leverage on financial assets of dubious value contributed significantly to the downward spiral of stock prices, which triggered the failure of numerous securities firms (many of which also accepted demand deposits) and commercial banks. And ultimately the loss extended all the way to individual depositors, whose bank accounts became worthless.

Having said that, it is unfair to issue a wholesale condemnation of the unregulated U.S. securities industry or to blame the Depression on its unregulated condition. Indeed, the industry served a primary purpose of a capital market quite admirably throughout the nineteenth century and for several decades into the twentieth century. On the one hand it sustained economic development by channeling or guiding investment capital into productive activities. Railroads, utilities, natural resources, and other basic industries developed rapidly prior to and during the 1920s, in part because they enjoyed a secure source of capital. And on the other hand, the unregulated securities industry provided savers and investors alike with a multitude of savings and investment instruments. Fortunes were made in this environment, demand for workers was robust, and companies that endure to the present day were well served by the investment banks of the time. However, in the late 1920s, U.S. capital markets failed to perform two of their primary functions—the allocation of capital to productive projects and the provision of viable investment opportunities to the owners of capital. The crash of October 1929, whose wreckage persisted into the early 1930s, created losses that would take another twenty-five years to recoup.[7] Ultimately, eight thousand banks failed between 1929 and 1933, wiping out the savings of untold numbers of individual savers.

The literature surrounding this debacle is vast and conflicts on some points, but a number of valuable insights are more or less agreed upon.[8] One is that no single event or market caused the Depression, although the failure of capital markets deserves special recognition. Also, there is no question but that a significant portion of the nation's storehouse of investment capital had been squandered.[9] Some losses were the result of outright shams, but others were simply marginal businesses that proved to be grossly overvalued by their promoters. And it is also largely agreed that this buying frenzy was fueled in part by the liquidity that was created by generous margin loans and the dearth of useful investment information.[10] Abruptly withdrawing that liquidity put irresistible downward pressure on stock prices. As described by Maury Klein, one of the longer-term consequences that would have a lasting impact upon national prosperity was the reluctance for investors, domestically and internationally, to participate in U.S. capital markets.[11] Restoring the integrity of those markets as well as ensuring that similar failures would not repeat themselves—at least not in the same way—became a primary objective of the regulatory regime that emerged in the Depression's wake.

Several legislative acts, not all of which are administered by the SEC, enabled the present regulatory framework. The focus here is on two primary acts, the Securities Act of 1933 (33 Act) and the Securities Exchange Act of 1934 (34 Act), although the purpose of those omitted is in concert with these two.[12] The first, the 33 Act, imposed strict disclosure requirements on issuers of securities. As discussed above, before the enactment of the 33 Act a company could sell its stock or bonds to the public with a minimum of financial or operational disclosures. The 33 Act not only imposed detailed periodic reporting requirements, but it also mandated that issuers of securities submit to annual audits by independent accountants, the results of which could determine whether the company would be permitted to access the public capital markets or whether its securities could continue to trade on secondary exchanges. The 34 Act gave rise to the SEC and placed the various private exchanges, including the New York Stock Exchange, under its direct supervision. Another feature of the 34 Act that bears mention is the regulation of credit for the purchase of securities. The Federal Reserve Board was granted the authority to establish limits on margin loans. Requirements were initially set between forty and ninety percent (depending on the security) of the value of the collateralized security, a serious increase from the ten percent prevailing at the time.

These two pieces of legislation—concerned primarily with the trading of securities and the administration of firms engaged in this business—were rounded out by a third. The National Banking Act of 1933 (or the Glass-Stegall Act, as it is popularly known) mandated structural changes in the overall financial services industry. Among other things, Glass-Stegall required that the industry be segregated into three discrete activities—commercial banking, insurance, and broker-dealer activities. This meant that a company involved in commercial banking could not also participate in investment banking or insurance. Fully integrated firms (e.g., First National Bank of Boston) were required to spin off independent organizations (e.g., First Boston) or else cease their investment banking and retail brokerage activities. In this way, bank deposits were insulated against losses from investment banking or retail brokerage. In return, the Glass-Stegall Act also gave rise to the Federal Deposit Insurance Corporation, which administered an industry-funded insurance program for small depositors.[13]

The cumulative effect of this legislation was to radically alter the securities industry and the operation of U.S. capital markets. The management of broker-dealers was brought under direct SEC supervision through the promulgation of regulations mandating daily tests of a firm's financial stability and liquidity. Moreover, the way in which securities were underwritten and sold to the public was radically altered. The idea of caveat emptor was by no means eliminated, but it was dealt a serious blow. The landmark Section 9 of the 34 Act, "Prohibition against Manipulation of Securities Prices," outlawed a number of previously accepted practices. In particular, "insiders" were prohibited from taking advantage of material nonpublic information for personal gain (see the section below entitled Insider Trading). By any standard, these acts represented a sweeping change in the way a major U.S. industry was structured and operated.

The moral principles of this regulatory effort can be gleaned from a phrase that occurs frequently in the legislative language and in present-day SEC literature—"in the public interest and for the protection of investors." As laudable as that goal may be, this regulatory regime is precisely the sort of commercial intrusion that many libertarians find so abhorrent. To paraphrase Robert Nozick's whimsical expression, contemporary securities law *can* prohibit capitalist acts between consenting adults and it incarcerates others for engaging in them.[14] It is therefore not surprising that some horrified opponents of this legislation described it as "authoritarian and socialistic."[15]

But libertarians were not alone in their revulsion to this legislation. Fighting its way through the legislative process, these acts encountered another sort of resistance. Some were disappointed by the tentative nature of the legislation and urged further restraint of the securities industry. These opponents argued that capital market oversight was an insufficient reaction to the stakes involved in capital market failures. As will be discussed, these objections were lodged in similar terms to contemporary communitarianism. The legislation that emerged from this debate disappointed libertarians and communitarians alike. It was, in the words of its most diligent chronicler, "a *conservative* response to the economic crisis known as the depression" (emphasis added), but it struck a balance between the two extremes of doing nothing and rationalizing the capital markets.[16] Understanding the different reasons advanced against this legislation provides an opportunity to counter these extremes in terms of the principles of this Regulatory Strategy. Generally speaking, the provisions of the legislation can be understood along two dimensions: antifraud and mandatory corporate disclosure. The antifraud provisions punish issuers for making false or misleading statements or for omitting material information in connection with the sale of securities. As every philosophical perspective acknowledges the deterrence of fraud as a legitimate government function, I will not focus much attention on these provisions. The information disclosure requirements imply that the antifraud provisions would not adequately constrain undesirable capital market behavior, and it is that portion of the legislation to which I turn.

Mandatory Information Disclosures and Their Discontents

The onerous disclosure requirements imposed on issuers represent a compromise between two extreme alternatives. One is to permit investors and issuers to freely negotiate the nature and extent of publicly available financial information. The other grants authority to the state (e.g., the SEC) to approve the public sale of any particular stock or bond. This alternative, requiring that the state opine on the merits of an investment, affects the flow of investment capital. In the debates surrounding the creation of the disclosure requirements in place today, both of these alternatives had their ardent advocates.[17] The shape of the final legislation could not fully satisfy either side, so what emerged continues to provide ample grist for libertarian and communitarian criticism mills regardless of the specific application. Whether the question is mandatory information disclosures, auditor independence, or insider trading, neither political outlook can warmly embrace the legislation. It has been criticized for its free-market bias and the resulting losses incurred by individual investors. And it has been savaged for the onerous demands and the criminal penalties it imposes on seemingly innocent (victimless) behavior. Either way, the moral justification for this sort of market intervention is in perennial dispute.

Consider the primitive case of an investment banking transaction whereby a company accesses the public capital markets by issuing shares of stock. In the preregulatory period, issuers were at liberty to raise capital without the myriad of rules and regulations that exist today. They did not file with the SEC a complex registration statement, or continue to file any of the periodic or episodically required statements that are required today. Subsequent to the enactment of the 33 and 34 Acts, issuers confront a dauntingly complex array of rules and regulations that necessitate the services of specialized and expensive attorneys, accountants, and other advisors. Among these rules is the one that requires an audit by independent accountants who attest that the firm's financial statements do not contain material departures from accounting principles whose legitimacy is sanctioned by the SEC. And the results of that audit must be included in the registration statement that is made public shortly after its submission to the SEC. This statement may run hundreds of pages, and must include a discussion of the issuer's business prospects and specific risks to purchasers of the security. Sanctions for misleading, incomplete, or fraudulent disclosures include fines, rescission of the underwriting and return of the investment proceeds, and incarceration.

One purpose of these rules is to reduce the information asymmetry between issuers and investors. Although it is impossible to eliminate information imbalances entirely, it is possible to ameliorate them by requiring disclosure of information vital to investors. In particular, insurers must reveal any "materially adverse" information, upon registration and continuously thereafter, that could reasonably influence an evaluation of the investment merits of the security—loss of a major customer, major litigation, senior management changes, and so forth. And a development-stage issuer without a history of operations is required to disclose its business plan and its prospects for future profitability. Referring to the 33 Act in an address to Congress, President Roosevelt said this:

> The Federal Government cannot and should not take any action which might be construed as approving or guaranteeing that newly issued securities are sound in the sense that their value will be maintained or that the properties which they represent will earn a profit. There is, however an obligation upon us to insist that every issue of new securities to be sold in interstate commerce shall be accompanied by full publicity

and information, and that no essentially important element attending the issue shall be concealed from the buying public. . . . This proposal adds to the ancient rule of caveat emptor, the further doctrine "let the seller also beware." It puts the burden of telling the whole truth on the seller. It should give impetus to honest dealings in securities and thereby bring back public confidence.[18]

President Roosevelt's sentiments would seem to provide a conclusive justification for mandatory disclosure requirements, but they do not. Such requirements were and are criticized as unnecessary and illegitimate invasions into the private matter of buying and selling securities. Or, given the importance Roosevelt places on public confidence, they can be criticized as too feeble, because they fail to protect investors in any thoroughgoing way. The libertarian objection could champion the issuer and note the risks, competitive or otherwise, of publicly disseminating proprietary information. Such risks could discourage otherwise qualified companies from accessing the public capital markets. To the extent that investors are willing to purchase securities without access to this information, perhaps because they trust the insurer's management, mandatory disclosure appears to be unnecessarily coercive. After all, the purchase and sale of securities is a voluntary transaction in which all parties are free to decline participation if the transaction is not to their liking. This may not be true of some issuers in desperate need of capital, but it is true of the investors whom the disclosure requirements are intended to benefit.

The gist of this libertarian objection is captured by an interchange between Thomas Phillips, a member of the ad hoc Congressional Industrial Commission, and Henry Havemeyer of American Sugar as he testified on the proposal for mandatory information disclosure:

> *Phillips:* You think, then, that when a corporation is chartered by the State, offers stock to the public, and is one in which the public is interested, that the public has no right to know what its earning power is or to subject them to any inspection whatever, that the people may not buy stock blindly?
> *Havemeyer:* Yes; that is my theory. Let the buyer beware; that covers the whole business. You cannot wet-nurse people from the time they are born until the day they die. They have got to wade in and get stuck and that is the way men are educated and cultivated.[19]

Havemeyer's response would not satisfy libertarian thinking if "getting stuck" included fraud. Libertarians support remedies for fraud but not the apparatus of securities regulation. Coercively demanding that information is morally wrong because it imposes the costs of compliance on businesses without regard to their wrongdoing or the exigencies of individual cases. For instance, it is conceivable that some issuers could raise large amounts of capital without disclosing much of anything to a large pool of investors willing to forego the information. In that case, these requirements do smack of the preemptive punishment that libertarians abhor. Alternatively, the regulatory framework of which the disclosure requirements are a part can be criticized for not going far enough. Subsequent to the market crash of October 1987, investors did not express any abiding confidence in U.S. equity markets. The same could be said at present of those experiencing the spectacular equity market declines of recent quarters.[20]

A Defense of Mandatory Information Disclosure

This Regulatory Strategy justifies market intervention to protect individual liberty and to remove obstacles to achieving commercial autonomy. These principles require that intervention proceed pragmatically, taking into account the goals of market participants and the special features of individual goods and services. It is far from obvious that securities regulation, information disclosures in particular, conforms to these principles. The process through which it emerged clearly satisfies the procedural requirements elaborated in chapter 1. The deliberations were open, transparent, and took account of every competing interest. But otherwise, this legislation raises serious questions: does it arbitrarily promote the interests of some groups, say, investors, over those of issuers? Would tort law discipline wrongdoers and rid the market of undesirable influences without burdening all market participants with the costs of compliance? If investment capital is so important, then why not impose a formal approval process similar to that of the pharmaceutical industry—why limit authority to information disclosures? Most importantly, there is a sense in which this regulatory regime hinders the Commercial Autonomy of issuers and encroaches on their Commercial Liberty. These and other vexing problems challenge a Regulatory Strategy rooted in a commitment to liberty and autonomy.

Information is clearly an important factor in making rational decisions, and it is reasonable to assume that investors prefer more as opposed to less of it. But this is not universally true, particularly when it comes to buying and selling securities; many ignore disclosures, and if the events of the past few years are any indication, this includes the explicit risk factors in a prospectus (see the section below entitled "The Efficacy of Information Disclosures"). But it is also quite possible that investors will demand whatever information they consider to be important and make their investment decisions accordingly. If such demands are not satisfied, then investors can decline to invest. As Machan and other libertarians rightly note, consumers have a right to refuse to purchase things, but they do not have an automatic right to information. So consider the case of a firm—call it Obscurity, Inc.— that offers its securities without any representations or warranties, without any financial or other disclosures, and without any assurances as to its future prospects. If a group of investors are willing to purchase the stock or bonds of Obscurity, fully knowledgeable that they are acting blindly, what, if any, moral principle or value do they offend against? Does not their voluntary consent to the conditions of the transaction justify morally Obscurity's actions?

I rehearsed this scenario to expose the structure of many of the arguments in opposition to market regulation—if a rule punishes a consensual transaction, then the reasoning behind the rule must be wrongheaded and the rule itself must be illegitimate. This sort of argument is particularly compelling with regard to securities regulation that subjects such seemingly innocuous behavior to criminal sanctions. And this is a helpful means of highlighting the unacceptable implications of some commercial regulation. But in the case of securities regulation, I want to argue that it is a defective objection because it abstracts and isolates behavior from the market in which it occurs and ignores the wider consequences that routine behavior of this sort could have on the market—its direct participants and others with a stake in the way capital markets function.

To appreciate the moral wrong of Obscurity's proposed underwriting, it is necessary to consider the way capital markets function when this behavior is widespread. And it is not speculative to imagine that market characterized by a paucity of investment information, because such a scenario describes preregulatory U.S. capital markets.[21] As discussed above, such market conditions contributed to an economic dislocation whose impact was enduring and widespread. Most importantly, the Depression affected those who were not a party to— did not consent to—the underwriting contract. Capital market failures radiate to anyone dependent upon commercial prosperity, be they wage earners, consumers, firms, or investors. But to be clear, efficiency, isolated from the consequences of a specific market failure, is not a sufficient reason for intervention. Many markets suffer from informational failures that could be improved upon by mandating more or higher-quality disclosures. There is no doubt but that entertainment purchases would proceed better if media firms were subjected to truth-in-advertising laws. But making such disclosures mandatory is not morally justified unless there is something else at stake. Regulating capital markets is consistent with government's protective role because it removes a considerable obstacle to living an autonomous (commercial) life. This claim cannot be made in the abstract through theoretical economic analysis that relates informational asymmetries to market inefficiencies simply because market participants might be willing to accept them the way moviegoers seem to accept the bogus representations by movie studios. That is, economic efficiency is not a moral end in itself. Nor does a casual reference to living an autonomous life suffice to justify the regulatory scheme of U.S. capital markets. However, when capital markets are understood as a primary factor in achieving nearly any notion of commercial autonomy by any market participant, intervention is justified.[22]

Unless a consistent requirement for information is made mandatory, the market in securities will be seriously lacking in meaningful investment information. And there are reasons to believe that the market will not naturally correct for this deficiency. There is instead a presumption—both empirical and theoretical—that the market will not provide useful investment information. From an empirical standpoint, the period of time before the advent of securities regulation demonstrated that useful investment information was not forthcoming. And this was not a young market. Many publicly traded companies did not issue periodic financial statements or disclose risks of "material adverse changes" in their businesses. And there is a reason to believe that this was not just a historical fluke or one that would naturally correct itself in any reasonable period of time. Rather, there are plausible reasons to believe that securities markets will not encourage but will instead discourage the dissemination of the most valuable information—the risks associated with investing. If the accepted practice within the market is to withhold such information, then the handful of companies that voluntarily disclose it can only hinder their access to capital. The sorts of disclosures that are vital to good investment decisions are often the most disparaging. They reveal problems and risks in the company and if some but not every firm is forthcoming with this information, they are likely to be punished vis-à-vis their coy competitors. Unless a uniform standard is maintained throughout the universe of issuers, it is not realistic to believe that individual issuers would or could bear the risk of voluntary disclosure. So while there is no denying that mandatory disclosure rules limit the contractual freedom of issuers, the limit is justified by the risks of unconstrained capital markets and the obstacles those risks pose for the autonomy of direct participants and nonparticipants alike.[23]

Mandatory information disclosure rules also satisfy the background conditions of liberal democracies discussed in chapter 1. For one, it is a method of intervention that balances the interests of those affected by it. It also requires that those benefiting most directly from the stability of capital markets shoulder the burden of compliance. The most crucial function of this market is to satisfy the capital needs of firms by providing a reliable outlet for selling their securities. And indeed, the costs of compliance are borne directly by issuers, indirectly by their shareholder–investors, and only tangentially by those outside the market but dependent upon it for jobs, products, or services. But no single interest dominates. Information disclosures do not protect investor interests for information and disregard the interests of firms (to profit or to operate unencumbered by complex rules). To the extent that information disclosers contribute to the stability and reliability of U.S. capital markets, then issuer interests are also served.

Second, mandatory information disclosures do not violate the requirement that states remain relatively neutral with regard to the meaning of a good commercial life. Securities regulation endorses the goal of national prosperity but does not otherwise attempt to influence the character of commercial life. As mentioned earlier, the debates surrounding the enactment of this legislation included an appeal for much more stringent regulatory controls. In particular, some advocated that underwriting be subjected to a pre-approval process whereby the SEC would determine whether insurers warranted access to the capital markets, similar to the Food and Drug Administration's protocols for approving a new pharmaceutical therapy. But securities are not pharmaceuticals, and rulings on the efficacy and safety of drugs do not map onto stocks and bonds. For the SEC to approve or disapprove of investments places the government in the position of directing capital flows, an untenable possibility. The reasons that justified information disclosure—the risks of financial market failures—do not also license the regulation of capital flows. Regulating capital flows is neither a proportionate response to the risks of capital market failures nor is it specifically designed to eliminate them.

Statutory Securities Regulation versus Tort Law Remedies

It is arguable that the foregoing discussion justifies some form of market intervention but not the current regulatory framework. One possibility is to acknowledge that information is vital to the operation of a capital market but to insist that there are noncoercive mechanisms to coax quality information out of issuers. It should be noted that by libertarian lights, the willingness of investors to participate in capital markets is by no means a legitimate concern of government. However, protection against force and fraud is. So libertarians could argue that it is morally justified to punish issuers for fraudulent statements, perhaps through a tort action. And, it might be further argued, this strategy is more appropriate because unlike its statutory cousin, tort actions only apply to those whose behavior is actually harmful. Tort actions do not burden honest and dishonest issuers alike because although everyone is disciplined by the possibility of litigation, only those committing fraud pay the price.

Such appeals to tort law are often right. Statutory regulation is a superfluous and clumsy nuisance if other legal remedies are effective in constraining pernicious commercial practices. However, it is overly general to apply this dictum to every instance of statutory regulation. Rather, practices within specific markets must be carefully examined in terms of the salient differences between the two approaches: Tort law remedies are only operable after harm has occurred and they are generally limited to money damages, but statutory regulation is operable before harmful behavior occurs and in addition to money damages it can include criminal sanctions. In the case of securities markets, there are several reasons to doubt the efficacy of tort law remedies. Most importantly, it is not usually the case that damages connected with securities fraud are recoverable. In the prototypical case of serious securities losses, the issuer is not able to restore investors. Indeed, the losses are usually related to the financial disappointment or failure of the issuer. Additionally, the magnitude of securities losses makes it improbable that others connected with an underwriting (e.g., investment banks or auditing firms) can afford to compensate investors. In many such cases it is doubtful whether plaintiffs can recover even a fraction of their losses.[24] Whether the defendant is an issuer or an investment banker, the threat of litigation does not influence commercial behavior of those "judgment-proof" actors whose resources are either limited or legally protected. But even those firms with substantial resources at stake are not automatically disciplined by the threat of litigation. The recent demise of Arthur Andersen demonstrated that while it is clearly irrational for firms to behave so opportunistically that they would endanger their financial viability, individuals are not similarly constrained. While tort law sends powerful signals to firms, it does not necessarily alter the incentives of individuals whose personal resources are not similarly vulnerable. However when the threat of money damages is coupled with the very real possibility of incarceration, the incentives of corporate and individual actors are aligned.

As this book goes to press and reports of managerial misconduct are daily occurrences this reasoning might not be convincing. Some might suggest that existing criminal sanctions have been ineffective. From personal experience in the securities and accounting industries, I would suggest that criminal sanctions are far superior deterrents although it is difficult to prosecute those presently in force. And although their relative efficacy cannot be measured scientifically, most executives (with some notable exceptions) responsible for signing SEC documents or for participating in their preparation will attest to the seriousness with which those tasks are undertaken. In particular, the mere possibility of criminal sanctions precludes considerations of cost-benefit or similar financial calculations. However, corrective measures of this sort cannot be achieved by way of a statute against fraud because not every capital market shortcoming involves fraud. For instance, the need for firms doing business with the public to maintain adequate capital is, I believe, fairly well demonstrated. But absent a mandatory capital rule it is hard to see where firms could be disciplined on the basis of fraud to maintain the appropriate levels of capital. And if history is any indicator, tort damages will not discipline the marginal firms.

The Efficacy of Information Disclosures

I have been arguing that mandatory information disclosures are justified on the basis of their intended effects on capital market and the people affected by their operation. And I have cited historical and theoretical reasons to believe that this is the case. But other evidence seems to belie this conclusion. First, consider what an effective capital market pricing mechanism should do with regard to the securities circulating in it. Ideally, it makes it possible for market participants to value the securities of firms with promising productive potential more highly than those with poor prospects. And, accordingly, those firms with the potential to profit by producing goods and services demanded by consumers will enjoy lower costs of capital than those with inferior prospects. The danger of chronic pricing errors is twofold: that productive projects will be hampered by unrealistically high capital costs or, in the worst case, be denied capital altogether; and that investors will squander their savings on unproductive projects or, at a minimum, receive unrealistically low returns in relation to their risks.

Now, do the information disclosure rules in place today make a difference? Better yet, on the heels of a rather spectacular misallocation of billions of dollars in capital to currently worthless Internet companies, did they make a difference? And if not, how can the costs of compliance be justified? This is a serious problem because the events of the past few years suggest that investors are not the rationally self-interested utility maximizers that economists suppose them to be. If they are not, if information has become unimportant, then mandating its dissemination and punishing those who fail to follow this mandate is not justified. A case in point is the prospectus for online retailer buy.com, whose prospectus (7 February 2000) contains more than twelve pages of boldly highlighted risk factors including this doozy: "Our business model is new and unproven, and we may not be able to achieve profitability." Notwithstanding this and other disquietingly dire warnings, the company raised $182 million though the sale of 14 million shares of common stock at $13 per share. The company never prospered, virtually all of the capital raised was lost, and shareholders recently agreed to sell the remnants of the business for seventeen cents per share. However, in the intervening eighteen months of the short and tragic life of buy.com, the shares traded considerably higher than their initial $13 offering price. It is a challenge beyond the scope of this writer's ability to make a positive connection between the SEC disclosure requirements operative before, during, and subsequent to the public trading of this company's shares and the accuracy of the pricing of its shares. Numerous counterparts to this story have contributed to losses estimated as high as $500 billion.[25]

If the quality of investment decisions depends upon the quality of information but investors routinely ignore it, why mandate its production? To argue for mandatory information requirements in light of the events of the past few years seems naïve or Pollyannaish in the extreme. At the risk of bearing either or both of those ascriptions, I venture a defense. Market participants, and their willingness to act upon the information made available to them, limit the efficacy of mandatory disclosure requirements. Investors have an opportunity to make informed decisions, but they are equally free to ignore publicly available information and speculate with wild abandon. The fact that they routinely do so is damaging to any theory of market regulation. It undermines the libertarian case that the best of all possible pricing systems emerges from unconstrained trade. The Internet bubble was an instance in which the invisible hand of free enterprise was all thumbs. The only theoretical approach vindicated is the one that would remove capital allocation decisions from individuals and vest them in some central decision-making forum. But there is no success-ful model of such an agency having succeeded in making successful investment allocation decisions. As flawed as individual investors might be, their results far outpace the dismal record of centrally planned economies. Indeed, notwithstanding the magnitude of the most recent debacle, it should not be exaggerated. It was not the case that this latest episode of investor dementia caused a systemic market crisis. Throughout the past several years, worthy commercial projects had access to ample capital at reasonable prices. The market distor-tions caused by high-technology or Internet stock trading were largely contained in what became a casino of trading in a single category of the equity markets. It did not infect every other category of equity investments and credit markets remained relatively unscathed. Nor was it the case that these losses did serious damage to the overall sup-ply of investment capital. By historical standards, interest rates on fixed income securities remained quite tame. Moreover, although this episode has produced an overabundance of useless websites and equally frivolous high-technology gadgets, it has not impaired in the least the supply of goods and services that are in demand. And finally, it would be wrong to presume that because one segment of the invest-ing public was oblivious to financial information that other segments were equally blind. Indeed, financial disclosures played a crucial role in the investment decisions of a great many individual and institu-tional investors who chose to avoid this sector. In sum, the events of the past few years are troubling reminders of the limits of financial information, but they do not warrant a reevaluation of its vital role.

Some have been more pointed in their criticism of the SEC and the value of mandatory information disclosures. Based on evidence compiled by George Benston,[26] Susan Phillips and Richard Zecher allege, "In fact no documentation by the SEC is available that shows that their regulatory programs have reduced the amount of price manipulation fraud and deceit."[27] To clarify, prior to this quote the authors refer to three categories of activity untouched by SEC regulation in which fraud is listed separately from price manipulation. Therefore it is fair to interpret this passage as referring to securities fraud and not only price manipulation. Benston had undertaken a study of newly issued securities and found that SEC rules do not affect positively or negatively the reception they receive in secondary trading markets. The findings of that study were disputed by Irwin Friend and R. Westerfield and were more or less dismissed by A. A. Sommer Jr. as an inappropriate use of mathematical techniques. This interchange repeats the pattern set a decade earlier when George Stigler claimed that the SEC rules had no effect on the market for new issues, a position that was roundly criticized by Sidney Robbins and Walter Werner.[28]

Homer Kripke recounts the above quarrel and comments on the difficulty of resolving it.[29] One could assume that regulation discouraged some capital market abuses, but measuring that impact requires evidence of something that never occurred. Consequently, it is unlikely that this dispute can be settled on the basis of empirical analysis. However, I would offer an observation that, although highly colored by personal experience, is nonetheless valuable. First, it is unrealistic to assume that the criminal sanctions contained in the securities legislation would have emerged out of the common law. As Irwin Friend and Edward Herman observe,

> Though many (but by no means all) manipulative and fraudulent activities may have been illegal under common law before the federal securities legislation administered by the SEC was enacted, it was not possible to enforce the law effectively. We doubt that any person reasonably well acquainted with the evolution of stock-market practices between the pre- and post-S.E.C. periods could lament or underrate the success of the new legislation in eradicating many of the weaknesses in our capital markets.[30]

Second, from examining the debate it is apparent that those who question the efficacy of SEC regulation have not had responsibility for making public disclosures subject to the securities legislation. And I do not attribute this to mere happenstance. Rather, I believe it is highly probable that anyone having signed documents that fall within the purview of the SEC would acknowledge a heightened sense of cautious seriousness. Most financial executives are far less likely to knowingly engage in activities that threaten criminal sanctions than they are to risk tort liability. But this is only the case if the threat is realistic. Although there are notorious exceptions, they are distinguished as exceptional cases. So from this less than rigorous but no less plausible standpoint, I am inclined to believe that SEC oversight of capital markets does filter some significant amount of financial chicanery.

Insider Trading

A test of this Regulatory Strategy would be incomplete without a brief examination of the persistent controversy surrounding insider trading. The practice—trading securities with benefit of material nonpublic information—has frustrated courts and scholars, not to mention capital market participants. The SEC and various courts have identified a vast array of actionable behavior from legislative language that, as legislative language goes, is fairly straightforward:

> It shall be unlawful for any person, directly or indirectly . . . [t]o use or employ, in connection with the purchase or sale of any security . . . any manipulative or deceptive device or contrivance in contravention of such rules and regulations as the Commission may prescribe as necessary or appropriate *in the public interest for the protection of investors* [emphasis added].
>
> Section 10(b) of the Securities and Exchange Act of 1934. 15 U.S.C § 78j (1934)

Subsequently, the SEC prescribed Rule 10b-5, which provides in pertinent part that

> It shall be unlawful . . .
>
> a) To employ any device, scheme, or artifice to defraud,
> b) To make any untrue statement of a material fact or to omit to state a material fact necessary in order to make the statements made, in light of the circumstances under which they were made, not misleading, or

c) To engage in any act, practice, or course of business which operates or would operate as a fraud or deceit upon any person, in connection with the purchase or sale of any security.

17 C.F.R. § 240.10b-5 (1992)

Note that the term *"insider"* does not appear in either the legislation or the Rule, leaving it to regulators and ultimately the courts to determine what behavior is actionable. It is intuitive that something untoward takes place when a corporate employee is enriched personally by trading in his or her employer's securities on the basis of privileged information. But it is difficult to specify the wrong, or to say precisely why it is wrong, in such a way that other intuitively wrong cases will be covered but whole classes of innocent behavior won't be condemned. In the prototypical case of insider trading the wrong can be described as a breach of fiduciary duty to shareholders. But the employee has no fiduciary duty to nonshareholders, so he or she could avoid the rule by simply trading with someone who does not yet own shares, an outsider. While this trade may not violate a fiduciary duty there is still something wrong about it. But what is it? In recent years the prohibition against insider trading has been expanded to so-called outside traders or those removed from the corporation but trading on privileged information obtained from insiders (e.g., friends of insiders or other "tippees"). The insider has breached some moral duty, but not to the tippee profiting from the news. And some offenses do not involve insiders at all. Printers, investment bankers, couriers, and other independent third parties have access to confidential information. When they do, the moral substance of their behavior resembles these others, but it is not clear how to characterize it. So if for no other reason than consistency of treatment and coherence of reasoning, it is desirable to construct a theoretical account of what makes these practices wrong. More importantly, in the context of this study, it is important to specify the reason why states are justified in punishing those engaging in them.[31]

A great number of explanations have been advanced and, in turn, more or less fatally criticized. I will not recount them in detail here.[32] Instead, I will describe the flaws that have hobbled prior attempts to construct a reasonable account of insider trading. In doing so I will create criteria that any successful account must satisfy. For one, many of the efforts to justify a legal prohibition against trading on nonpublic information have affixed moral blameworthiness to behavior that is not necessarily criticized in other areas of commercial life. Indeed, the advantage gained through superior knowledge is often rewarded. So a successful account needs to specify why profiting from inside information is wrong without also impugning informational advantages in other commercial settings. Similarly, it is overly general to condemn a trading relationship, say, because it violates trust or because it exploits another's vulnerability. Commercial life presents far too many examples in which exploiting vulnerabilities is not blameworthy, much less actionable under criminal law. For such instances of exploitation to be actionable, it is usually necessary that they occur within a relationship characterized by reasonable expectations about fair play and due consideration of someone else's interests. Securities trading relationships cannot be described this way. The parties are anonymous and trades are consummated with minimal representations and warranties (e.g., delivery, payment, and negotiability). Another challenge is to characterize the wrong that attaches to the trading of securities on privileged information and not to the illicit acquisition of the information. A theory that calls out "misappropriation" as the source of wrongness captures only what occurs between the owner of the information and the one absconding with it. The moral wrong of misappropriation is obvious. But trading on it, especially by a third party unconnected to the misappropriation, is probably wrong for another reason. And one final flaw has hobbled these efforts: it is not clear whether insider trading harms anyone. Of course, so-called victimless crimes are not necessarily morally innocent.[33] But they are particularly nettlesome when some allege that insider trading is socially beneficial.

These and other similarly perplexing difficulties have kept debates over insider trading alive far longer than would be expected.[34] Two of the most thoroughgoing and promising attempts to overcome the problem are worthy of examination. I do so with the intention of illustrating the profound difficulty of this challenge and not to idly criticize these efforts. And I will suggest modifications in both of these projects, based on this Regulatory Strategy, that cure their weaknesses. The first, Strudler and Orts's "equitable disclosure rationale," derives its normative force through an appeal to a moral principle. They claim that trading on material nonpublic information is morally wrong because it violates the autonomous choices of individual investors by interfering with their rational decisions. They claim that withholding crucial information is blameworthy, unless those withholding it have valid rights to it. This is a good strategy insofar as it is explicit enough to serve as a guide to regulatory and judicial decision making. But also, even though it is justified on the basis of individual autonomy, it does not impose an unrealistically high standard on traders. According to Strudler and Orts, it is morally permissible to exploit one's superior knowledge to the disadvantage of someone else so long as that knowledge was not "illicitly acquired" or "morally tainted." So the informal maxim of capital market justice, to each according to his or her superior knowledge, requires only a minor amendment— that he or she came by this knowledge rightfully.

Market intervention to remove an obstacle to personal autonomy is consistent with this Regulatory Strategy. However, whether a practice is an impediment to autonomous decision making or not requires some empirical spadework. Strudler and Ort are obliged to show that instances of insider trading are highly likely to compromise someone's autonomy. This, I will argue, is difficult to demonstrate on a case-by-case basis. Consider their example:

> Suppose that Ralph steals the information that he uses to get a bargaining advantage over Alice in their sales transaction. Ralph's advantage does not derive from his rights in information, and it follows that Ralph's use of that information wrongly interferes with Alice's autonomous choice. Ralph has an unfair advantage over Alice by using stolen information. Thus, the use of stolen information ordinarily compromises autonomy and triggers a duty to disclose before trading.[35]

Now, if this were true—that the source of information can affect the autonomy of a counterparty to a securities transaction—then their argument is cinched. But it is not true. Assume this hypothetical sequence of events:

1. At T_1 Alice decides, based on rational reasons, to sell 1,000 shares of Acme, Inc. at $50 per share.
2. Unbeknownst to Alice, Acme is a takeover target of Beta, Inc. at a price of $100 per share.
3. Fred is also oblivious to this eventuality although he suspects, based on his diligent research, that a takeover is probable, so at T_1 he places an order to buy 1,000 shares of Acme at $50 per share.
4. Ralph, having recently broken into the offices of Beta, Inc. and read confidential documents, places an order to buy 1,000 shares of Acme at $50 per share at T_1.

Now, at T_2, when trading occurs, it is possible that Alice's order is transacted with, or in industry jargon, "crossed," with Ralph's, Fred's, or some combination of the two. Strudler and Orts claim that if it is crossed with Ralph's, then the moral taint of his ill-gotten information wrongly tampers with her autonomy. But if, instead, her order were crossed with Fred's, then she has acted autonomously (although presumably some other party would be acting heteronomously). And if 500 of her shares were crossed equally with Ralph and Fred, then it is not clear how to describe her action because a single decision cannot be both autonomous and heteronomous.

The absurdity of these possibilities suggests something wrong with the model that treats Alice's autonomy as the morally salient factor in Ralph's blameworthiness (with respect to her as opposed to Beta or Acme). It is noteworthy that Ralph did not encroach upon her autonomy by compelling her to sell—they are anonymous to one another, and her sale would have taken place whether Ralph was a party to it or not. Indeed, equity markets for highly liquid issues (where insider trading is generally focused) rarely afford the possibility to link individual sellers with the buyers of their shares. The settlement of trades occurs on a consolidated basis through a complex jumble of counterparty brokerage firms and other financial intermediaries. Alice's shares are fungible with all other shares of Acme, Inc., and as they snake their way through this system they are commingled with thousands and sometimes millions of other shares until they ultimately find their way into someone else's securities account. They are rarely acquired directly by Ralph or any other individual trader. Whether they remain intact or not, as Ralph's purchase of Alice's shares, is a metaphysical question that need not deter us here. What is of significance is this: the only reasonable construal of this situation is that at T_1 it is impossible to specify exactly whose autonomy was violated or upon what basis someone's rational self-interested decision was compromised. It might be suggested that Ralph encroached upon the autonomy of everyone selling stock on that day. But it is implausible that his 1,000-share purchase wreaked so much havoc on a single day's activity that includes vast numbers of trades and even larger volumes of shares.[36] Alternatively, it could be acknowledged that the source of Ralph's knowledge is irrelevant in determining whether Alice behaved autonomously or not. Either way there is something flawed in this interpretation of the wrongfulness of insider trading.

But Strudler and Orts's intuition stands; even if Ralph did not breach a duty, commit a fraud, or, as has been argued, violate Alice's autonomy, it seems as though he did something wrong. The second project draws its normative force from social contract theory. Kim

Scheppele emphasizes the moral importance of the consent manifest in fully informed contractual relationships. For Scheppele, market intervention is legitimate if it comports with "what potential contractors would say were they asked for their views under conditions that ensured they were free from coercion and other contaminating influences."[37] She subjects insider trading to this contractarian test by pondering the rules that market participants would insist upon and arrives at these two conditions: "a roughly calculable chance to win" and "a level playing field." The first condition requires that one can determine with some level of accuracy the probability of success. And the second requires that every market participant have similar access to information—trading on privileged information would only be acceptable if everyone "began on a level playing field."[38]

Scheppele believes that trading on confidential information violates both of these conditions and is therefore morally wrong. Whether she is right or not turns on whether it is plausible to believe that contractors would or would not choose these rules and, moreover, whether those rules would indeed single out morally obnoxious cases of insider trading without also condemning innocent behavior. There are reasons to doubt whether either condition can be satisfied. First, under the calculable chance to win condition, Scheppele says that inside information presents a "hidden danger" whose risk cannot be quantified because it cannot be known. Since participants insist on being able to calculate their chances of winning, they will prohibit the information from being "deployed against them."[39] However, it is not plausible that fully informed contractors would press for this rule because it does not follow from: (1) the fact that there are hidden dangers in the market, and (2) an insistence on calculable risks, that (3) trading on nonpublic information should be prohibited. Hidden dangers in securities markets (e.g., earnings shortfalls, litigation, impending loss of a major customer) are not caused or even affected by whether someone trades on them or not. If hidden risks impair one's ability to calculate the probability of winning, and if calculating such probability is a necessary condition for participation, then market participation in securities markets is problematic, separate and apart from insider trading. Scheppele's first rule says too much. It is unreasonable to preclude insider trading on the basis that it impairs one's ability to calculate one's chances of winning if such a calculation remains problematic in the absence of insider trading. And such is the case with most information that inside traders would use. That is, it is

an unknown danger (or windfall) of the market. But imperfect knowledge does not preclude participation.

Scheppele's second rule—a level playing field—suffers a similar fate
when it sets limits on the "sorts of inequalities in access to knowledge
people will be willing to tolerate."[40] Obviously investors accept some
inequality, and Scheppele draws the line at the point where someone
has a clear chance of winning that precludes the chance that others
can win. She gives the example of a lottery that is rigged so that the
lottery master is also a player. Of course this character always wins,
generating considerable ill will among the other players. It is fair to
assume that hypothetical contractors would endorse a prohibition
against rigging a zero-sum game in which one participant's gain
means that counterparties will loose. But this example does not map
onto securities trading, and the rule it endorses would not apply to
instances of insider trading. Most capital markets are not zero-sum
games, because it is not necessary for one party (much less every other
party) to lose when another party wins. In the above example, it
would be wrong to assume that Ralph's gain caused Alice to suffer a
loss. It is conceivable that both of them will profit from their ownership of Acme, Inc. stock. So a rule constructed along the lines of this
level playing field condition is a reasonable one, and it is plausible to
assume that contractors would opt for it. However, it would not apply
to instances of insider trading.

Make no mistake, both of these projects are excellent ones and have
been examined because they get as close to resolving the insider trading conundrum as any others. Does the Regulatory Strategy formulated here fare any better? Recall that it endorses a prohibition against
practices that could conceivably contribute to the failure of U.S. capital
markets. Such a failure would be plausible if insider trading were so
widespread that investors were reluctant to participate. As discussed
earlier in this chapter, investor confidence is a legitimate regulatory
concern for the same reasons that justify mandatory information disclosures—capital market failures compromise indirectly individual
autonomy. Strudler and Orts also emphasize personal autonomy, but
they do so at a different level where this risk is not always apparent.
As was true of information disclosures, the wrongness of insider trading is not apparent from an examination of isolated transactions.
Focus on Alice and Ralph does not reveal a compromise of autonomy.
Only when that transaction is generalized and its deleterious consequences are observed (or reasonably predicted) does the evil of insider
trading become apparent. So Strudler and Orts are right: insider trad-

ing is a threat to personal autonomy, and the defense of autonomy justifies market intervention. But this threat should be understood as a consequence of the contamination of U.S. capital markets.

Scheppele's contractarian approach can be similarly modified to include this understanding of the wrong of insider trading. But doing so is complicated by the emphasis she places on the *consent* to *rational* rules as a test for moral legitimacy. An opponent of the insider trading laws might counter that irrational rules are not necessarily immoral so long as they are consensual. Alternatively, this critic might make a case for the rationality of insider trading. Either way, insider trading appears to be morally permissible. Consider that Scheppele arrived at her two conditions for capital market rules by assuming that fully informed rationally self-interested deliberators would choose them. And this is reasonable to believe, because they are rules that seem to protect their self-interests. But other social contractarians might wonder whether it would be immoral for these parties to construct their rules on other than a fully rational basis. That is, suppose they favored rules that permitted insider trading because they thought it was more efficient or fun. Would regulators be justified in punishing them? There is nothing inherently wrong with a game in which the chances of winning are stacked disproportionately so long as everyone is fully informed of the risks and no one is coerced into playing it. The gaming industry and state lotteries tilt playing fields to the extreme in favor of casinos and state treasuries, respectively. Participating in these games commits a grievous sin against human reason and the laws of probability, but it is hardly cause for moral condemnation. What moral reason prevents the hypothetical contractors from agreeing to laissez-faire capital markets bereft of any rules governing the source of one's information?

Again, this question cannot be answered adequately without considering the special nature of capital markets and their place in modern commercial life. In particular, it is vital that these markets be differentiated on the basis of their reach. Generally speaking (leaving aside the families of habitual gamblers), the manner in which the gaming industry operates does not reverberate throughout commercial life in the same way that capital market failures do. A legitimate social contract relative to capital markets must therefore include everyone at risk of a market failure and not just the "potential contractors" engaged in trading securities. Now, although many traders might seek the entertainment value of trading and abhor any intervention, it is unrealistic to believe that innocent outsiders with nothing to win from trading but a great deal to lose from a capital market failure (e.g., wage earners or corporate issuers) would approve. Regulatory intervention is justified when these interests are taken into consideration. But without these innocent third parties—if the consequences of capital market failures were confined to securities traders, each of whom were sanguine about insider trading—prohibitions against insider trading cannot be justified.

So, if the group of deliberators were expanded to include everyone affected by capital market operations, they would probably consent to something along these lines: A prohibition against trading practices that, if widespread, would likely contaminate the integrity of capital markets and discourage investor participation. This rule would seem to cover insider-trading practices. But moreover, it is reasonable to believe that the relevant group would consent to this if group members did not know in advance whether they were direct market participants (honest, avaricious, or otherwise) or bystanders whose interests were vulnerable to the operation of the capital market. This rule and the first approximation Scheppele formulated both depend on rational consent as the justification for the rule. The difference is that this formulation takes account of the special purpose and risks of capital markets. As with Strudler and Orts's appeal to autonomy, without considering the special implications of capital market failures, the moral wrongness of insider trading defies an uncontroversial explanation as well as a straightforward justification for coercively prohibiting it.

Notes

1. James Willard Hurst, *Law and Markets in United States History* (Madison, Wis.: University of Wisconsin Press, 1982), 68.

2. Martin Feldstein, ed., *The Risk of Economic Crisis* (Chicago: Chicago University Press, 1991), 2.

3. Jonathan Glover, *Humanity: A Moral History of the Twentieth Century* (New Haven, Conn.: Yale University Press, 2000), 43.

4. Perhaps the most even-handed account of securities regulation is Joel Seligman, *The Transformation of Wall Street* (Boston: Northeastern University Press, 1995). Largely critical accounts are more readily available, including Roberta Karmel, *Regulation by Prosecution* (New York: Simon and Schuster, 1982); Homer Kripke, *The S.E.C. and Corporate Disclosure: Regulation in Search of a Purpose* (New York: Law and Business, Inc., 1979); and Susan Phillips and J. Richard Zecher, *The S.E.C. and the Public Interest* (Cambridge, Mass.: MIT Press, 1981).

5. In 1998, the SEC employed 3,039 people with total spending authority

of $297.4 million, all of which was funded by user fees and fines (*S.E.C. GPRA Report: Position and Cost Data for 1996–1998*). According to Seligman, *The Transformation*, 13, the agency employed 879 people in 1936, its first full year of operation.

6. As Joel Seligman, *The Transformation*, xv, explains, "Few have suggested seriously that the SEC has been a 'captive' of the industries it regulates." A glaring exception is the way the accounting industry, for a time, was able to fend off SEC initiatives regarding the provision of consulting services. However, this was less a case of regulatory capture as it was political override of the Agency's will. And, as events have played out, that override was only temporary.

7. Specifically, the Dow Jones Industrial Average peaked at 381 in 1929 but did not return to that level until 1954. More dramatically, perhaps, is this: "Between September 1, 1929, and July 1, 1932, the value of all stocks listed on the New York Stock Exchange shrank from a total of nearly $90 billion to just under $16 billion—a loss of 83 percent. In a comparable period, bonds listed on the New York Stock Exchange declined from a value of $49 billion to $31 billion" (Seligman, *The Transformation*, 2).

8. For a particularly able and engaging account, see Charles Kindleberger, *The World in Depression, 1929–1939* (Berkeley: University of California Press, 1973) and, more generally, his *Manias, Panics, and Crashes* (New York: Basic Books, 1978). For a conflicting account that puts the blame on monetary decisions by the Federal Reserve, see Milton Friedman, *The Great Contraction, 1929–1933* (Princeton, N.J.: Princeton University Press, 1965). But Barrie Wigmore argues, "macro-fiscal and monetary policies had slight opportunity to affect the course of events in this chain of disasters [meaning the interrelated failures of stock markets and the banking system, international trade and finance]." See *The Crash and Its Aftermath: A History of Securities Markets in the United States, 1929–1933* (Westport, Conn.: Greenwood Press, 1985).

9. Seligman (*The Transformation*, 3) explains that in the post–World War I decade, $50 billion of new securities were underwritten and that approximately half would prove "near or totally valueless." Considering that at their peaks the stock and bond markets totaled only $139 billion, the new issues represented (at least) a staggering 36 percent of the market capitalization of the public equity and debt markets.

10. It is fashionable to compare recent stock market debacles such as the crash of 1987 or the high-technology Internet stock bubble to the 1929 crash. Although there are enough similarities to make a comparison, there are important differences. Most importantly, the losses in the most recent frenzies were limited to purchasers of securities—regulatory controls prevented those losses from pouring over and infecting banks. A similar result was observed in the savings and loan failures of the 1970s and early 1980s. The widespread collapse of that industry did not spread to other portions of the financial services industry. Again, the regulatory regime in place at that time contained the problem, albeit at a very high price.

11. Maury Klein, *Rainbow's End: The Crash of 1929* (New York: Oxford Uni-

versity Press, 2001). However, David Kennedy claims that there is not a cause and effect relationship between the crash and the Depression and that, indeed, the two events are separated in time. Other events such as monetary policy vie for prominence as causal factors for the Depression, although Kennedy observes that all of them are controversial for one reason or another. See *Freedom from Fear: The American People in Depression and War, 1929–1945* (New York: Oxford University Press, 1999).

12. The others being the Public Utility Holding Company Act of 1935, the Trust Indenture Act of 1939, the Investment Company Act of 1940, and the Investment Advisers Act of 1940.

13. Recent legislation has overhauled some elements of the Glass-Stegall Act. The primary thrust of this legislation is to relax the rules requiring that discrete activities be carried out in separate organizations. However, the legislation did nothing to relax other supervisory aspects of the Glass-Stegall Act. Indeed, the Federal Reserve and the SEC continue to maintain capital requirement rules that provide the safety features that were previously realized through the segregation of activities in independent corporate solution.

14. To be precise, he says, "[t]he socialist society would have to forbid capitalist acts between consenting adults." Nozick, *Anarchy, State, and Utopia* (New York: Basic Books, 1974), 163.

15. Klein, *Rainbow's End*, 73.

16. Seligman, *The Transformation*, 37.

17. A thorough, blow-by-blow recount of these rather spectacular debates is detailed in the first five chapters of Seligman, *The Transformation*.

18. Seligman, *The Transformation*, 53–54.

19. Thomas K. McCraw, *Prophets of Regulation*. (Cambridge, Mass.: Harvard University Press, 1984), 166.

20. A period marked by a plunge of the technology-rich NASDAQ Index from a high of 5,049 on 10 March 2000 to 1,639 on 5 April 2001 for a loss of 67 percent.

21. Economic theory has fairly well coalesced around the notion that information is a crucial component of an effective capital market. In a study of economic crises, Joseph Grundfest describes information as "the lifeblood of the market." See "When Markets Crash: The Consequences of Information Failure in the Market for Liquidity" in Martin Feldstein, ed., *The Risk of Economic Crisis* (Chicago: University of Chicago Press, 1991), 67. Some dispute the extent to which the paucity of financial information contributed to the events of 1929, but this is secondary to the fact that there was a lack of information and that more would be needed to restore investors' willingness to participate in U.S. capital markets. As Joseph Auerbach and Samuel Hayes note, "Much to the detriment of public investors, a true 'information gap' developed as accurate and timely information became (by the 1920s) more crucial than ever before. But traditional business practice, exacerbated by the competitive circumstances of the time, made the distribution of such information impossible, and the great crash of 1929 produced a special crisis of legitimacy. Afterward, neither the confidence nor the faith upon which legitimacy

rests could be restored by simple acts of belief; better information was required, but it was not forthcoming" ("Underwriting Regulation and the Shelf Registration Phenomenon," in *Wall Street and Regulation*, ed. Samuel Hayes III, [Boston, Mass.: Harvard Business School Press, 1987], 131).

22. Parenthetically, government has another vital interest in the way capital markets perform. Market historian Robert Sobel documents eleven crises in U.S. capital markets, from the Duer panic in 1792 to the Kennedy slide in 1962. Many of these episodes produced civil unrest on a scale that posed a threat to national stability. See *Panic on Wall Street: A History of America's Financial Disasters* (New York: Macmillan, 1969). However, it is noteworthy that similar fallout cannot be associated with the crises and panics occurring subsequent to the 1933–34 Securities Acts and the restructuring of the Federal Reserve.

23. This argument results in a moral assessment of individuals' behavior in virtue of their membership in a group. For a carefully argued defense for such a perspective, see Larry May, *The Morality of Groups: Collective Responsibility, Group-Based Harms, and Corporate Rights* (Notre Dame, Ind.: University of Notre Dame Press, 1987).

24. Commenting on litigation associated with underwriting initial public offerings of Internet-related business by U.S. investment banks, the actual losses of which are estimated at between $10 and $50 billion, Shawn Tully says, "Typically, class-action suits in this business settle for around 10% of the alleged damages." Shawn Tully, "Will Wall Street Go Up in Smoke?" *Fortune*, 3 September 2001, 37.

25. Tully, "Will Wall Street Go Up in Smoke?" 37.

26. George J. Benston, "Required Disclosure and the Stock Market: An Evaluation of the Securities Exchange Act of 1934," *American Economics Review* 63 (March 1973), 132–55.

27. Phillips and Zecher, *The S.E.C.*, 19.

28. For a recapitulation of portions of the Stigler–Friend/Herman–Benston debate, see chapter 11 of *Economics of Corporation and Securities Regulation*, ed. Richard A. Posner and Kenneth E. Scott (Boston: Little, Brown and Company, 1980).

29. Kripke, *The S.E.C.*, 10–11.

30. Posner and Scott, *Economics*, 352.

31. Scholarly research that includes an article by Roberta S. Karmel, "Outsider Trading on Confidential Information—A Breach in Search of a Duty," 20 *Cardozo L. Rev.* 83 (1998) gives some sense for the urgency in establishing a theoretical framework. James D. Cox, in "Insider Trading and Contracting: A Critical Response to the Chicago School," 1986 *Duke L.J.* 628–34, finds the state of affairs so unsettling that he condemns the active prosecution of such cases.

32. Two excellent articles that thoroughly detail the various projects and their shortcomings are Alan Strudler and Eric W. Orts, "Moral Principle in the Law of Insider Trading," *Texas Law Review* (December 1999): 375–438; and Kim Lane Scheppele, "'It's Just Not Right': The Ethics of Insider Trading," *Law and Contemporary* Problems 56, no. 3 (Summer 1993): 123–73.

33. For an insightful explanation (with particular bearing on insider trading) of why this is the case, see Leo Katz, *Ill-Gotten Gains: Evasion, Blackmail, Fraud, and Kindred Puzzles of the Law* (Chicago: University of Chicago Press, 1996).

34. And these debates do not occupy legal and other scholars alone. On the popular front, it is not uncommon for those accused of 10-b(5) violations to question the authority to punish what they take to be innocuous behavior. One of the late twentieth century's most spectacular instances even had a book written about its injustice: Daniel R. Fischel, *Payback: The Conspiracy to Destroy Michael Milken and His Financial Revolution* (New York: Harper Business, 1995).

35. Strudler and Orts, "Moral Principle in the Law of Insider Trading," 411.

36. Insider trading is typically perpetrated in highly liquid markets and in small enough quantities that it does not arouse suspicion.

37. Kim Lane Scheppele, "'It's Just Not Right': The Ethics of Insider Trading," 152.

38. Kim Lane Scheppele, "'It's Just Not Right': The Ethics of Insider Trading," 160.

39. Kim Lane Scheppele, "'It's Just Not Right': The Ethics of Insider Trading," 158.

40. Kim Lane Scheppele, "'It's Just Not Right': The Ethics of Insider Trading," 161.

5

Agricultural Biotechnology

Monsanto and Agricultural Biotechnology

THIS CHAPTER PROBES the moral justification of commercial regulation through the perspective of a firm, Monsanto, and its biotechnology business. Agricultural biotechnology (i.e., genetically modified or GM crops) and this firm in particular have been the focus of passionate criticism and even violent protests. Unlike the previous case this one involves environmental and human health risks attendant to novel technology. But also, the agricultural biotechnology controversy is a significant target in the antiglobalization movement. Therefore, this is a good case to examine and to use in further probing the adequacy of this Regulatory Strategy. I begin with some brief background information on Monsanto and the agricultural biotechnology industry. Next I explain and critically examine the precautionary principle, a proposal for regulating environmental risk. Then I consider some international dimensions of this controversy by exploring the European reaction to GM corps and processed food products containing GM ingredients. I will conclude by reconsidering the role of communitarian values in regulating GM risks, an approach being urged by some European activists.

Monsanto and the Agricultural
Biotechnology Controversy

Monsanto enjoys a leadership position in agricultural productivity (e.g., herbicides and hybrid seeds) and proprietary plant genomic discoveries. Two such discoveries, first commercialized in 1997, were crop varieties resistant to insect predation (e.g., Bollgard® cotton, Maisgard® corn, and NewLeaf® potatoes) and other varieties resistant to broad-spectrum glyphosate herbicides (e.g., Roundup Ready® corn, soybean, canola, and cotton, sometimes "stacked" with pest protection in a single seed). Pest-protected crop varieties are attractive to growers because they reduce the use and cost of pesticides. Herbicide resistance is attractive because it allows growers to safely manage weeds with a broad-spectrum herbicide after the seed has germinated.

Biotechnology has made commercial inroads in the agricultural sector that are both stunning and disappointing. On the one hand, after only five years of commercial production, GM crops were planted to 109 million acres worldwide in 2000[1] (90 percent of which were produced by Monsanto).[2] But on the other hand, adoption has been grossly uneven. Growers in the United States embraced it, planting 75 million acres to GM varieties in 1998 that accounted for more than 40 percent of domestic cotton, soybean, and corn acreage.[3] But these plantings represented 69 percent of worldwide GM cultivation with (in decreasing order) Argentina, Canada, and China ranking far behind. And although worldwide biotech plantings increased 11 percent in 2000, virtually all of that growth came from developing countries as plantings in the developed world stalled to a 2-percent increase.[4]

Such irregular adoption of a commodity product is curious when early adopters report near universal satisfaction, as is the case with agricultural biotechnology.[5] This anomaly can be traced to the European Union (EU) where resistance to GM technology has been staunch. Spurred on by activists' claims of environmental and human health risks, European regulators threw up roadblocks to the widespread adoption of GM crop technology and the importation of GM food products. Early in 1999, after years of hesitantly approving only a handful of GM crop applications, several EU member states announced their refusal to participate in the regulatory approval process, creating a de facto moratorium on new product approvals ever since.[6] And the problem is not limited to the dearth of GM crop cultivation in Europe.[7] Rather, this resistance affects any grower whose harvested products would enter international food channels. I will not rehearse this dispute in any detail but will simply outline the salient factors relevant to the present discussion.[8]

The widespread cultivation of GM plants raises at least three different sorts of environmental risks, all of them concerned in one way or another with agro-diversity. The first is a worry that the engineered trait (e.g., the protection against pest predation by causing plant tissue to emit a bacterial insecticide) will harm nontarget species (e.g., monarch butterflies). Reduced populations of nontarget species could upset the regulatory mechanisms that naturally constrain pest populations. The second worry is gene flow, or the risk that the special trait of a GM plant will be conferred on wild relatives through cross-pollination. In the case of protection against insect predation, the wild relatives would inherit a reproductive advantage that could give rise to so-called super-weeds at the expense of any natural balance in the neighboring ecosystem.[9] Third is the concern that the pests targeted by the genetic modification will evolve resistance to the protective feature (e.g., the insecticide bacterium called Bt), making them impervious to conventional controls and giving rise to so-called killer bugs and the possibility for widespread damage to cultivated crops and surrounding plant life alike.

Any of these risks could be good reasons to curtail the commercial cultivation of GM plants. And none of them should be dismissed out of hand. No less of a passionate advocate of agricultural biotechnology than former Monsanto CEO, Robert Shapiro, warned that:

> [w]hen you start talking about large-scale introduction of dramatic traits in combination with each other, you are dealing with systems that are so complicated that no one can effectively model them. You can start with running field trials, just as when you introduce a new drug you run clinical trials to see if people really keel over. But, just as the human body is a subtle and complicated thing, it may be that only one time in a million some side effect happens.[10]

But neither should these risks be exaggerated to the point of ignoring the regulatory regimes that must approve new GM crops. In the United States, GM plants are subject to the Regulatory Framework for the Regulation of Biotechnology Products[11] administered by the Food and Drug Administration, the Environmental Protection Agency, and the Animal and Plant Health Inspection Service (APHIS) of the U.S. Department of Agriculture. For purposes of this discussion, it is only important to note that U.S. regulators have identified and considered each of the three categories of environmental risk with respect to each plant that is approved for commercialization and that different but similarly stringent protocols exist in Canada and the EU.[12] Also, it is noteworthy that this regulatory protocol has been evaluated favorably by the National Research Council on several occasions.[13]

Moreover, it should be borne in mind that many extant agricultural practices are environmentally hostile. Regulatory approval of a GM plant for commercial production in the United States or in Europe has meant accepting its environmental risks in virtue of some environmental benefit that is deemed to outweigh them.[14] The environmental risks of current agricultural practices played an important role in the acceptance of some GM crops as substitutes for other more environmentally pernicious practices. That is, regulators concluded that the possibility of diminished agro-diversity from cultivating GM plants was acceptable in comparison to the harmful affects of chemical pesticides that extract a higher toll on agro-diversity, surface and subsurface water, wildlife, and so forth. Without belaboring the point, regulators treat GM technology as a substitute for or a replacement of some more pernicious technology or practice.[15]

The human health worries over GM technology focus on two risks. One is the possibility of allergic reactions to any proteins contained in the GM plant that are not present in the unmodified variety. Second, some have raised concerns over the "pesticide" (Bt) contained in the plant tissue that is subsequently consumed. To address these concerns, U.S. regulators have adopted a "substantial equivalence" test whereby food products derived from genetically modified plants must behave in a physiologically identical way as their nonmodified cousins in terms of toxicity and allergenicity.[16]

There is a sense in which this regulatory approval process reduces environmental and human health risks to a subjective determination in the political process. Indeed, some would claim that risk is after all a socially constructed concept and therefore any assessment of it is inherently corrupted by personal bias. Conceding that there is an unavoidably subjective element in this process, I reject the radical implications that some would attach to this. As Kristen Shrader-Frechette explains,

> But even though risk evaluation is not wholly objective, neither is it merely evaluative nor only a construct. Constructs don't kill people; faulty reactors, improperly stored toxins, and poor risk evaluations do. At least some hazards are real, and many of these are measurable. Hence, the cultural relativists are wrong in overemphasizing value judgments in risk assessment and evaluation. Risk evaluations assess real hazards, not just constructs.[17]

Notwithstanding the satisfaction of U.S.[18] and EU regulatory protocols that are equally or in some cases more stringent, GM technology has endured savage criticism. Protests have been waged internationally, but unlike in the United States and Canada and elsewhere, they gained serious popular and regulatory traction in the EU. Initially leveled at environmental risks, some of the harshest condemnations have raised worries over dangers to human health. And this has persisted in the face of mounting scientific evidence of the safety of GM technology and the paucity of critical findings.[19] Moreover, this criticism has remained buoyant during a period of time when GM crops have been widely cultivated and consumed without *any* documented environmental or human health harms.[20] Quite to the contrary, GM plantings have reduced the use of environmentally unfriendly pesticides and encouraged no-till soil conservation cultivation. Notwithstanding the lack of evidence—ecological or physiological—GM plants have received particularly onerous regulatory and trade restrictions.[21] Perhaps most importantly, the fears that were originally directed at regulators have been redirected to consumer markets where some food processing, retailing, and restaurant firms have rejected GM crops as potential food ingredients.

Precautionary Regulation: An Overview

The Precautionary Principle (hereafter, "PP") is a relatively new concept for regulating environmental and, to a lesser extent, the health risks of novel technology. I will explicate the doctrine and then critically analyze it with respect to Monsanto's efforts to commercialize[22] genetically modified pest-protected and herbicide-tolerant crops. I concede that my findings may not be applicable to other sorts of environmental or human health risks. However, this example does coax out into the open the regulatory framework suggested by PP advocates, and it therefore sets the stage for other such analyses.

Unfortunately, the PP has several different meanings, and users do not always specify which one they have in mind. Accordingly, I will first clarify the concept by proposing weak and strong categories for grouping the various formulations.[23] Weak versions specify highly flexible or pragmatic guidelines that afford significant leeway in determining the relative relevancy of any particular consideration.[24] Strong formulations restrict regulators to considerations of environmental risk. I will explain that weak formulations of the PP are largely consistent with the conceptual framework for approving GM crops in the United States. And I will argue that this framework is justifiable—

morally, politically, and otherwise. While the weak PP has few, if any, domestic regulatory implications, it could have some undesirable consequences when incorporated into international trade agreements like the Cartagena Protocols on Biosafety, some of which undermine the cause of environmental protection. And finally I will argue for rejecting strong formulations of the PP as a conceptual framework for regulating the environmental risks of GM crops.

The PP has emerged as a response to perceived weaknesses in traditional regulatory regimes, particularly the willingness to pragmatically accept an environmental risk in virtue of a putative benefit. But it is not a clear response insofar as different writers and regulatory bodies use the concept in different ways. However, nearly every version embraces two core beliefs.[25] First is the belief that scientific certainty is not a necessary condition for deciding matters of environmental risk. Said another way, scientific ambiguity or controversy in the scientific community should not preclude a finding that some commercial practice is environmentally risky. I do not interpret this as licensing capricious decisions unconnected with science. Rather, it is a recognition that the best available science is not usually capable of rendering an unimpeachable cause and effect relationship between a commercial practice and an environmental hazard. The PP urges that regulators not be held hostage to scientific certainty but instead that they should accept the best available science, albeit tentative, inconclusive, or in dispute.

Second is the belief that environmental risks should sometimes be avoided—notwithstanding other desirable features of the technology. Risk avoidance, when invoked, rejects an evaluation of environmental risk in relation to nonenvironmental factors, or perhaps even countervailing environmental risks. So risk avoidance stands in stark opposition to risk management protocols that pragmatically balance environmental risk against other factors. Combining environmental risk avoidance with the first belief (scientific uncertainty) produces the following regulatory principle: *sometimes* regulators should prohibit (or constrain) the commercialization of environmentally risky technology, even though the science that identifies the risk is uncertain and even though economic or other factors might recommend otherwise. I emphasize "sometimes" because different versions of the PP invoke risk avoidance differently.

These core beliefs only define the spirit of precautionary regulation; they are too general to specify actual duties of an environmental regulator. To get at those duties I now turn to the details of the PP in official documents and in the literature. However, insofar as this is also a critical undertaking, it behooves me to organize this material in some coherent fashion and not critically analyze the various formulations individually. O'Riordan[26] and Jordan[27] suggest that the PP can be understood along a continuum from very weak to very strong formulations. Their thinking is useful and, to a large extent, I will take advantage of it. However, my reading of the rather sparse PP literature and government documents invoking it suggests two formal categories: weak and strong. I base these categories on the range of factors that are recognized as legitimate regulatory concerns and the different emphasis they place on environmental risk.

The Weak Precautionary Principle

Formulations of the PP in this category do not seriously restrict the factors that decision makers should take into account. Moreover, regulators do not receive any specific guidance on the relative weighting of any given factor. The weak PP is pragmatic, insofar as environmentally risky technology can be evaluated in terms of economic efficiency or by way of trade-offs against some other environmental risk. In the weak PP formulations, staunch risk avoidance vies for regulatory attention with cost and risk-benefit analysis. If the weak PP does anything at all, it is this: it provides the authority to override other factors and make environmental risk the paramount and deciding concern. Regulators might consider all the factors of a practice and judge the environmental hazards to be so profound that they dismiss as secondary any findings of a cost or risk-benefit analysis.[28] But the weak PP does not *mandate* that regulators treat environmental risk this way because it is agnostic as to the relative importance of environmental risk.

A good example of the weak PP is the *Communication from the Commission of the European Communities: On the Precautionary Principle*.[29] This document proposes rules for applying the PP both within the EU and internationally (presumably in connection with EU or member state treaties). I highlight here only two portions of the report.

> Recourse to the precautionary principle presupposes that potentially dangerous effects deriving from a phenomenon, product, or process have been identified, and that scientific evaluation does not allow the risk to be determined with sufficient certainty.[30]

Where action is deemed necessary, measures based on the precautionary
principle should be, inter alia:
[fourth bullet point] based on an examination of the potential benefits
and costs of action or lack of action (including, where appropriate and
feasible, an economic cost/benefit analysis.[31]

Another instance is the Rio Declaration of the 1992 United Nations
Conference on the Environment and Development. Although invoking the precautionary "approach" and not "principle," the fifteenth
principle states that

> in order to protect the environment, the precautionary approach shall be
> widely applied by States according to their capability. Where there are
> threats of serious or irreversible damage, lack of full scientific certainty
> shall not be used as a reason for postponing cost-effective measures to
> prevent environmental degradation.

In both cases, scientific certainty is rejected as a necessary condition
for regulatory action. But also, regulators are urged to evaluate environmental risk in terms of its acceptability. In the first case, benefits
are relevant and in the second, action of a "cost effective" nature is
urged. I describe formulations in this category as weak because they
sanction pragmatic judgments to accept environmental risks in virtue
of some putative benefit.

The PP was recently invoked in an EU document providing eight
guiding principles for future GM crop regulation.[32] The second principle provides:

> Risk assessment should continue to be science-based and in cases where
> scientific evidence is insufficient, inconclusive or uncertain, and where
> possible risks to human health, animal health or the environment are
> judged to be unacceptable, measures should be based on the precaution-
> ary principle.[33]

But this reference is an example of the weak PP in virtue of the following qualification in its third principle:

> Decisions to authorize GMO's, including seeds, and GM derived food
> and feed should be based on the outcome of the risk assessment. As with
> all risk management measure, other legitimate factors, such as societal,
> economic, traditional, ethical and environmental and the feasibility of
> controls, may be relevant to and taken into account in reaching such
> decisions.[34]

The Weak Precautionary Principle: Critical Assessment

There is a profound inconsistency between the two principles in this last elaboration. If risk is to be determined on the basis of science, it is not clear why "tradition" is included on this laundry list of legitimate factors. But I charitably assume that as a theory about environmental and human health risks, any action required by the PP must originate in a credible scientific story. If a "potentially dangerous effect" or some "serious or irreversible damage" did not have a scientific basis, then the PP—in any formulation—is at risk of being arbitrary if not dogmatic.[35] But assuming that an environmental risk is in some sense scientifically grounded, the question is whether GM crops threaten harms that states should legitimately constrain. And it appears that they are at least candidates. The above risks identified not only threaten to diminish biodiversity but could also undermine agricultural productivity. And they are the sorts of risks that cannot be contained between contracting parties who might individually choose to assume them. Rather, if these risks should materialize, they could harm innocent bystanders (e.g., adjoining farmers) who, for a variety of reasons, might not be able to redress their damages through tort actions.[36] Consequently, states have a legitimate interest in the commercial use of GM technology.

And it is not morally (or otherwise) problematic that the weak PP authorizes regulatory action based on something less than scientific "certainty." The idea that states should be restrained from taking protective action without incontrovertible (cause and effect) science seems to impose too high a standard. In most any case of public safety, there is some ambiguity in the science or some division in the scientific community.[37] But protecting the public requires regulators to make judgments based on a variety of scientific disciplines, none of which speak in one voice, and none of which are so intellectually arrogant as to ascribe timeless truth or irreversibility to their claims. Yet science provides the raw material for regulatory restraint if it can muster a compelling case of probable harm—something far short of certainty but, as John Dewey described it, "the best authenticated knowledge we have."[38]

The more interesting question is what, if anything, the weak PP adds to the prevailing regulatory framework in the United States. I would suggest two possibilities. One is to place environmental risk on a more even playing field with cost-benefit analysis. Economic efficiency dominates some areas of environmental regulation, and the weak PP represents a chink in that armor. However, it is not clear how important this factor is with respect to GM crops. Critics of GM crops have sought regulatory reforms that put more emphasis on environmental risk, but at least in the PP's weak formulations there is no reason to believe that it will. So long as environmental risk avoidance is optional and not required, there is no guarantee that the outcome of regulatory deliberations will be as risk averse as some would urge them to be. Indeed, I would suggest that the Coordinated Framework for the Regulation of Biotechnology is an example of the weak PP. That is, none of the environmental risks of GM crops have been "proven," and yet they were a factor in the regulatory approval process. But as there is no guidance for weighing the various factors, environmental risk was pragmatically reduced in importance vis-à-vis other concerns. So at least domestically, weak formulations of the PP represent somewhat innocuous or feeble additions to the regulatory landscape.

The second significant modification of prevailing regulatory doctrine occurs in the area of international trade. The recently released Cartagena Protocol on Biosafety[39] (an extension of the Rio Declaration) provides that states can refuse shipments of GM crops even though there is a "[l]ack of scientific certainty due to the insufficient relevant scientific information and knowledge regarding the extent of the potential adverse effects of a living modified organism on the conservation and sustainable use of biological diversity." The Protocol belongs in my weak category because such refusal is optional; parties can decide to accept environmental risk based on other factors they deem relevant.[40] The significance of the Protocol is that if a country rejects GM crops on the basis of their environmental risks, they are sheltered from charges (and penalties) of nontariff protectionism.

Why is this significant and what are the implications for environmental protection? On the surface, this language is unobjectionable—states should be free to reject environmentally hazardous products. However, individual states already enjoy this right, although they must defend using it against charges of unfair protectionist trade masquerading behind unjustified environmental fears. The Cartagena Protocol removes the possibility of recriminations and, in doing so, removes a vital political check on domestic producers. Absent the Cartagena Protocol, the refusal to accept shipments of GM crops could at least be challenged as unfair protectionism. The political influence of domestic producers whose products (e.g., agrichemical or non-GM crop varieties) are threatened by Monsanto's technology is checked in the context of an international trade dispute. However the debate that accompanies such disputes is potentially quieted by the weak PP language of the Cartagena Protocol. So long as GM crops are the least bit environmentally risky, the Protocol not only insulates domestic producers, it also perpetuates environmentally hazardous practices that GM technology is replacing elsewhere in the world.[41]

The Strong Precautionary Principle

Strong formulations of the PP stand in sharp contrast to the pragmatic balancing of risks and benefits of their weak cousins. These formulations endorse instead that risk be avoided by elevating the importance of environmental risk. Indeed, such risks are determinative of regulatory action. The following excerpt from the Wingspread Statement[42] is an example:

> Therefore, it is necessary to implement the Precautionary Principle: When an activity raises threats of harm to human health or the environment, precautionary measures should be taken even if some cause and effect relationships are not fully established scientifically.

The key feature of this doctrine is the lack of consideration for any factor except environmental risk. Here, the risks of GM crops should be evaluated in isolation from the hazards of extant agricultural practices that they might ameliorate. Risk avoidance rejects choosing the lesser of two (environmental) evils. As the Wingspread Statement provides, a regulatory decision maker bound by the strong PP should not treat environmental risks as something to be bartered off against other factors. And, he or she should act on environmental risks by taking "precautionary measures" and not accept them in virtue of greater agricultural yields or because the risks of pesticides and fungicides might be abated by them.

I do not mean to portray advocates of the strong PP as arbitrarily or maniacally focused on the risk side of the risk–reward equation and to thereby make a straw man out of the doctrine. Risk avoidance is grounded in the very real appreciation for two things. First is the sheer weight of cases of environmental degradation under the watchful eye of pragmatic regulatory protocols. Second is the primitive state of ecological science. Echoing Robert Shapiro's comments, Carolyn Raffensberger, an advocate of strong PP policies, says,

[E]ven basic knowledge about the impacts of the most widely used toxic chemicals is unavailable. Analysis of the impacts of human activities on health and the environment is wrought with uncertainty. This ignorance leads to an important question for decision makers, "How can science establish an 'assimilative capacity' (a predictable level of harm from which an ecosystem can recover) or a 'safe' level when the exact effect, its magnitude, and interconnectedness are unknown?"[43]

Of course, the question posed in this passage is a rhetorical one. But it expresses a profound appreciation for the impoverished state of environmental science. This problem is exacerbated with GM crops because the technology raises questions of genetics, evolutionary biology, *and* environmental science. Consequently, predictions about future environmental impacts are hobbled by the indeterminacies that characterize each of these disciplines.[44] Moreover, although it is widely understood that agricultural chemicals pose serious environmental risks, those hazards are not fully understood. If one seriously takes to heart this level of scientific uncertainty, it is understandable why supporters of the strong PP reject pragmatic decision making and why they think that comparisons between GM crops and present agricultural practices are bogus.

Legislative examples of the strong PP are hard to come by. Jordan and O'Riordan[45] cite but two, and I quote them as they appear. The first is part of a 1984 report on air quality by the German federal government.

The principle of precaution commands that the damages done to the natural world . . . should be avoided in advance and in accordance with opportunity and possibility. [Precaution] further means the early detection of dangers to health and environment by comprehensive, synchronized . . . research . . . [I]t also means acting when conclusively ascertained understanding by science is not yet available. (31)

The other is from the 1990 Third Ministerial Declaration on the North Sea. It urges governments to

Apply the precautionary principle, that is to take action to avoid potentially damaging impacts of [toxic] substances . . . even where there is no scientific evidence to prove a causal link between emissions and effects. (31)

In comparison to the above instances of the weak PP, these formulations *require* action in the face of environmental hazards, without appeal to any mitigating factors. It is in this sense that I describe the strong PP as a risk avoidance strategy and not as an instrument of pragmatic risk management.

The Strong Precautionary Principle: Critical Analysis

First it is necessary to dispel a variety of criticism that has been leveled against strong formulations of the PP.[46] Some have ridiculed the theory and countered that if environmental science is so impoverished that we cannot tell a compelling story about safety, then likewise we should be equally unable to say anything interesting about risk. And if risk cannot be verified, then there is no legal or moral basis for blocking the activity. This counterargument, advanced as a reductio ad absurdum of the strong PP, concludes that GM crops (and other environmentally risky technology) ought to be commercially exploited until such time as science can substantiate their environmental dangers.

I assume that no one seriously considers this conclusion as a live option for environmental regulatory policy. As a reductio, the argument is only intended to show the absurdity of the strong PP. That is, it spins out a ludicrous conclusion based on the same scientific indeterminacy upon which the strong PP is based. But like any reductio it is troubling, and it raises the question as to why this is so easily done and whether it is fair to do so. I believe it is unfair, but my defense will expose some frailties in reasoning that infect the strong PP doctrine. The defense requires harmonizing two seemingly paradoxical beliefs. First is the notion that environmental regulation ought to be predicated upon good science. Second is the belief that there are cases in which science can credibly identify an environmental risk although that same science is not up to the task of confirming or disconfirming worries about environmental safety. These two beliefs seem to conflict, insofar as in the first one (risk assessment) science is credible but in the second (demonstrating safety) it is not. Harmonizing them requires that a distinction be made between the evidentiary demands for assessing risk and those for demonstrating safety. And this sounds as though the strong PP commits an epistemological sleight of hand or that it is trafficking in an unfair double standard of evidence—one for risk assessment and a higher one for demonstrating safety.

But it is not necessarily unreasonable to expect that more evidence is needed to demonstrate safety than is needed to identify a risk. Assessing risk only involves identifying one potentially harmful effect of an activity. However, very few commercial practices have only one effect. Rather, they have many effects, and demonstrating safety involves showing that none of them pose serious hazards. Simply put, there is just more involved in demonstrating safety than in identifying risk. Because safety requires more in the way of evidence and research, it is not unusual that verifying safety would come later in the game than risk assessment. In the meantime, the best available science might support precautionary regulatory action. The above reductio is unfair because it glosses over this evidentiary or epistemic difference. The strong PP is not absurd because it is based on a reasonable epistemic intuition.

But as reasonable as this intuition might be, it is not clear how far it goes or whether it has anything interesting or important to say about the regulation of GM crops. As a regulatory protocol the strong PP can be diagrammed as the following argument:

1. States are morally justified to protect citizens against the uninvited harms of others.
2. There is credible scientific evidence that GM crops pose environmental hazards.
3. Attempts to demonstrate the safety of GM crops are inconclusive.
   Conclusion: The commercial cultivation of GM crops should be *prohibited* (until such time as their safety can be demonstrated conclusively).

Now, consider the following sketch of the argument that constitutes the U.S. Coordinated Framework for the Regulation of Biotechnology.

1. States are morally justified to protect citizens against the uninvited harms of others. *Sometimes this entails approving something that is hazardous if it relieves the risks of something that is more dangerous.*
2. There is credible scientific evidence that GM crops pose environmental hazards.
3. Attempts to demonstrate the safety of GM crops are inconclusive.
4. There is credible scientific evidence that extant agricultural practices pose environmental risks.

5. The environmental risks of GM crops are preferable to those associated with present-day agricultural practices.
   Conclusion: The commercial cultivation of GM crops should be permitted.

My fourth premise is not contentious; both sides to the GM crop debate agree that U.S. agricultural practices are fraught with environmental risks. Of course, my fifth premise and the italicized addition to the first premise are controversial. The strong PP is significant because it dictates the terms of environmental debates by rejecting the legitimacy of even considering these factors I have inserted. But do they have good reasons for doing so?

Advocates of the strong PP advance epistemic and practical reasons why the environmental risks of GM crops should be evaluated and regulated in isolation from any other factor—including the environmental risks they would ameliorate. For one, as discussed above, they claim that we lack the science to compare and choose between environmental risks. Second is their claim that pragmatic trade-offs degrade the environment. Indeed, the hazards of present-day agricultural practices can be understood as a trade-off against something less desirable—either some other environmental risk or economic efficiency. And third, they worry that if present practices constitute the baseline against which new risks are compared, then our standard will be too permissive.

I will now argue that none of these reasons mount a particularly compelling case against a pragmatic evaluation of the environmental risks of GM technology. I begin with the assertion that science cannot evaluate the relative riskiness of GM and extant agricultural practices. This is a flawed claim because it cannot be the case that we could know enough about the risks of GM crops to forbid their cultivation but not enough to *compare* those risks to the prevailing risks of pesticides, fungicides, top soil erosion, and so forth. A higher epistemic standard should not be invoked for purposes of comparison. Unlike a safety claim, comparing two risks should not require any additional scientific evidence. My understanding of an environmental risk is this: a credible scientific warning about what could possibly go wrong—perhaps a list of environmental harms with rough probabilities of occurrence. Comparing such a list to another one and deciding which is preferable is *not* hampered by scientific uncertainty. To claim that such a comparison is prima facie impossible on the grounds of scientific indeterminacy is to confuse the nature of what takes place in comparing and choosing between two risks. A judgment as to which risk is more desirable, although scientifically informed, is not a scientific decision. It is an expression of preferences and in this context it is a political or a moral decision.[47] This is not to suggest that the comparison is easy or that a winner will clearly emerge.[48] But if GM crops are candidates for regulatory constraint, then it must be the case that certain environmental risks have been identified. Whether those risks are more desirable than those of extant agricultural practices cannot be decided by science. And it is wrong to preclude judgments of this nature on grounds of scientific indeterminacies.

Friends of the strong PP would disagree and refer me back to the murky science of ecology and evolutionary biology. However, they are well advised to not push this point too hard. If they could succeed in showing that the relevant science is too impoverished to say anything interesting about the risks of GM crops, then they lose the basis for state regulatory action. That is, the ground for legitimately invoking regulatory restraints is a story in science that GM crops could trigger harmful ecological events of a certain kind (e.g., killer bugs, super-weeds, etc.). If the suspicion is not grounded in science, if it is simply a hunch or suspicion, then the regulatory effort cannot get started.[49] Science, albeit tentative or incomplete, must be the starting point for determining that there is a credible risk, and strong PP advocates cannot have it both ways. They cannot simultaneously argue that there are good (scientific) reasons upon which to base state intervention but at the same time claim that the science is too impoverished to have identified them. The science must at least be developed to the point that possible harms can be identified. This is not the same as demonstrating safety and should not be required to jump a higher epistemic hurdle. And notwithstanding the indeterminacies in ecology and evolutionary biology, the risks of GM crops have been identified. Indeed, it is because of these risks that there is a controversy in the first place. The next step, choosing between two sets of risks, does not require additional scientific evidence.

Although scientific indeterminacy does not impede a choice between the risks of GM crops and, say, the risks of chemical pest controls, there might be moral reasons against even entertaining such judgments. Comparisons between risks might be morally problematic if they involved incommensurable harms or if they affected different people differently. Incommensurable harms (e.g., between the loss of life and increased economic efficiency) raise notoriously difficult moral problems. They involve comparing and trading off harms that morally *should not* be bartered. But that is not the case with GM crops and extant agricultural practices. The risks of GM crops and the technologies they replace are not incommensurable—they both involve environmental perils. Moreover, a choice between the two does not shift the risk between different groups. Both alternatives involve hazards that are imposed on the same groups of people. So the moral reasons that might preclude a choice between two potentially harmful practices are not operative in the case of GM crops.

The second reason for rejecting a pragmatic evaluation of GM crops claims that environmental trade-offs lead to environmental degradation. There is obvious truth to this claim, but it is not clear that it is a compelling reason for rejecting every instance of environmentally remedial technology. Environmental conditions are not simply a consequence of trading off extant harms for seemingly less pernicious ones that turned out to be worse than anticipated. Although there are clear cases in which this has occurred, it is not universally true. It might be more accurate to blame the influence of economic trade-offs or simple dereliction of regulatory attention to environmental risks. These are good reasons to perhaps qualify the use of economic cost-benefit analysis or to enforce environmental regulations more diligently. But reforms of this nature are not the same as a risk avoidance approach to environmental regulation. An argument for risk avoidance would have to go much further and show that risk management invariably, or at least usually, results in worse outcomes. But the history of replacement risks is not one of constant exacerbation of environmental harms. Rather, the history is something of a mixed bag—some ameliorated, others exacerbated, and yet others had no demonstrable effect on environmental conditions. This mixed experience is not sufficient to reject out of hand a comparative evaluation of the environmental risks of GM crops.

The third reason why risk comparisons should not be pursued holds that present commercial practices provide too high a baseline to realistically screen out seriously dangerous environmental risks. Although this might be true with respect to some toxic compounds, there is no good reason to generalize it to every commercial practice. At least with regard to GM crops, the fact that existing agriculture technology poses serious environmental risks is not a good reason to reject an attempted amelioration with GM crops. Indeed, it would seem that the more environmentally pernicious a commercial practice is, the more compelling are the reasons to consider friendlier alternatives. A claim that this sets the threshold for acceptable risk too high ignores the fact that these are precisely the sorts of risks that deserve remedial attention.

A final factor argues against strong versions of the PP. Although any regulatory policy is subject to opportunistic manipulation, a stringent interpretation of the PP is particularly vulnerable. If the determining factor is environmental safety in isolation from any other factor then regulators are unlikely to approve any technological innovation. Monsanto and other GM seed producers confronted this problem in trying to establish a level of testing that would satisfy their critics as to the safety of the technology. Consider the responses of Lord Peter Melchett at a hearing by the House of Lords regarding the safety of GM technology:

> *Question 101:* Lord Melchett, in relation to genetic modification, what do you object to and why?
> *Lord Melchett:* My Lord Chairman, the fundamental objection is that there are unreliable and unpredictable risks.
> *Question 105:* How far are you prepared to carry your objections to these developments?
> *Lord Melchett:* I am happy to answer for Greenpeace [. . .] Greenpeace opposes all releases to the environment of genetically modified organisms.
> *Question 107:* Your opposition to the release of GMOs, that is an absolute and definite opposition? It is not one that is dependent on further scientific research or improved procedures being developed or any satisfaction you might get with regard to the safety or otherwise in the future?
> *Lord Melchett:* It is a permanent and definite and complete opposition based on a view that there will always be major uncertainties. It is the nature of the technology, indeed it is the nature of science, that there will not be any absolute proof. No scientist would sit before your Lordships and claim that if they were a scientist at all.[50]

The strong PP accommodates Lord Melchett's intransigence and, as such, it is almost assured that any novel technology would fail to satisfy a regulatory protocol based on risk avoidance. Some might argue to relieve this rigidity by taking into account existing environmental conditions, but nothing else. However, the choice between two technologies might legitimately involve factors other than their relative environmental risks. For instance, it is arguable that GM crops contribute to an affordable and abundant food supply.[51] And it is dogmatic to claim that this is not a legitimate regulatory concern. To the extent that extreme precautionary thinking precludes such considerations is evidence of a profound flaw in the doctrine: the commercial world is simply too complex for any single regulatory rule—cost-benefit or environmental risk avoidance—to contend with. Of course there are cases where environmental risk should prevail as the most important regulatory consideration. But these cases do not license regulators or activists to generalize these isolate cases to the exclusion of every other human concern.

The European Reaction to Biotechnology

Given what is presently known about agricultural biotechnology, it is difficult to explain Monsanto's difficult European experience vis-à-vis their more favorable treatment in the United States. Before providing what I take to be a reasonable explanation and the regulatory implications, a few others deserve consideration. For instance, some commentators view Europe as naturally hostile to American firms and treat European resistance to GM technology as just one more instance. However, this explanation ignores the historical success of American technology (including agricultural innovations) in Europe. It also ignores the fact that although Monsanto has dominated the market, agricultural biotechnology is not exclusive to U.S. firms. When Monsanto encountered the furious reaction to genetic technology, their competitors included Novartis (Swiss), Zeneca (British), AgrEvo (German), and Rhône-Poulenc (French), each of whom shared a similar fate in the European regulatory regime. Another explanation attributes the European disdain for GM technology to psychological differences, saying that in contrast to North Americans, Europeans have a fear of new technology. Not only does this explanation fly in the face of conflicting evidence (e.g., the European embrace of nuclear energy or the British acceptance of human stem cell research) it is a variety of social explanation that does not warrant serious consideration.[52]

Another explanation issues an indictment of management: that in its arrogance, Monsanto failed to respond adequately to European fears of environmental risk.[53] Although this may have been a contributing factor, it cannot explain entirely the disparate experiences. For one, early field trials of GM plants kindled environmental protests in the United States and Canada as well as in Europe. And Monsanto's organizational response was similar on both sides of the Atlantic,[54] although they did much more to accommodate European concerns. Specifically, permits for cultivation were sought in North America, but

initially they were not pursued in Europe. The most virulent environmental protests erupted in the fall of 1996 when soybean-laden ships
entered British ports. But environmental worries should have been
assuaged by management's decision to forego European cultivation.

Another explanation is that Europeans have poignant memories of
Nazi eugenics during World War II. And indeed, the protests against
GM technology originated in Germany. However, it should be noted
that the opposition quickly spread to France and was particularly pro-
nounced in England. Yet England has shown a greater acceptance of
human applications of biotechnology (e.g., embryonic stem cell
research) than has the United States. So not only does this explanation
assume that Europeans are too obtuse to distinguish between genetic
manipulation of plants and people, it also treats all Europeans as
being similarly disposed toward genetic research.

Other explanations are equally speculative, including the one that
posits U.S. environmental and food safety regulation as feeble and
captured in comparison to European regimes. It is fair to describe EU
environmental regulation as more cumbersome than that in the
United States, but it would be wrong to treat it as more rigorous.[55]
Both systems are designed to protect against the same human health
and environmental risks, and Monsanto's experience confirms the
lack of meaningful differences. The firm's first request to the EU was
to import into the EU Roundup Ready® soybeans that had been cultivated elsewhere. U.S. regulators had accepted the product for cultivation and consumption in the United States. The application was
presented to U.K. authorities in their role as rapporteur. The application was approved and forwarded to the European Commission (E.C.)
for consideration by other member states. In April of 1996, it received
EU-wide approval. Likewise, in April of 1998, Monsanto received EU-
wide approval for cultivating pest-protected corn, with France acting
as their rapporteur. This evidence (plus the 1998 approval of three
other varieties) belies the notion that EU regulation was either more
rigorous or that the technology could not satisfy EU regulators.

Key to understanding Monsanto's European experience are events
that transpired during the application process for cultivating Yield
Guard® pest-protected corn. French regulatory authorities had proposed the product for EU-wide approval in 1997 but then refused to
vote for its approval in 1998. Why the change? French environmental
authorities had advanced the initial proposal, but in the face of
increased environmental activism, political authorities overruled
them when the time came for a vote. France's reaction was taken up

by other member states such that a defacto moratorium on GM technology was in place by early 1999.

Meanwhile, U.S. regulators were unfazed by the European events and by similar environmental protests in the United States. Importantly, unlike their North American counterparts, European activists succeeded in influencing the political process. But their success, and the explanation of Monsanto's disparate treatment, is not related to superior tactics, most of which were identical on both sides of the Atlantic. Environmentalists gained political traction in Europe but not in the United States (nor in Canada) because of differences between the preferences of the electorate within these two democratic jurisdictions.[56] For instance, at a crucial point during this controversy—the year overlapping 1996 and 1997—Eurobarometer surveys indicated that, although 22 percent of Europeans could be described as supporters of GM food, 30 percent described themselves as opponents. In contrast, 37 percent of Americans were supporters, but only 13 percent were opponents.[57] A similar divergence existed with respect to cultivating GM crops. Whereas 35 percent of Europeans supported and 18 percent opposed cultivation, among U.S. respondents 51 percent supported but only 10 percent opposed it.

These different voter preferences are in turn explained by striking differences in public trust in the regulatory authorities in the two territories. In 1996, only 4 percent of Europeans identified their national regulators as their favored source for learning "the truth about genetically modified crops . . . ," slightly more than the food industry (1 percent) but considerably less than farming organizations (16 percent). Environmental organizations rated the highest, with 23 percent of Europeans identifying them as the most trustworthy source of information on GM crops. In contrast, 90 percent of U.S. respondents in 1997 had confidence in USDA statements about biotechnology, with the FDA garnering a similarly high 84 percent. Although it is not crucial for these purposes, these differences in attitudes could be attributed to European worries over food safety and, in particular, to spectacular events like the 1996 episode that connected Mad Cow Disease in livestock with new variant Creutzfeldt-Jakob disease in humans.

The above discussion was intended to demystify the European regulatory resistance to GM food technology and to relate it to voter fears about environmental and human health risks. As a matter of scientific evidence those fears are overblown, particularly those concerned with the consumption of GM food products. So, are regulators justified in blocking the importation of GM food products or of prohibiting the cultivation of GM crops under circumstances where public opinion is firmly coalesced around what David Byrne, European Commissioner for Health and Consumer Protection, described as an "irrational attitude?"[58] In the context of this study, can market intervention that emerges through a democratic political process be justified morally if it is not affected for the sake of Negative Commercial Liberty or Commercial Autonomy?

The answer urged here is no, that such intervention is an illegitimate use of regulatory power. An important consideration in this episode was the way political power was used to override the conclusions of environmental and food safety regulatory authorities. However, the decision to override and place a moratorium on new GM plants was not predicated upon a failure or even an inadequacy of these agencies. Rather it was (ostensibly) based on the need for further testing without credible evidence of risk. The EU action tracks the logic of the strong precautionary policies that were rejected in the above discussion.

My condemnation of the EU moratorium on GM technology would seem to elevate the importance of scientific findings over the will of a democratic electorate. After all, this action was a response to voter concerns over the safety of GM technology. The question could be asked, "Why should the scientific community be allowed to prevail?" The answer, I believe, is threefold. First, science did not prevail in the sense of determining the basis for regulatory intervention. Rather, protocols were established politically on the basis that it is unreasonable to constrain someone's contractual freedom on the basis of a safety risk unless that risk has a basis in science. Science only serves to cull the legitimate from the frivolous risks. If science were removed from the equation there is every reason to expect that health and safety rules would be used opportunistically.[59] Second, a first approximation of product safety is best left to the administrative authorities charged with the oversight of regulatory standards. Regulatory agencies are subject to judicial review so there is ample opportunity to challenge their findings. Political interference on the other hand is a prescription for opportunistic manipulation and, ultimately, regulatory capture. Third, the market provides an effective mechanism for realizing the popular will in cases such as this one. Indeed, the market for GM food products has been bludgeoned throughout Europe to the point that many large retailers refuse to sell them and many restaurants boast that their menu items are free of GM ingredients. And the market is a more appropriate mechanism insofar as it is not clear whether a majority or just a large (and vocal) segment of Europeans would avoid purchasing them if given the chance.

Reasons to Regulate: Values Revisited

GM technology has encountered other varieties of criticism, some of which are unrelated to human health and environmental safety. Some criticize GM crops on the basis that they offend against religious precepts or that they are "unnatural." These sorts of objections have been surveyed and largely dismissed by the Nuffield Council on Bioethics and will not be addressed here.[60] Another criticism is specifically directed at varieties of corn and soybeans that have been modified to express Bt toxins as a protection against insect predation. Organic farmers use Bt but claim that they do so in limited quantities and only in reaction to serious infestation. They worry that the widespread cultivation of Bt-modified crops that constantly omit high dosages of the toxin will trigger insect resistance and thereby eliminate the efficacy of a safe method of insect control they depend upon. Insect resistance to pesticides is not a new problem, but it is a novel controversy in this context. Pesticide producers typically respond to insect resistance by altering their formulations. And, presumably, Monsanto and other producers of Bt seeds will alter the genetic code of Bt seeds in the event that resistance occurs. However, from the organic farmer's perspective, the damage will have been done, irrevocably.

This criticism can be restated in the following generic format: Farmers depend upon certain environmental conditions and if those conditions were intentionally disturbed to the detriment of a crop's yields, then a good case could be made to either prohibit the offending practice or to impose the cost of the disturbance on the agent that brought it about. However, the issue at hand is nowhere near that simple. For one thing, organic farmers describe their use of Bt as though its effectiveness will be sustainable indefinitely. However, this assumes that every organic grower applies the pesticide properly and judiciously; otherwise, organic farming is also a source of potential insect resistance to Bt. But this is not a realistic assumption. Consequently, the risk of Bt-resistant insects cannot be attributed to GM technology alone. Indeed, advocates of GM technology argue that Bt-modified plants produce the toxin uniformly within the plant tissue and at levels that kill insects before they have an opportunity to reproduce resistant offspring. Accordingly, although this is a factual matter and ripe for additional research, it is not presently a good reason to constrain GM technology.

Some have urged measures that would mandate the labeling of GM produce as well as processed foods with GM ingredients.[61] Product labeling is a complicated affair and this is not the place to vet it thoroughly. However, it would be mistaken to assume that there is a moral imperative to label food ingredients or that states are morally justified in mandating the disclosure of ingredients. For one, consumers do not have a limitless moral right to know the contents of their food and producers are under no correlative duty to disclose these details. Consumers have a moral right to be warned of the presence of a dangerous ingredient (e.g., known allergens) or similar risks. But this right cannot be generalized without generating some intuitively ludicrous results. Evidence of this intuition is embodied in the two controlling principles for mandatory food labeling contained in the Codex Alimentarius: "protection of consumer health and fair practices in the food trade."[62] So if the precise formula for Coca-Cola syrup or the spices in Kentucky Fried Chicken are harmless then they need not be disclosed. Likewise, packaged breakfast cereals contain microscopic traces of insect parts and rodent hair (yes, they are in there) but since it has been shown that they are harmless, Kellogg's is not obliged to list them as ingredients.

The safety of consuming GM foods should exempt them from mandatory labeling. Alternatively, if the causal history of a food product represents a genuine health risk then GM food products should not be singled out for special treatment. Instead, every food product derived from a mutated plant (virtually every commercial cultivar) should be labeled accordingly. To do otherwise, to legislate mandatory food labeling statutes on a basis other than consumer protection, is an invitation to the competitive gaming that has marred the food industry historically.

French activist José Bové levels another variety of criticism against GM technology.[63] Best known for his 1999 destruction (or, as he prefers, "dismantling") of a McDonald's restaurant under construction outside of Millau in Normandy, Bové also led groups that destroyed GM corn in a Novartis storage facility in Nerac in 1997. And in January of 2001 he was expelled from Brazil after his involvement in activities that resulted in the uprooting of GM corn and soy crops. An overriding theme in his project is the preservation of traditional farming techniques, communities, and values. If his use of violence is removed from the equation, he justifies his cause with reasons that are redolent of philosophical communitarianism. Bové's stance against GM technology is a proxy for a cluster of similar efforts to curtail the influence of multinational corporations. These positions provide much of the intellectual impetus to the antiglobalization movement of which Bové is a leader. In the interest of examining the regulatory goals of this movement I will critically examine Bové's case against GM technology.

Bové resents GM technology as the latest entry on a long list of agricultural innovations that altered the lives of farmers, agricultural communities, and the way consumers traditionally related to food.[64] Consider these excerpts from a statement he read at his 8 February 1998 trial for the Nerac incident:[65]

> For some decades productionism [large-scale or "industrial" farming] has served to enslave farmers. From being a producer, the farmer has now become someone who is exploited, who can no longer decide on her or his way of managing the land, nor freely choose her or his [production] techniques . . . Either we accept intensive production and the huge reduction in the number of farmers in the sole interest of the World Market, or we create a farmer's agriculture for the benefit of everyone. Genetically modified maize is also the symbol of a system of agriculture and a type of society which I refuse to accept . . . Agricultural production has now become the agro-industry.

And consider his comments from an extensive interview:

> With its scientific organization of work, industry became the reference point for measuring economic efficiency. But it was felt that in agriculture, in contrast to industry and commerce, these transformations could be assimilated to the social objective of maintaining the family farm. In fact, this objective was difficult to reconcile with the overall project and its reliance on specialization, the key concept in modernization.[66]

> . . . agriculture has adopted a production-line organization involving segmentation . . . Mechanization has played a crucial role in the intensification of agriculture.[67] The size of a plot of land has now been adapted to the machine, often to the detriment of the natural topography and the needs of proper drainage.[68]

> Nowadays, food is rarely eaten in anything like the state in which it leaves the farm. It's reconstructed—often several times over—to produce easily prepared, ready-made meals that can be consumed with little work in the home. The food industry regards the farmer as merely the

supplier of raw commodities to meet the need of the manufacturers, rather than those of the consumer . . . The art of cooking and eating will soon not be passed on to new generations; this has resulted in a loss of family cohesion and of the ties that bind us to the land or place where we live.[69]

Bové is an activist, so hyperbole and distortion of facts are to be expected in his communications. But since his goals include the mobilization of political power, the interesting question is whether his sentiments can be reformulated into sound arguments. Stated another way, is there a regulatory instantiation of his project that is consistent with the moral principles of liberal democracies? First, to clarify and classify Bové's project, recall the previous discussion of communitarianism and the role of values in a regulatory framework. Bové urges that the values expressed in a certain "way of life" be afforded regulatory importance. He believes that this mode of life and the community in which it is situated are vulnerable to the influences of international trade and technological innovation. By barring regulatory intervention he fears that something of great value will be lost. Whether this is true or not need not deter us here. What is of interest is whether any way of life can serve as a legitimate end of commercial regulation.

The moral principles of this Regulatory Strategy are not proposed with or designed for the creation or preservation of any particular way of life. Rather, they are instruments of individual liberty and it is assumed that valuable ways of life will be constructed with the benefits of these freedoms. If there is a genuine interest in more intimate modes of food production or preparation then, presumably, people will pursue them. Such is the case with the burgeoning organic food industry, microbreweries, and the like. But although market mechanisms address many of Bové's concerns, they cannot address them all. There is no denying that technological change is socially disruptive and that there are losers sometimes. For instance, Alan McHughen, a molecular geneticist and an advocate for the ag-biotech industry observes that "with genetic modification to and market domination by vegetable oils from the northern temperate zone (e.g., maize, rapeseed), traditional market for oil products such as palm oil and coconut oil, grown mainly in poorer topical countries, will diminish."[70] Likewise, Bové notes that mechanized equipment has altered the economy of scale in agriculture to the point that many small farmers can no longer compete. The question is not whether destabilizing dislocations have occurred or whether there are more to come, but whether they constitute a justifiable reason to regulate agricultural practices. In what follows I will argue that they do not, and in so doing I hope to capture a range of objections that are raised on the basis of values or of preserving a certain way of life.

To instantiate Bové's project in law would necessitate one of two regulatory initiatives; particular ways of life could be protected or they could be subsidized. Protection implies that states would ban disruptive technology, a remedy that is urged with regard to GM technology. However actually carrying this out is difficult because the long-term social impacts of novel technology cannot be predicted with any degree of accuracy. Although social change is an inevitable consequence of most technology, neither the extent nor the nature of change can be determined ex ante. Of course there is great interest in understanding the consequences of new technology; witness the creation in 1973 of the Congressional Office of Technology Assessment (subsequently closed on 29 September 1995). Donella Meadows is an optimist regarding the possibility of predicting the "side effects of various technologies on the world's physical and economic systems."[71] In contrast, efforts to accurately predict the future consequences of economic phenomena prompt Frederick Prior to invoke the aphorism, "When mortals speak of the future, the gods smile."[72] And even Meadows admits that her models cannot predict the "social side effects of new technologies." But these "side effects" must be understood if ways of life are to be insulated against technological encroachment. Worse yet, it is not obvious when an agricultural innovation will be disruptive of social life because they are so subtle and incremental. In these cases, social change is not triggered by any particular innovation but by the cumulative effect of a continuum of small improvements. For instance, early tractors did little more than emulate the function of draft animals by dragging a plow. Farmers continued to trudge behind the plow and guide it through furrows. The behemoths in use today have radically altered the economy of scale of farming. But they developed incrementally such that there was no particular model change or point in time where the social impacts of mechanized farm equipment would have been obvious. In sum, if the social consequences of novel agricultural technology cannot be known then regulating on this basis is speculative.

And speculative regulatory excursions raise social dangers that cannot be overlooked. A primitive economic assumption is that human welfare (i.e., individual and national prosperity) is a function of available endowments (i.e., resources, natural or otherwise) and the knowledge to transform resources into goods and services. Measurements of economic welfare—standard of living and the like—are notoriously difficult and contentious terms that are not easily squared with philosophically rigorous notions of well-being.[73] But whatever metric is employed, there can be no denying that some minimal level of material prosperity is vital to living a good life regardless of how one cashes out its precise meaning. And the relationship between the adoption of technology and economic prosperity is not an abstraction. Rather, it has been documented in a literature that looks at the history of economic growth through the lens of technological adoption.[74] The relationship is robust enough to support Mancur Olson's concurrence that "the rate at which a country grows is not pre-determined by its endowments and depends much more on the extent to which it adopts superior technologies."[75] Olson does not argue that technology adoption is the only causal factor in economic growth and, indeed, he emphasizes the crucial role of national governance and other institutional arrangements in general.[76] But because endowments are relatively fixed or, in some cases, diminishing, the store of knowledge or technology will largely determine whether economic output will satisfy the needs of any given society. Attempts to preserve ways of life by regulating technology must be mindful that social life generally is imperiled whenever the mechanisms of material prosperity are blindly tampered with.

Now, if states should not resist technological innovation on the basis that it disrupts a way of life then the only remaining way to achieve Bové's project is through state subsidization. Doing so raises the obvious question of why one group's interest in pursuing a particular way of life should be someone else's burden. But it also raises intractable difficulties in implementation. First, upon what basis could states determine the ways of life that deserve public largess? Bové advocates on behalf of small farmers but such groups are ubiquitous. Opera companies, fixtures in many small nineteenth-century American towns, were destroyed by the recording industry. What about these and other such groups that suddenly succumb to technological forces? The lack of economic viability of a practice is often addressed privately, as in the case of symphony orchestras in major U.S. cities. Likewise, the Amish have preserved their special agricultural production methods and the way of life these sustain by segregating themselves from the forces of modern agriculture. But they do so without public support. Russell Hardin provides a compelling argument against subsidizing ways of life that is germane to Bové's project. He notes that farming supports

> are universalistic in the sense that anyone who goes into farming in relevant ways is entitled to them. It is not the community of farmers as such, but the individual farmers who are supported. And the supports are essentially straight cash . . . Genuinely to protect the way of life of farmers might eventually require the production of vastly too much food that then, would have to be destroyed rather than consumed. This has marginally been the effect of American farm supports, but it would have to be carried to much greater extreme if most farmers and their children did not leave the farm, thereby giving up their way of life. Alternatively, government could simply pay farmers to stay on the farm without producing food, as the American government does in part. But if carried to extremes, this policy would finally destroy the supposed way of life of farmers even while keeping them on the farm.[77]

The foregoing discussion highlights the moral and practical impediments to instantiating a communitarian-based regulatory policy. Of course, communitarian thinkers have waged a similar criticism of liberal regulation based on managing risk. For instance, communitarian author Richard Hiskes believes (plausibly) that today's risks cannot be understood in terms of individual behavior because they emerge from the collective actions of groups of people and institutions. And he believes that these emergent risks "threaten [liberalism and democracy] because it brings liberal democracy face to face with a value and social fact it has ignored or relegated to the second tier of political virtues for three hundred years, the idea of community."[78] More specifically, he claims, "the emergent nature of risk befuddles the liberal epistemological reduction of all phenomena to their individual components, even to the extent of making the concept of agency unintelligible in totally individualistic terms."[79] This is a serious charge, but he levels it without any specific remedies except a call for "new conceptualizations"[80] of the liberal ideals of individual autonomy, democracy, and so forth along communitarian lines.

It is questionable whether Hiskes succeeds in condemning the tradition of liberal writers, any specific liberal thinker, or extant societies organized according to liberal democratic ideals. It is possible that his broadside attack of liberalism commits what A. John Simmons calls the "communitarian fallacy."[81] That is, Hiskes criticizes liberalism for overemphasizing individualism to the detriment of the communal aspects of life. And he indicts this neglect as a moral wrong in virtue of the constitutive property of communities, that individual selves are formed by them. So it follows that rectifying this moral wrong requires a political reorientation in which communities supplant in importance the role of the individual in liberal thought.

However, as Simmons points out, Hiskes' argument is an abstraction, and for it to go through, a great deal more sociology, psychology, history, and other such evidence is needed. Most importantly, Hiskes needs to contend with the evidence he proffers in criticizing the liberal project. By his own account, liberalism has been overemphasizing the individual for "three hundred years." One would think that communities, political or social, would have withered after such a prolonged assault. And yet if the international controversy over GM technology has proven anything, it is that many communities—democratic states, supranational organizations, nongovernmental organizations, and other assemblies of people—are potent forces. The fact that environmentalists were free to function as a community, express themselves, and influence the outcome of government policy is a piece of evidence that Hiskes and other communitarians should not overlook. The fact that the risks of GM technology are not individual risks seems irrelevant to the finding that many liberal states have contended admirably with them. The liberal tradition presents a large target for a great deal of criticism, but in this case it appears to have been missed.

Notes

1. Clive James, "Global Status of Commercialized Transgenic Crops: 2000," *International Service for the Acquisition of Agri-Biotech Applications 21–2000*, at www.isaaa.org/publications/briefs/Brief_21.htm (accessed 30 January 2002).

2. Monsanto Internal Document: *Plant Biotechnology 2000*, 1. As for the most recent data, the National Agricultural Statistics Service of the United States Department of Agriculture reports in the publication *Acreage* (Washington, D.C.: USDA, 2002) that the following percentages of U.S. acres were cultivated to GM crops in 2002: 34 percent of corn, 69 percent of upland cotton, and 75 percent of soybeans, http://usda.mannlib.cornell.edu/reports/nassr/field/pcp-bba/acrg0602.txt (accessed 2 July 2002). Considering that the first GM seeds came to market in 1996 this represents a stunning rate of adoption. National Agricultural Statistics Service.

3. Jorge Fernandez-Cornejo and William McBride, with contributions from Cassandra Klotz-Ingram, Sharon Jans, and Nora Brooks, "Genetically Engineered Crops for Pest Management in U.S. Agriculture," *Agricultural Economics Report* No. 786. May 2000, table 13, p. 13.

4. Monsanto, *Plant Biotechnology 2000,* 1

5. According to Monsanto's internal studies, "Grower satisfaction with Monsanto's biotech crops remained high. For instance, about 96 percent of surveyed U.S. Roundup Ready® corn growers and more than 95 percent of surveyed U.S. Roundup Ready® soybean growers reported satisfaction with our products" (www.biotechbasics.com/biotech01/intro.html) (accessed 30 January 2002).

6. A recent EU directive (2001/18/EC OJ L 106 of 17.4.2001) attempts to break this impasse. However, this new policy is as incomplete as it is onerous, and it is too soon to tell whether it will succeed or not.

7. In 1999, transgenic crops accounted for only .03 percent of all the cultivated acreage in the European Union (Commission of the European Communities, Directorate-General for Agriculture, 2000, *Economic Impacts of Genetically Modified Crops on the Agri-Food Sector: A First Review,* working document rev. 2, http://europa.eu.int/comm/agriculture/publi/gmo/summary.htm (accessed 30 January 2002).

8. For an excellent explanation of the technology, its risks, and its benefits, see Alan McHughen, *Pandora's Picnic Basket: The Potential and Hazards of Genetically Modified Foods* (New York: Oxford University Press, 2000). For an analysis of the regulatory issues surrounding the pest-protected variety of genetically modified plants, see my article, "Assessing the Precautionary Principle," *Public Affairs Quarterly* 14, no. 4 (October 2000): 309–28.

9. In a letter to *Nature,* researchers claimed to have identified gene flow in Mexico. See David Quist and Ignacio Chapela, "Transgenic DNA Introgressed into Traditional Maize Landraces in Oaxaca, Mexico," *Nature* 414 (November 2001): 541–43. However, others, including colleagues of Quist and Chapela at the University of California-Berkeley, are doubtful of these results. See John Hodgson, "Maize Uncertainties Create Political Fallout," *Nature Biotechnology* 20, no. 2 (February 2002): 106–7.

10. Michael Specter. "The Pharmageddon Riddle," *The New Yorker* (10 April 2000): 10.

11. Published 26 June 1986 in 51 Fed. Reg. 23,303. This regulation provides in pertinent part that risks of GM crops are to be regulated pursuant to the Federal Insecticide, Fungicide, and Rodenticide Act (FIFRA) and the Federal Food, Drug, and Cosmetic Act (FFDCA). For an overview of the regulatory process as well as the duties and responsibilities of the Biotechnology Science Coordinating Committee, see Federal Register vol. 50, no. 220, 14 November 1885.

12. For a comprehensive discussion of what is required to gain approval of GM plants throughout the world, see McHughen, *Pandora's Basket,* 136–59.

13. National Research Council: Committee on Genetically Modified Pest-Protected Plants, Board on Agriculture and National Resources, *Genetically Modified-Pest Protected Plants: Science and Regulation* (Washington, D.C., National Academy Press, 2000) provides an in-depth discussion and evaluation of this regulatory protocol.

14. Basing acceptability on tolerable risk, or tolerable risk on whatever is

acceptable, can be vacuously circular. William Lowrance's classic analysis of this problem provides a way out with his definition of risk as "a measure of the probability and severity of harm to human health." See *Of Acceptable Risk: Science and the Determination of Safety* (Los Altos, Calif.: William Kaufmann, 1976), 8. So long as there is some objective measurement in determining acceptability, the concept involves a subjective determination but not ncessarily an empty one.

15. Indur M. Goklany contrasts the benefits and risks of GM technology in "Applying the Precautionary Principle to Genetically Modified Crops," in *Center for the Study of American Business: Policy Study Number 157* (August 2000): 4–19.

16. Substantial equivalence is the food safety equivalent of the "bioequivalence" standard that the FDA has applied to generic pharmaceuticals since passage of the Hatch-Waxman Act in 1984.

17. Kristen Shrader-Frechette, *Risk and Rationality* (Berkeley, Calif.: University of California Press, 1991), 30. See also, Lee Clark and James F. Short Jr., "Social Organization and Risk: Some Current Controversies," *Annual Review of Sociology* 19 (1993): 375–99.

18. The adequacy of these protocols is reviewed in National Research Council, *Modified Pest-Protected Plants: Science and Regulation.* And the U.S. General Accounting Office recently issued a report on the overall adequacy of the FDA's GM food safety regulations. See, "Genetically Modified Foods: Experts View Regime as Adequate, But FDA's Evaluation Process Could Be Enhanced" (GAO-02-566, May 2002).

19. Anthony Trewavas and Christopher Leaver survey the relevant research in "Is Opposition to GM Crops Science or Politics? An Investigation into the Arguments That GM Crops Pose a Particular Threat to the Environment," *EMBO Reports* 2, no. 6 (2001): 455–59, at www.embo-reports.oup journals.org/cgi/content/full/2/6/455 (accessed 30 January 2002).

20. Citing U.S. government officials, Robert Paarlberg explains "that in no instance to date has any GM plant approved for field testing by APHIS created an environmental hazard or exhibited any unpredictable or unusual biosafety behavior, compared with similar corps modified through conventional breeding methods." *The Politics of Precaution: Genetically Modified Crops in Developing Countries* (Baltimore, Md.: Johns Hopkins University Press, 2001).

21. Such as the Cartagena Protocols on Biosafety which remove GM plants from the typical World Trade Organization (WTO) strictures against protectionism.

22. Stephen Stich makes several compelling arguments against what I would call the strong PP in the context of the recombinant DNA research debate of the 1970s. However, commercialization and not research projects are at stake in the GM crop debate. See Stephen Stich, "The Recombinant DNA Debate: Some Philosophical Considerations," in *The Recombinant DNA Debate*, ed. David Jackson and Stephen Stich (Englewood Cliffs, N.J.: Prentice-Hall, 1979), 183–202.

23. There is another version of the precautionary principle that I will not

address. Groups loosely identified as deep or neo-Darwinians believe that exposure to substances that were not present during our evolutionary past are prima facie risky and are candidates for regulatory restraint. As there is little immediate chance that neo-Darwinian views will find their way into regulatory policy anytime soon, I will not address them here.

24. My use of the term *pragmatic* is not a specific reference to philosophical pragmatism. Rather, I mean it to describe a regulatory process that evaluates novel technology in terms of comparative risks and benefits and decides what to do without reference to any fixed weighting of any particular factor. For an account of environmental regulation specifically designed in terms of philosophical pragmatism, see Daniel Farber, *Eco-Pragmatism* (Chicago: University of Chicago Press, 1999).

25. A third core belief holds that producers of environmentally risky technology should bear the burden of demonstrating its safety. Insofar as GMO producers are already subject to a regulatory regime that assumes environmental risk until demonstrated otherwise, I will not pursue this tenet of the doctrine.

26. Timothy O'Riordan and Andrew Jordan, "The Precautionary Principle in Contemporary Environmental Policy and Politics," *Environmental Values* 4 (1995): 191–212.

27. Andrew Jordan and Timothy O'Riordan, "The Precautionary Principle in Contemporary Environmental Policy and Politics," in *Protecting Public Health and the Environment: Implementing the Precautionary Principle,* ed. Carolyn Raffensperger and Joel Tickner (Washington, D.C., Island Press, 2000), 15–35.

28. For instance, this position stands in sharp contrast to Ronald Reagan's Executive Order mandating cost-benefit analysis or the Unfunded Mandates Reform Act of 1995 (§ 201, 2 U.S.C. § 1531) requiring selection of the least costly approach to achieving a given environmental outcome.

29. Commission of the European Communities, *Communication from the Commission of the European Communities: On the Precautionary Principle,* COM (2000) 1, Brussels, 2.2.2000.

30. Commission, *Communication,* 4.

31. Commission, *Communication,* 4.

32. Commission of the European Communities, *Communication from the Commission: Towards a Strategic Vision of Life Sciences and Biotechnology,* COM (2001) 454 final, Brussels, 4.9.2001.

33. Commission, *Communication—Strategic Vision,* 20.

34. Commission, *Communication—Strategic Vision,* 20.

35. This is not to suggest that science is the only basis for intervention. However, the PP is a theory about environmental safety, and in this limited realm science is crucial. Admitting hunches, superstitions, or other such inclinations opens the door to regulatory fiat.

36. Two possibilities come to mind. One is that the damages could be so significant that no GM crop producer or grower could pay them. But secondly, the harms could be irreversible and therefore not something easily remedied with money damages.

37. Such cases are ubiquitous. After the crash of an Alaska Airline jet, a theory emerged about problems in the horizontal stabilizer of some aircraft. The theory is not scientifically certain, but there is reason to be suspicious. Notwithstanding the lack of scientific certainty, the Federal Aviation Administration required airlines to inspect every relevant aircraft in their fleet, upon penalty of grounding. Prudence would seem to demand this action. Awaiting certainty would seem to undermine the FAA's ability to satisfy public concerns about safety.

38. John Dewey, *Freedom and Culture* (Buffalo, New York: Prometheus Books, 1989), 107.

39. Conference of the Parties to the Convention on Biological Diversity, Montreal, 24–28 January 2000.

40. Specifically, Annex II to the Protocol allows a member to make a determination "as to whether or not the risks are acceptable or manageable, including where necessary, identification of strategies to manage these risks."

41. There are reasons to believe that such an outcome is not only possible but that it is designed into the Cartagena Protocol. The provisions of the document are limited to "living modified organisms" brought about through the processes of "modern biotechnology." In defining "modern biotechnology," the agreement is further limited to transgenic and DNA techniques, technology that has been commercialized by only a handful of firms and one in particular. But one of the striking conclusions of the National Research Council (p. 6) study is that the environmental risks of this technology are indistinguishable from the risks of conventionally bred plants. And given the precision of rDNA technology, GM plants are environmentally safer than plants bred through chemical and radiological means, both of which are exempted from the treaty. Consequently, there is a suspicion that whatever environmentally sincere motivations might have been operative, the Protocol also contains the seeds of protectionism.

42. From a press release of the Science and Health Network dated 2 February 1998. This, along with several other provisions, is referred to as the Wingspread Statement. The principle has since been formalized in the introduction to *Protecting Public Health and the Environment: Implementing the Precautionary Principle*, ed. Carolyn Raffensperger and Joel Tickner (Washington, D.C.: Island Press, 1999), 1–11.

43. Raffensperger and Tickner, *Protecting*, 3.

44. W. Von Wartburg and Julian Liew highlight this problem in their discussion of the public discourse of genetically modified organisms. See *Gene Technology and Social Acceptance* (Lanham, Md.: University Press of America, 1999), 17.

45. Andrew Jordan and Timothy O'Riodan, "The Precautionary Principle in Contemporary Environmental Policy and Politics," in Raffensperger and Tickner, *Protecting*, 15–35.

46. A classic case is the editorial "Fear of the Future," *Wall Street Journal* 10 February 2000.

47. For a good discussion of the complex interrelationship between science

and environmental policy, see David V. Bates, *Environmental Health Risks and Public Policy: Decision Making in Free Societies* (Seattle: University of Washington Press, 1994) and Kristin Shrader-Frechette, *Risk Analysis and Scientific Method* (Boston: Dordrecht, 1985).

48. Supreme Court Justice Stephen Breyer provides a provocative account of how this decision might be institutionalized in *Breaking the Vicious Circle: Toward Effective Risk Regulation* (Cambridge, Mass.: Harvard University Press, 1993), 55–81.

49. The Administrative Procedures Act instantiates this requirement by barring administrative agencies from actions that are either "arbitrary" or "capricious" [5 U.S.C. §706(2)(A)]. In other cases, courts have interpreted this standard to require "substantial evidence." See *AFL-CIO v. OSHA*, 965 F.2d 962 (11th Cir. 1992).

50. House of Lords Select Committee on European Communities 2nd Report: EC Regulation of Genetic Modification of Agriculture. Cited in Trewavas and Leaver, "Opposition."

51. Klaus Leisinger, Karin Schmitt, and Rajul Pandya-Lorch, *Six Billion and Counting: Population Growth and Food Security in the Twenty-First Century* (International Food Policy Research Institute, Washington, D.C., distributed by the Johns Hopkins University Press, 2002) argue that biotechnology can, at a minimum, buy time to cope with the devastating consequences of worldwide population growth. For the potential of GM technology in underdeveloped regions, see J. deVries, *Securing the Harvest: Biotechnology, Breeding, and Seed Systems for African Crops* (New York: Rockefeller Foundation, 2001).

52. I refer here to such hazy notions as "computer phobia." See Martin Bauer, "'Technophobia': A Misleading Conception of Resistance to New Technology," in Martin Bauer, ed., *Resistance to New Technology: Nuclear Power Information Technology and Biotechnology* (New York: Cambridge University Press, 1995), 87–122.

53. See K. Eichenwald, G. Kolata, and M. Petersen, "Biotechnology Food: From the Lab to a Debacle," *New York Times*, 25 January 2001. However, Daniel Charles provides evidence of serious efforts to bridge differences between Monsanto and hostile environmentalists in *Lords of the Harvest: Biotech, Big Money, and the Future of Food* (Cambridge, Mass.: Perseus Books), 102.

54. Details of these episodes were obtained from personal correspondence (25 September 2001) and subsequent interviews (28 September 2001) with Thomas J. McDermott, director of industry relations for Monsanto.

55. European protocols in place at the time (Directive 90/220/EEC) involve the "competent authorities" (e.g., environmental or health regulators) of each member state as part of a mechanism for gaining EU-wide approval. Applications to release new GM crops must first satisfy the regulatory authorities of some member state, referred to for these purposes as a "rapporteur." If the rapporteur approves the application, then it is forwarded to the European Commission (EC) for consideration and approval by other member states. It has been noted that the details of the formal approval process in the EU differs substantively from that in the United States. But, the aims of the processes are identical, as have been the outcomes.

56. In making this leap, I assume the merits of the account of electoral market efficiency in the political science literature. See S. A. Baba, "Democracies and Inefficiency," *Economics and Politics* 9 (July 1997): 99–114; and D. Wittman, "*The Myth of Democratic Failure: Why Political Institutions Are Efficient*," (Chicago: University of Chicago Press, 1995). One line of work shows that, even if voters are rationally ignorant concerning key issues, they still have their policy preferences reflected in legislation because politicians in contested political markets learn to anticipate what the policy preferences of the median voter would be. See J. A. Stimson, R. S. Erikson, and M. B. MacKuen, "Dynamic Representation," *American Political Science Review* 89 (1995): 543–65; and R. D. Arnold, *The Logic of Congressional Action* (New Haven, Conn.: Yale University Press, 1990).

57. All references to eurobarometer surveys and other data are from G. M. Gaskell, J. Durant, and N. C. Allum, "Worlds Apart? The Reception of Genetically Modified Foods in Europe and the U.S.," *Science* 285 (16 July 1999): 384–87. For similar findings see Mark Cantley, Thomas Hobin, and Albert Sasson. "Regulations and Consumer Attitudes in Biotechnology," *Nature Biotechnology* 17 (March 1999 supplement): 37–38.

58. National Press Club, Washington D.C., 9 October 2001, EU Commission: SPEECH 01/442.

59. This is not a hypothetical worry. Legal historian Lawrence Friedman chronicles a period of U.S. commercial history when regulators curtailed the production of goods for reasons other than

> the sour, the putrid, and the diseased. But in the aggregate, the tremendous volume of "health" laws, snowballing between 1850 and 1900, meant that free enterprise theory had failed significantly to win and hold its true believers. Good goods should, ultimately, drive out bad ones in the market, or barter down the price. But the public and the producers of good goods were not willing to wait so long. (*A History of American Law* [New York: Simon & Schuster, 1973], 400)

A classic example he cites is a dispute between Pennsylvania dairymen and corn growers over "butterine or oleomargarine." Citing what were obviously bogus health concerns the dairy industry curtailed the production of this newfangled foodstuff for a period and then hobbled its acceptance with onerous labeling requirements.

60. Nuffield Council on Bioethics, *Genetically Modified Crops: The Ethical and Social Issues* (London: author, 1999), available for online download at nuffieldbioethics.org/publications (accessed 30 January 2002). Also, Gregory Pence analyzes and trenchantly criticizes appeals to naturalism in the domain of GM food in chapter 6 of *Designer Food: Mutant Harvest or Breadbasket of the World?* (Lanham, Md.: Rowman & Littlefield, 2002). Some of the religious objections having to do with dietary laws have been negated by Monsanto's "pledge" that reads in pertinent part, "We will respect the religious, cultural and ethical concerns of people throughout the world by not using genes from animals or humans in products intended for food or feed" (www.monsanto.com/monsanto/about_us/monsanto_pledge/default.htm) (accessed 12 June 2002).

61. In the EU, the rules are contained in Directive 2001/18/EC of the Committee of the Environment, Public Health and Consumer Policy, A5–0229/2002, Final 12 June 2002. The European Parliament and the Council of Ministers accepted the Committee report on 3 July 2002 with an amendment exempting meat and dairy products from animals that had consumed GM feed. A similar effort is afoot domestically where Oregon voters will be asked to approve a GM labeling law in the fall of 2002.

62. Food and Agricultural Organization of the United Nations; World Health Organization, *Understanding the Codex Alimentarius* (New York: Food & Agriculture Organization, 1999), 3. The Codex Alimentarius Commission is a joint endeavor of the Food and Agricultural Organization of the United Nations and the World Health Organization.

63. See José Bové and François Dufour, *The World Is Not for Sale: Farmers against Junk Food*, from an interview by Gilles Luneau, translated by Anna de Casparis (London: Verso, 2001).

64. He also has doubts about the safety of GM technology and urges regulators to respect the strong PP described above.

65. Bové's protests against McDonald's stems from a tit-for-tat trade dispute between France and the United States. It began when France prohibited the importation of hormone-treated beef, an action that the WTO would declare illegal. (Also, McDonald's serves French beef that is processed in Orléans.) In the meantime, the United States imposed tariffs on French cheese that fell heavily on Bové and other French sheepherders.

66. Bové and Dufour, *The World*, 63.

67. Bové and Dufour, *The World*, 64.

68. Bové and Dufour, *The World*, 65.

69. Bové and Dufour, *The World*, 56.

70. McHughen, *Pandora's Basket*, 144.

71. Donella H. Meadows et al., "Technology and the Limits to Growth," in Albert H. Teich, ed., *Technology and the Future*, 4th ed., (New York: St. Martin's Press, 1997): 154–92, 171.

72. Frederick L. Pryor, *Economic Evolution and Structure: The Impact of Complexity on the U.S. Economic System* (Cambridge, U.K.: Cambridge University Press, 1996), 242.

73. This difficulty is explored in Geoffrey Hawthorn, ed., *The Standard of Living* (Cambridge, U.K.: Cambridge University Press, 1987).

74. For insight into this literature, see Joel Mokyr, *The Lever of Richs* (New York: Oxford University Press, 1990).

75. Mancur Olson and Satu Kähkönen, eds., *A Not-so-Dismal Science: A Broader View of Economies and Societies* (New York: Oxford University Press, 2000), 12.

76. Mancur Olson, "Distinguished Lecture on Economics in Government," *Journal of Economic Perspectives* 10, no. 2 (Spring 1996): 3–24.

77. Russell Hardin, "Communities and Development: Autarkik Social Groups and the Economy," in Mancur Olson and Satu Kähkönen, eds., *A Not-so-Dismal Science*, 210–11.

78. Richard P. Hiskes, *Democracy, Risk, and Community: Technological Hazards and the Evolution of Liberalism* (New York: Oxford University Press, 1998), 10.

79. Hiskes, *Democracy*, 31.

80. Hiskes, *Democracy*, 133.

81. A. John Simmons, *On the Edge of Anarchy: Locke, Consent, and the Limits of Society* (Princeton, N.J.: Princeton University Press, 1993), 37; also see his *Lockean Theory of Rights* (Princeton, N.J.: Princeton University Press, 1992), 109–16.

Bibliography

Adler, Matthew. "Expressive Theories of Law: A Skeptical Overview." 148 *U. Pa. L. Rev.* 1363 (2000).

Anderson, Elizabeth. "Comment on Dawson's 'Exit, Voice and Values in Economic Institutions.'" *Economics and Philosophy* 13 (1997): 101–5.

———. *Value in Ethics and Economics.* Cambridge, Mass.: Harvard University Press, 1993.

Anderson, Elizabeth, and Richard H. Pildes. "Expressive Theories of Law: A General Restatement." 148 *U. Pa. L. Rev.* 1503, 1564–65 (2000).

Arneil, Barbara. *John Locke and America: The Defence of English Colonialism.* Oxford, U.K.: Clarendon Press, 1996.

Arnold, R. D. *The Logic of Congressional Action.* New Haven, Conn.: Yale University Press, 1990.

Arthur, W. Brian. "Competing Technologies, Increasing Returns, and Lock-In by Historical Events." *The Economic Journal* 99 (1989): 116–31.

Baba, S. A. "Democracies and Inefficiency." *Economics and Politics* 9 (July 1997): 99–114.

Auerbach, Joseph, and Hayes, Samuel. "Underwriting Regulation and the Shelf Registration Phenomenon." In *Wall Street and Regulation*, edited by Samuel Hayes, III. Boston, Mass.: Harvard Business School Press, 1987, 127–55.

Baier, Annette. "Some Thoughts on How We Moral Philosophers Live Now." *The Monist* 67, no. 4 (October 1984): 490–97.

Baron, Marsha, Phillip Petitt, and Michael Slote. *Three Methods of Ethics—A Debate: For and Against: Consequences, Maxims, and Virtues.* Oxford, U.K.: Blackwell Publishers, 1997.

Barry, Brian. *Culture and Equality: An Egalitarian Criticism of Multiculturalism.* Cambridge, Mass.: Harvard University Press, 2001.

Bates, David V. *Environmental Health Risks and Public Policy: Decision Making in Free Societies.* Seattle: University of Washington Press, 1994.

Bauer, Martin. "'Technophobia': A Misleading Conception of Resistance to New Technology." In *Resistance to New Technology: Nuclear Power Information Technology and Biotechnology*, ed. Martin Bauer. New York: Cambridge University Press, 1995, 87–122.

Beauchamp, Tom. "On Eliminating the Distinction between Applied Ethics and Ethical Theory." *The Monist* 67, no. 4 (October 1984): 514–31.

———. "Reply to Strong on Principlism and Casuistry." *Journal of Medicine and Philosophy* 25, no. 3 (June 2000): 342–47.

Beauchamp, Tom, and James Childress. *Principles of Biomedical Ethics*, 4th ed. New York: Oxford University Press, 1994.

Becker, Gary. *The Economic Approach to Human Behavior*. Chicago: University of Chicago Press, 1976.

———. *The Economics of Discrimination*. Chicago: University of Chicago Press, 1971.

———. *A Treatise on the Family*. Cambridge, Mass.: Harvard University Press, 1991.

Benston, George J. "Required Disclosure and the Stock Market: An Evaluation of the Securities Exchange Act of 1934." *American Economics Review* 63 (March 1973): 132–55.

Berlin, Isaiah. *Two Concepts of Liberty*. Oxford, U.K.: The Clarendon Press, 1958.

Blair, Roger, and David Kaserman. "The Economics and Ethics of Alternative Cadaveric Organ Procurement Policies." *Yale Journal of Regulation* 8, no. 2 (Summer 1991): 403–52.

Blaug, Mark. *Economic Theory in Retrospect*. Cambridge, Mass.: Cambridge University Press, 1996.

Bowie, Norman. *Business Ethics: A Kantian Perspective*. Malden, Mass.: Blackwell Publishers, 1999.

Bové, José, and François Dufour. The World Is Not for Sale: Farmers against Junk Food, interviewed by Gilles Luneau, translated by Anna de Casparis. London: Verso, 2001.

Brace, Laura. *The Idea of Property in Seventeenth Century England, Tithes and the Individual*. Manchester, England: Manchester University Press, 1998.

Bradley, Phillips, ed. *Democracy in America*, 2d vol. 1835. Reprint, 1945, New York: Alfred A. Knopf.

Breyer, Stephen. *Breaking the Vicious Circle: Toward Effective Risk Regulation*. Cambridge, Mass.: Harvard University Press, 1993.

Buchanan, Allen E. "Assessing the Communitarian Critique of Liberalism." *Ethics* 99, no. 4 (1989): 852–82.

Buchanan, James. *Fiscal Theory and Political Economy*. Chapel Hill: University of North Carolina Press, 1960.

———. *The Limits of Liberty*. Chicago: University of Chicago Press, 1975.

———. *The Reason of Rules*. Cambridge, Mass.: Cambridge University Press. 1985.

Buchanan, James, and Gordon Tullock. *The Calculus of Consent*. Ann Arbor: University of Michigan Press, 1962.

Buchholz, Rogene, and Sandra Rosenthal. *Business Ethics: The Pragmatic Path, Beyond Principles to Process.* Upper Saddle River, N.J.: Prentice-Hall, 1998.
———. *Rethinking Business Ethics: A Pragmatic Approach.* New York: Oxford University Press, 2000.
Cantley, Mark, Thomas Hobin, and Albert Sasson. "Regulations and Consumer Attitudes in Biotechnology." *Nature Biotechnology* 17 (March 1999 supplement): 37–38.
Chan, Joseph. "Legitimacy, Unanimity, and Perfectionism." *Philosophy and Public Affairs* 29, no. 1 (Winter 2000): 5–42.
Charles, Dan. *Lords of the Harvest: Biotech, Big Money, and the Future of Food.* Cambridge, Mass.: Perseus Books, 102.
Christman, John, ed. *The Inner Citadel: Essays on Individual Autonomy.* New York: Oxford University Press, 1989.
Clark, Lee, and James F. Short Jr. "Social Organization and Risk: Some Current Controversies." *Annual Review of Sociology* 19 (1993): 375–99.
Coase, R. "The Federal Communications Commission." *Journal of Law and Economics* 2 (October 1959): 1–40.
———. "The Problem of Social Cost." *Journal of Law and Economics* 3 (October 1960): 1–44.
Coase, R., and Nicholas Johnson. "Should the Federal Communications Commission Be Abolished?" In *Regulation, Economics, and the Law,* ed. Bernard H. Siegan. Lexington, Mass.: D.C. Heath and Co., 1979, 41–56.
Cohen, G. A. *If You're an Egalitarian, How Come You're so Rich?* Cambridge, Mass.: Harvard University Press, 2000.
———. *Self-Ownership, Freedom, and Equality.* Cambridge, Mass.: Cambridge University Press, 1995.
Cohen, Joshua. "Review of Walzer's *Spheres of Justice.*" *Journal of Philosophy* 83 (1986): 457–68.
Collins, James C., and Jerry I. Porras. *Built to Last.* New York: Harper Business, 1997.
Commission of the European Communities. *Communication from the Commission: Towards a Strategic Vision of Life Sciences and Biotechnology,* COM (2001) 454 final, Brussels, 4.9.2001.
Commission of the European Communities. *Communication from the Commission of the European Communities: On the Precautionary Principle,* COM (2000) 1, Brussels, 2.2.2000.
Cox, James D. "Insider Trading and Contracting: A Critical Response to the Chicago School." *Duke L.J.* (1986): 628–34.
Dahl, Robert. *Democracy and Its Critics.* New Haven, Conn.: Yale University Press, 1989.
Daniels, Norman. "Review of Walzer's *Spheres of Justice.*" *Philosophical Review* 94 (1985): 142–8.
Daniels, Norman, Donald W. Light, and Ronald L. Caplan. *Benchmarks of Fairness for Health Care Reform.* New York: Oxford University Press, 1996.
Danley, John. "Community and the Corporation in Contemporary Communitarianism." In *Proceedings of the Ninth Annual Meeting of the International*

Association for Business and Society, ed. Jerry Carlton and Kathleen Rehbein, 1998, 371–76.

Dawson, Graham. "Exit, Voice, and Values in Economic Institutions." *Economics and Philosophy* 13 (1997): 87–100.

de Tocqueville, Alexis. *Democracy in America,* ed. Phillips Bradley, 2 vols. 1835. Reprint, New York: Alfred A. Knopf, 1945.

Dewey, John. *Moral Principles in Education.* New York: Houghton Mifflin, 1909.

———. *Creative Democracy—The Task before Us.* In *The Later Works, 1925–1953,* ed. Jo Ann Boydston, vol 14. Carbondale, Ill.: University of Southern Illinois Press, 1981–1990.

———. *Freedom and Culture.* Buffalo, New York: Prometheus Books, 1989.

DiMagio, Paul. "The Relevance of Organization Theory to the Study of Religion." In *Sacred Companies,* ed. N. J. Demerath, Peter Dobkin, Terry Schmitt, and Rhys Williams. New York: Oxford University Press, 1998, 7–23.

Donaldson, Thomas, and Thomas Dunfee. "Toward a Unified Conception of Business Ethics: Integrative Social Contracts Theory." *Academy of Management Review* 19, no. 2 (1994): 252–84.

———. "Integrative Social Contracts Theory: A Communitarian Conception of Economic Ethics." *Economics and Philosophy* 11, no. 1 (1995): 85–112.

———. *Ties That Bind: A Social Contracts Approach to Business Ethics.* Boston: Harvard Business School Press, 1999.

Dreier, Peter, John Mollenkopf, and Todd Swanstrom. *Places Matter.* Lawrence, Kans.: University of Kansas Press, 2001.

Dworkin, Ronald M. "Is Wealth Maximization a Value?" *Journal of Legal Studies* 9, 191 (1980).

———. *A Matter of Principle.* Cambridge, Mass.: Harvard University Press, 1985.

———. *The Theory and Practice of Autonomy.* Cambridge, U.K.: Cambridge University Press, 1995.

Easterbrook, Frank, and Daniel Fischel. *The Economic Structure of Corporate Law.* Cambridge, Mass.: Harvard University Press, 1991.

Eggertsson, Thrainn. *Economic Behavior and Institutions.* Cambridge, U.K.: Cambridge University Press, 1990.

Ehrlich, Walter. *Zion in the Valley.* Columbia, Mo.: University of Missouri Press, 1997.

Eichenwald, K., G. Kolata, and M. Petersen. "Biotechnology Food: From the Lab to a Debacle." *New York Times* (25 January 2001).

Emmons, Willis. *The Evolving Bargain: Strategic Implications of Deregulation and Privatization.* Cambridge, Mass: Harvard Business School Press, 2000.

Farber, Daniel. *Eco-Pragmatism.* Chicago: University of Chicago Press, 1999.

Feldstein, Martin, ed. *The Risk of Economic Crisis.* Chicago: Chicago University Press, 1991.

Fernandez-Cornejo, Jorge, and William McBride, with contributions from Cassandra Klotz-Ingram, Sharon Jans, and Nora Brooks. "Genetically Engineered Crops for Pest Management in U.S. Agriculture." *Agricultural Economics Report* No. 786. May 2000, table 13, p. 13.

Fins, Joseph J., Franklin G. Miller, and Mathew D. Bachetta. "Clinical Pragmatism: Bridging Theory and Practice." *Kennedy Institute of Ethics Journal* 8, no. 1 (March 1998): 37–42.

———. "Clinical Pragmatism: A Method of Moral Problem Solving," *Kennedy Institute of Ethics Journal* 7, no. 2 (June 1997): 129–46.

Fischel, Daniel R. *Payback: The Conspiracy to Destroy Michael Milken and His Financial Revolution.* New York: Harper Business, 1995.

Fischhoff, Baruch. *Acceptable Risk.* New York: Cambridge University Press, 1983.

Frankena, W. *Ethics.* Englewood Cliffs, N.J.: Prentice-Hall, 1970.

Friedman, Lawrence. *A History of American Law.* New York: Simon & Schuster, 1973.

Friedman, Marilyn. "Feminism and Modern Friendship: Dislocating the Community." *Ethics* 99 (1989): 275–90.

Friedman, Milton. *Bright Promise, Dismal Performance.* New York: Harcourt Brace Jovanovich, 1983.

———. *Capitalism and Freedom.* Chicago: University of Chicago Press, 1962.

———. *The Great Contraction, 1929–1933.* Princeton, N.J.: Princeton University Press, 1965.

———. "The Methodology of Positive Economics." In *Essays in Positive Economics.* Chicago: University of Chicago Press, 1953, 3–43.

Friedman, Milton, and Rose Friedman. *Free to Choose.* New York: Harcourt Brace Jovanovich, 1980.

Friedman, Milton, and Paul A. Samuelson. *The Economic Responsibility of Government.* College Station, Tex.: The Center for Education and Research in Free Enterprise at Texas A&M University, 1977.

———. *Milton Friedman and Paul A. Samuelson Discuss the Economic Responsibility of Government.* College Station, Tex.: The Center for Education and Research in Free Enterprise at Texas A&M University, 1980.

Friend, Irwin, and R. Westerfield. "Required Disclosure and the Stock Market: Comment." *American Economic Review* 65, no. 3 (June 1975): 467–72.

Gaskell, G. M., J. Durant, and N. C. Allum. "Worlds Apart? The Reception of Genetically Modified Foods in Europe and the U.S." *Science* 285 (16 July 1999): 384–87.

Gattuso, James. "Life, Liberty, and Cell Phones." *Competitive Enterprise Institute Update* 14, no. 6 (August 2001).

Gewirth, Alan. *The Community of Rights.* Chicago: University of Chicago Press, 1996.

Gibbard, Alan. "What's Morally Special about Free Exchange." In *Ethics and Economics,* ed. Ellen Frankel Paul, Fred D. Miller, Jr., and Jeffrey Paul. Oxford: Basil Blackwell, 1985, 20–28.

Gilpin, Robert, and Jean Gilpin. *Global Political Economy: Understanding the International Economic Order.* Princeton, N.J.: Princeton University Press, 2001.

Glover, Jonathan. *Humanity: A Moral History of the Twentieth Century.* New Haven, Conn.: Yale University Press, 2000.

Goklany, Indur M. "Applying the Precautionary Principle to Genetically Modified Crops." Center for the Study of American Business: Policy Study Number 157 (August 2000): 4–19.

Graham, Katharine. *Personal History*. New York: Random House, 1998.

Gray, John, ed. *On Liberty and Other Essays*. 1859. Reprint, Oxford, U.K.: Oxford University Press, 1991.

———. *Beyond the New Right*. New York: Routledge, 1993.

Greer, Mark R. "Assessing the Soothsayers: An Examination of the Track Record of Macroeconomic Forecasting." *Journal of Economic Issues* 33, no.1 (March 1999): 77–94.

Grundfest, Joseph. "When Markets Crash: The Consequences of Information Failure in the Market for Liquidity." In *The Risk of Economic Crisis*, ed. Martin Feldstein. Chicago: University of Chicago Press, 1991, 62–83.

Haack, Susan. *Manifesto of a Passionate Moderate: Unfashionable Essays*. Chicago: University of Chicago Press, 1998.

———. "Vulgar Rortyism." *The New Criterion* (November 1997): 67–70.

Hall, Stuart. *Democratic Values and Technological Choices*. Stanford, Calif.: Stanford University Press, 1992.

Hanafin, John J. "Morality and the Market in China." *Business Ethics Quarterly* 12 (January 2002): 1–18.

Hardin, Russell. *Morality within the Limits of Reason*. Chicago: University of Chicago Press, 1988.

———. "Communities and Development: Autarkik Social Groups and the Economy." In *A Not-So-Dismal Science: A Broader View of Economies and Societies*, ed. Mancur Olson and Satu Kähkönen. New York: Oxford University Press, 2000, 206–227.

Hartwell, Ronald M. *The Industrial Revolution in England*. London: Historical Association, 1965.

Hausman, Daniel, and Michael McPherson. "Taking Ethics Seriously: Economics and Contemporary Moral Philosophy." *Journal of Economic Literature* 31 (June 1993): 671–731.

Hawthorn, Geoffrey, ed. *The Standard of Living*. Cambridge, Mass.: Cambridge University Press, 1987.

Held, Virginia. *Rights and Goods*. Chicago: University of Chicago Press, 1998.

———. "John Locke on R. Nozick." *Social Research* 43 (Spring 76): 169–95.

———. *The Public Interest and Individual Interests*. New York: Basic Books, 1970.

Herzog, Don. "Public Choice and Constitutional Law: Externalities and Other Parasites." 67 *University of Chicago Law Review* (Summer, 2000): 895.

Hirschman, Albert O. *Exit, Voice, and Loyalty*. Cambridge, Mass.: Harvard University Press, 1970.

Hiskes, Richard P. *Democracy, Risk, and Community: Technological Hazards and the Evolution of Liberalism*. New York: Oxford University Press, 1998.

Hochschild, Jennifer. *What's Fair? American Beliefs about Distributive Justice*. Cambridge, Mass.: Harvard University Press, 1981.

———. *Facing up to the American Dream*. Princeton, N.J.: Princeton University Press, 1995.

Hodgson, John. "Maize Uncertainties Create Political Fallout." *Nature Biotechnology* 20, no. 2 (February 2002): 106–7.

Hundert, E. J. "The Achievement of Motive in Hume's Political Economy." *Journal of the History of Ideas* 35 (1974): 139–43.

Hurst, James Willard. *Law and Markets in the United States.* Madison, Wis.: University of Wisconsin Press, 1982.

Hursthouse, Rosalind. *On Virtue Ethics.* New York: Oxford University Press, 2000.

Huyler, Jerome. *Locke in America: The Moral Philosophy of the Founding Era.* Lawrence: University of Kansas Press, 1995.

Hyde, Lewis, ed. *The Essays of Henry D. Thoreau.* New York: North Point Press, 2002.

Iversen, Karen Vaughn. *John Locke: Economist and Social Scientist.* Chicago: University of Chicago Press, 1980.

James, Clive. "Global Status of Commercialized Transgenic Crops: 2000." *International Service for the Acquisition of Agri-Biotech Applications 21–2000,* at www.isaaa.org/publications/briefs/Brief_21.htm (accessed 30 January 2002).

Jansen, Lynn A. "Assessing Clinical Pragmatism." *Kennedy Institute of Ethics Journal* 8, no. 1 (March 1998): 23–36.

Johnston, David. *The Idea of Liberal Theory.* Princeton, N.J.: Princeton University Press, 1994.

Jones, Eric L. "Extensive Growth in the Pre-Modern World." In *Human History and Social Process,* ed. J. Goudsblom, E. L. Jones, and S. J. Mennell. Exeter, England: University of Exeter Press, 1989, 27–45.

———. "Patterns of Growth in History." In *Capitalism in Context: Essays on Economic Development,* ed. John James and Mark Thomas. Chicago: University of Chicago Press, 1994, 15–28.

Jordan, Andrew, and Timothy O'Riordan. "The Precautionary Principle in Contemporary Environmental Policy and Politics." In *Protecting Public Health and the Environment: Implementing the Precautionary Principle,* ed. Carolyn Raffensperger and Joel Tickner. Washington, D.C.: Island Press, 2000, 15–35.

Kahneman, Daniel, Paul Slovic, and Amos Tversky, eds. *Judgment under Uncertainty: Heuristics and Biases.* Cambridge, Mass.: Cambridge University Press, 1982.

Karmel, Roberta. "Outsider Trading on Confidential Information—A Breach in Search of a Duty." 20 *Cardozo L. Rev.* 83 (1998).

———. *Regulation by Prosecution.* New York: Simon and Schuster, 1982.

Kasserman, D., and J. Mayo. *Government and Business: The Economics of Antitrust and Regulation.* New York: Dryden Press-Harcourt Brace College Publishers, 1995.

Katz, Leo. *Ill-Gotten Gains: Evasion, Blackmail, Fraud, and Kindred Puzzles of the Law.* Chicago: University of Chicago Press, 1996.

Kekes, John. *Against Liberalism.* Ithaca, N.Y.: Cornell University Press, 1997.

Kelly, Patrick Hyde, ed. *Locke on Money.* Oxford, U.K.: Clarendon Press, 1991.

Kennedy, David. *Freedom from Fear: The American People in Depression and War, 1929–1945.* New York: Oxford University Press, 1999.

Kindleberger, Charles. *Manias, Panics, and Crashes.* New York: Basic Books, 1978.

———. *The World in Depression, 1929–1939.* Berkeley, Calif.: University of California Press, 1973.

Klein, Maury. *Rainbow's End: The Crash of 1929.* New York: Oxford University Press, 2001.

Kloppenberg, James T. "Pragmatism: An Old Name for Some New Ways of Thinking?" In Morris Dickstein, ed. *The Revival of Pragmatism.* Durham, N.C.: Duke University Press, 1998, 83–127.

Kripke, Homer. *The SEC and Corporate Disclosure: Regulation in Search of a Purpose.* New York: Law & Business, Inc., 1979.

Kronman, Anthony T. "Wealth Maximization as a Normative Principle." 9 *Journal of Legal Studies* 227 (1980).

Kymlicka, Will. *Liberalism, Community, and Culture.* Oxford, U.K.: Clarendon Press, 1989.

Lamore, Charles. *Patterns of Moral Complexity.* Boston: Cambridge University Press, 1987, 131–52.

Landes, William, and Richard Posner. *The Economic Structure of Tort Law.* Cambridge, Mass.: Harvard University Press, 1987.

———. *The Economics of Justice.* Cambridge, Mass.: Harvard University Press, 1981.

Larkin, Paschal. *Property in the Eighteenth Century: With Special Reference to England and Locke.* London: Cork University Press, 1930.

Leisinger, Klaus, Karin Schmitt, and Rajul Pandya-Lorch. *Six Billion and Counting: Population Growth and Food Security in the Twenty-First Century.* International Food Policy Research Institute, Washington, D.C., distributed by the Johns Hopkins University Press, 2002.

Lindbloom, Charles E. *Politics and Markets.* New York: Basic Books, Inc., 1977.

Locke, John. *Two Treatises of Government,* ed. Peter Laslett. Cambridge: Cambridge University Press, 1997.

Lowrance, William. *Of Acceptable Risk: Science and the Determination of Safety.* Los Altos, Calif.: William Kaufmann, 1976.

Luhmann, Niklas. *Social Systems.* Stanford, Calif.: Stanford University Press, 1995.

Macey, Jonathan R. "From Fairness to Contract: The New Direction of Rules against Insider Trading." 13 *Hofstra Law Review* 9, 10 (1984).

Machan, Tibor. "Government Regulation of Business." In *Commerce and Morality,* ed. Tibor Machan. New York: Rowman & Littlefield, 1988, 161–79.

———. *Individuals and Their Rights.* LaSalle, Ill.: Open Court, 1989.

———. "The Petty Tyranny of Government Regulation." In *Rights and Regulation,* ed. Tibor Machan and M. Bruce Johnson. Cambridge, Mass.: Ballinger Publishing Company, 1983, 259–88.

———, ed. Introduction to *The Commons: Its Tragedies and Other Follies.* Stanford, Calif.: Hoover Institution Press, 2001.

Maitland, Ian. "Virtuous Markets: The Market as School of Virtues." *Business Ethics Quarterly* 7, no. 1. (1997): 17–31.

May, Larry. *The Morality of Groups: Collective Responsibility, Group-Based Harms, and Corporate Rights.* Notre Dame, Ind.: University of Notre Dame Press, 1987.

McAdams, Richard H. "The Origin, Development, and Regulation of Norms," *Michigan Law Review* 96 (1997): 338–443.

McCraw, Thomas K. *Prophets of Regulation.* Cambridge, Mass.: Harvard University Press, 1984.

McHughen, Alan. *Pandora's Picnic Basket: The Potential and Hazards of Genetically Modified Foods.* New York: Oxford University Press, 2000.

McKeon, Richard, ed. *The Basic Works of Aristotle.* New York: Random House, 1971.

McRae, A. "Husbandry Manuals and the Language of Agrarian Improvement." In *Culture and Cultivation,* ed. M. Leslie and T. Raylor. Leicester and London: Leicester University Press, 1992.

Meadows, Donella H. "Technology and the Limits to Growth," In *Technology and the Future,* 4th ed., ed. Albert H. Teich. New York: St. Martin's Press, 1997, 154–92.

Mill, John Stuart. *Autobiography.* Indianapolis, Ind.: Bobbs-Merrill, 1957.

———. *On Liberty.* Indianapolis, Ind.: Hackett, 1978.

———. *Principles of Political Economy.* New York: August M. Kelley, 1969.

Miller, David. *Principles of Social Justice.* Cambridge, Mass.: Harvard University Press, 1999.

Miller, David, and Michael Walzer, eds. *Pluralism, Justice, and Equality.* New York: Oxford University Press, 1995.

Mokyr, Joel. *The Lever of Richs.* New York: Oxford University Press, 1990.

Morgenstern, Oscar. *On the Accuracy of Economic Observations.* Princeton, N.J.: Princeton University Press, 1963.

Morrison, Alan B., and Arthur A. Shenfield. "Government Regulation and the Consumer." In *Regulation, Economics, and the Law,* ed. Bernard H. Siegan. Lexington, Mass.: D.C. Heath and Company, 1979, 57–80.

Mulgan, Tim. *The Demands of Consequentialism.* New York: Oxford University Press, 2001.

National Research Council: Committee on Genetically Modified Pest-Protected Plants, Board on Agriculture and National Resources. *Genetically Modified-Pest Protected Plants: Science and Regulation.* Washington, D.C., National Academy Press, 2000.

North, Douglass. "The Evolution of Efficient Markets." In *Capitalism in Context: Economic Development and Cultural Changes,* ed. John James and Mark Thomas. Chicago: University of Chicago Press, 1994, 257–78.

———. *Institutions, Institutional Change, and Economic Performance.* Cambridge: Cambridge University Press, 1990.

Nozick, Robert. *Anarchy, State, and Utopia.* New York: Basic Books, 1974.

———. *The Examined Life.* New York: Simon and Schuster, 1989.

Nuffield Council on Bioethics. *Genetically Modified Crops: The Ethical and Social*

Issues. London: Nuffield Council on Bioethics, 1999. Available for download at nuffieldbioethics.org/publications (accessed 30 January 2002).

Okin, Arthur. *Prices and Quantities: A Macroeconomic Analysis*. Washington D.C.: Brookings Institution, 1981.

Oldenquist, Andrew. "Rules and Consequences." *Mind* 75 (April 1966): 180.

Olson, Mancur, and Satu Kähkönen, eds. *A Not-So-Dismal Science: A Broader View of Economies and Societies*. New York: Oxford University Press, 2000.

———. "Distinguished Lecture on Economics in Government." *Journal of Economic Perspectives* 10, no. 2 (Spring 1996): 3–24.

O'Riordan, Timothy, and Andrew Jordan. "The Precautionary Principle in Contemporary Environmental Policy and Politics." *Environmental Values* 4 (1995): 191–212.

Ossipow, William. "Niklas Luhmann's Sociology and the Economic System: Some Moral Implications." In *Ethics in Economic Affairs*, ed. Allan Lewis and Karl-Erik Warneryd. London: Routledge, 1994.

Osterfeld, David. *Freedom, Society, and the State*. Lanham, Md.: University Press of America, 1983.

Paarlberg, Robert. *The Politics of Precaution: Genetically Modified Crops in Developing Countries*. Baltimore, Md.: Johns Hopkins University Press, 2001.

Pence, Gregory. *Designer Food: Mutant Harvest or Breadbasket of the World?* Lanham, Md.: Rowman & Littlefield, 2002.

Phillips, Derek. *Looking Backward: A Critical Appraisal of Communitarian Thought*. Princeton, N.J.: Princeton University Press, 1993.

Phillips, Susan, and J. Rischard Zecher. *The SEC and the Public Interest*. Cambridge, Mass.: MIT Press, 1981.

Piper, Adrian. "Sense of Value." *Ethics* 106, no. 3 (1996): 525–37.

Posner, Richard. "The Problematics of Moral and Legal Theory: The 1997 Oliver Wendell Holmes Lectures." *Harvard Law Review* 111, no. 7 (May 1998): 1638–1717.

———. *Economic Analysis of Law*, 5th ed. New York: Aspen Publishers, 1998.

Posner, Richard, and Kenneth E. Scott, eds. *Economics of Corporation and Securities Regulation*. Boston: Little, Brown and Company, 1980.

Powell, G. B., Jr., and G. D. Whitten. "A Cross-National Analysis of Economic Voting: Taking Account of the Political Context." *American Journal of Political Science* 37 (1993): 391–414.

Pryor, Frederick L. *Economic Evolution and Structure: The Impact of Complexity on the U.S. Economic System*. Cambridge, Mass.: Cambridge University Press, 1996.

Quinn, D. P., and J. T. Woolley. "Democracy and National Economic Performance: The Preference for Stability." *American Journal of Political Science* 45 (2001): 634–57.

Quist, David, and Chapela, Ignacio. "Transgenic DNA Introgressed into Traditional Maize Landraces in Oaxaca, Mexico." *Nature* 414 (November 2001): 541–43.

Raffensperger, Carolyn, and Joel Tickner, eds. *Protecting Public Health and the Environment: Implementing the Precautionary Principle*. Washington, D.C.: Island Press, 1999.

Rawls, John. *Political Liberalism*. New York: Columbia University Press, 1993.
———. *A Theory of Justice*. Cambridge, Mass.: Harvard University Press, 1971.
Rescher, Nicholas. *Realistic Pragmatism*. Albany, N.Y.: State University of New York Press, 2000.
Richardson, Henry. "Specifying, Balancing, and Interpreting Bioethical Principles." *Journal of Medicine and Philosophy* 25, no. 3 (June 2000): 285–307.
———. "Specifying Norms as a Way to Resolve Concrete Ethical Problems." *Philosophy and Public Affairs* 19, no. 4 (Fall 1990): 279–310.
Rifkin, Jeremy. *The Age of Access: The New Culture of Hypercapitalism, Where All of Life Is a Paid-For Experience*. New York: J. P. Tarcher, 2000.
Ruch, Richard S. *Higher Ed, Inc*. Balitmore: Johns Hopkins University Press, 2001.
Ryan, Alan. *John Dewey and the High Tide of American Liberalism*. New York: W. W. Norton & Company, 1995.
Sandel, Michael. *Liberalism and the Limits of Justice*. New York: Cambridge University Press, 1982.
Scheppele, Kim Lane. " 'It's Just Not Right': The Ethics of Insider Trading." *Law and Contemporary Problems* 56, no.3 (Summer 1993): 123–73.
Scott, Richard W. *Organizations: Rational, Natural, and Open Systems*, 3rd ed. Englewood Cliffs, N.J.: Prentice-Hall, 1991.
Seligman, Joel. *The Transformation of Wall Street*. Boston: Northeastern University Press, 1995.
Sen, Amartya. "The Moral Standing of the Market." In *Ethics and Economics*, ed. Ellen Frankel Paul, Fred D. Miller Jr., and Jeffrey Paul. Oxford, U.K.: Basil Blackwell, 1985, 1–19.
———. "Isolation, Assurance, and the Social Rate of Discount." *Quarterly Journal of Economics* 81, no. 1 (February 1967): 112–24.
———. *Choice, Welfare, and Measurement*. Cambridge, Mass.: MIT Press, 1982.
Sennett, Richard. *The Corrosion of Character: The Personal Consequences of Work in the New Capitalism*. New York: W. W. Norton & Company, 1998.
Shrader-Frechette, Kristen. *Risk Analysis and Scientific Method*. Boston: D. Reidel, 1985.
———. *Risk and Rationality*. Berkeley, Calif.: University of California Press, 1991.
Simmons, A. John. *Lockean Theory of Rights*. Princeton, N.J.: Princeton University Press, 1992.
———. *On the Edge of Anarchy: Locke, Consent, and the Limits of Society*. Princeton, N.J.: Princeton University Press, 1993.
Singer, Marcus. *Generalization in Ethics*. New York: Knopf, 1961.
Sobel, Robert. *Panic on Wall Street: A History of America's Financial Disasters*. New York: Macmillan, 1969.
Soule, Edward. "Managerial Moral Strategies: In Search of a Few Good Principles." *Academy of Management Review* 27, no. 1 (January 2002): 114–24.
———. "David Hume and Economic Policy." *Hume Studies* 26, no. 1 (April 2000): 143–57.
———. "Assessing the Precautionary Principle." *Public Affairs Quarterly* 14, no. 4 (October 2000): 309–28.

Specter, Michael. "The Pharmageddon Riddle." *The New Yorker* (10 April 2000): 58–71.

Stich, Stephen. "The Recombinant DNA Debate: Some Philosophical Considerations." In *The Recombinant DNA Debate*, ed. David Jackson and Stephen Stich. Englewood Cliffs, N.J.: Prentice-Hall, Inc., 1979, 183–202.

Stigler, George. "Public Regulation of the Securities Markets," 73 *Journal of Business*, 117.

Stimson, J. A., R .S. Erikson, and M. B. MacKuen. "Dynamic Representation." *American Political Science Review* 89 (1995): 543–65.

Strong, Carson. "Specified Principlism: What Is It, and Does It Really Resolve Cases Better than Casuistry?" *Journal of Medicine and Philosophy* 25, no. 3 (June 2000): 323–41.

Strudler, Alan, and Eric Orts. "Moral Principle in the Law of Insider Trading." *Texas Law Review* (December 1999): 375–438.

Sturgeon, Nicholas. "Anderson on Reason and Value." *Ethics* 106, no. 3 (1996): 509–24.

Summers, Lawrence. "Macroeconomic Consequences of Financial Crises." In *The Risk of Economic Crisis*, ed. Martin Feldstein. Chicago: University of Chicago Press, 1991, 135–58.

Sunstein, Cass. "Disrupting Voluntary Transactions." In *Nomos XXXI*, ed. John Chapman and J. Roland Pennock. New York: New York University Press, 1989, 279–302.

———. *Free Markets and Social Justice*. New York: Oxford University Press, 1997.

———. "On the Expressive Function of Law," 144 *U. Pa. L. Rev.* 2021 (1996).

Taylor, Charles. *Sources of the Self*. Cambridge, Mass.: Cambridge University Press, 1990.

Titmus, Richard. *The Gift Relationship*. New York: Pantheon, 1971.

Trewavas, Anthony, and Christopher Leaver. "Is Opposition to GM Crops Science or Politics?: An Investigation into the Arguments that GM Crops Pose a Particular Threat to the Environment." *EMBO Reports* 2, no. 6 (2001): 455–59. Also at emboreports.oupjournals.org/cgi/content/full/2/6/455 (accessed 30 January 2002).

Tully, Shawn. "Will Wall Street Go Up in Smoke?" *Fortune*, 3 September 2001, 36–38.

United Nations Food and Agriculture Organization. *Codex Alimentarius Commission Procedural Manual*, 11th ed. Rome, Italy: Food and Agriculture Organization, 1999.

Van Staveren, Irene. *The Values of Economics: An Aristotelian Perspective*. New York: Routledge, 2001.

Von Wartburg, W., and Julian Liew. *Gene Technology and Social Acceptance*. Lanham, Md.: University Press of America, 1999.

Vries, J. de. *Securing the Harvest: Biotechnology, Breeding, and Seed Systems for African Crops*. New York: Rockefeller Foundation, 2001.

Walsh, Adrian. "Teaching, Preaching, and Queaching about Commodities." *The Southern Journal of Philosophy* 36, no. 3 (1998): 433–52.

Walzer, Michael. *Spheres of Justice.* New York: Basic Books, 1983.

————. *Thick and Thin: Moral Argument at Home and Abroad.* Notre Dame, Ind.: University of Notre Dame Press, 1994.

Warnock, G. J. *The Object of Morality.* London: Methuen & Co., 1971.

Weiss, Leonard, and Michael Klass, eds., *Regulatory Reform: What Actually Happened.* Boston: Little, Brown and Company, 1986.

Wigmore, Barrie. *The Crash and Its Aftermath: A History of Securities Markets in the United States, 1929–1933.* Westport, Conn.: Greenwood Press, 1985.

Will, George. "Reading China." *Washington Post,* 5 April 2001, 27(A).

Wittman, D. "Why Democracies Produce Efficient Results." *Journal of Political Economy* 97 (1989): 1395–1424.

————. *The Myth of Democratic Failure: Why Political Institutions Are Efficient.* Chicago: University of Chicago Press, 1995.

Wolff, Jonathan. *Robert Nozick.* Stanford, Calif.: Stanford University Press, 1991.

Wood, Neal. *John Locke and Agrarian Capitalism.* Berkeley: University of California Press, 1984.

Index

About the Author

Edward Soule, CPA, teaches managerial ethics at the McDonough School of Business at Georgetown University where he was the 2002 winner of the Joseph F. Le Moine Award for Undergraduate and Graduate Teaching Excellence. Prior to his teaching career he practiced public accounting and served as the CFO of a national securities firm. He received his Ph.D. in moral and political philosophy in 1999 from Washington University in St. Louis. Professor Soule publishes widely on issues in corporate ethics, public policy, and economic history; and he is a frequent contributor to national and international media reports on corporate ethics.